THE ETHNOLOGY OF INDIA

THE ETHNOLOGY OF INDIA

GEORGE CAMPBELL

GYAN

Published by

Gyan Publishing House
5, Ansari Road
Daryaganj, New Delhi-110002
Phone: 011-47034999, 9811692060
E-mail: books@gyanbooks.com

Distribution Network
gyanbooks.com
India, USA, Canada, UK, Australia

ISBN: 978-93-7169-068-3 (PB)

First Published, 1866

2nd Impression 2025

Printed at: Gyan Press, Delhi.

THE ETHNOLOGY OF INDIA
Author: GEORGE CAMPBELL

NEW SERIES. NO. CXXXVI.

JOURNAL

OF THE

ASIATIC SOCIETY OF BENGAL:

EDITED BY

THE NATURAL HISTORY SECRETARY.

PART II.—1866.

SPECIAL NUMBER.

ETHNOLOGY.

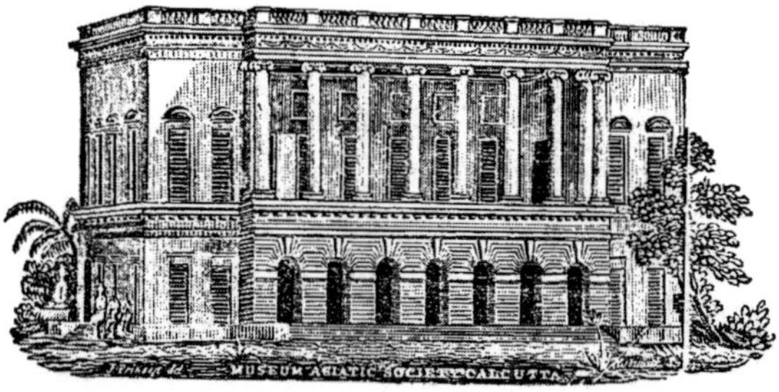

"The bounds of its investigation will be the geographical limits of Asia: and within these limits its inquiries will be extended to whatever is performed by man or produced by nature."—SIR WILLIAM JONES.

Price to Subscribers, per Number, 1-8 Rs.——To Non-Subscribers, 2 Rs.——Spare Numbers of Vols. XII. to XXIV. on sale at the Society's Rooms in Park Street, to Subscribers, at 1 R. per Number;——to Non-Subscribers, at 1-8 Rs., per Number.

*** *Communications should be sent under cover to the Secretaries As. Soc., to whom all orders for the work are to be addressed in India; or in London, to Messrs. Williams and Norgate, 14, Henrietta Street.*

CALCUTTA:

PRINTED BY C. B. LEWIS, AT THE BAPTIST MISSION PRESS,

CIRCULAR ROAD.

1866.

CONTENTS.

JOURNAL
OF THE
ASIATIC SOCIETY.

PART II.—1866.

SPECIAL NUMBER.

ETHNOLOGY.

CONTENTS.

ETHNOLOGY OF INDIA, BY MR. JUSTICE CAMPBELL.

EDITOR'S NOTE.

It is hoped that farther communications on Ethnological subjects may be received and published in continuation of the present special number, so as to form in all a separate and special Ethnological volume of the Journal of the Society. The paging is therefore kept distinct.

JOURNAL

OF THE

ASIATIC SOCIETY.

SUPLEMENTARY NUMBER.

Vol. XXXV. Part II.

The Ethnology of India.—By Mr. Justice Campbell.

[Received 4th June, 1866.]

I trust that the great subject of Indian Ethnology has been taken up by the Society in a serious and earnest manner, with a view to that actual observation and practical inquiry which is only possible in the countries and on the spots where the various races are found, or where specimens of them may be collected together. The Government has already consented to take the first step in aid of the movement by collecting from its officers, in all parts of India, lists of the races and classes existing in the various districts. The present paper is designed to assist both Government officers and private persons in making classified and descriptive lists in such a uniform manner, and with such a uniform nomenclature and arrangement, that it may be afterwards possible to weld together the whole of the information thus obtained. Without some common plan and nomenclature, without, as it were, some Ethnological skeleton to serve as the guide and model into which the various details may be fitted, and by which they may be classed, I fear that there may be much confusion and error in bringing together lists which must necessarily often be made by officials who have little knowledge of Ethnology as a science, and whose practical knowledge and nomenclature are limited to their own particular parts of India. My object then is, to supply a sort of rough hand book of existing information on the subject, particularly as regards the North of India, and my hope is, that such a guide may render much more easy, intelligible, and uniform, the collection of a mass of details, which will render our knowledge ample and complete. It happens that my personal experience has been wider than that of most officers; I have also travelled much in those parts of India in which I have not served, and have made the people a constant subject of observation and inquiry. I have farther, for some time past, noted the information on this subject which I could collect from books. And lastly, I have received much aid in my inquiries from many kind friends. During a late visit to the Punjaub frontier, I was under great obligations to many of the officers employed there, and feel that I can always look for assistance in that quarter. Recent papers by Colonel Dalton, Commissioner of the Chota-Nagpore territories, have given much information respecting several of the tribes of that locality of which I have made free use, and I had looked also to use another paper on the Coles promised by Colonel Dalton. It has not been received, but I hope that it will soon add to the information which I am now able to give. During a tour in the Bombay Presidency, I was fortunate enough to make the acquaintance and to obtain the assistance of Mr. Perceval of the Civil Service there, since Private Secretary to His Excellency Sir B. Frere, and through Mr. Perceval I have received a series of very interesting notes on the aborigines of that part of India by Captain Probyn, Major Keatinge, Mr. Ashburner, Mr. Probert, and the Rev. Messrs. Moore and Taylor, containing information not elsewhere procurable. During a former tour in the Mysore country and in some of the Madras districts adjoining, I received much kind assistance, and Mr. Bowring has since been good enough to point out to me some very interesting additional information. With respect, however, to the Telinga country, and the extreme South of India, I have not been fortunate enough to obtain all the information that I could desire.

It will be understood, moreover, that as respects every part of India, I by no means profess to give a complete sketch. I have not the necessary information, and have not time for the necessary study to enable me to attempt that. Indeed, in this as in so many other things, the more one learns, the more one sees one's ignorance and the vast amount of inquiry that still remains. I only desire to tell so much as I know, and to suggest points on which inquiry is desirable. Although I have always been much interested in the people, I have usually not had time and opportunity to commit all that I have observed to writing; it is in fact only of late years that I have in some degree done so. I am obliged therefore frequently to use such expressions as 'I think,' not because I do not speak from personal observation, but because, writing from memory, I must give my impressions subject to the chance of error. In attempting too so wide and general a subject without great opportunities of study, I am at every turn liable to error. I would at once avow that I warrant nothing, even when I do not specially qualify my phrases. I only give my impressions for what they are worth. It is true that it would have been possible to verify many doubtful points, to fill up many gaps, and to solve some difficulties which occur to me in writing this paper, by farther enquiries in the proper quarters; but looking to the character of my paper, as an avowedly imperfect sketch, designed to elicit the information which may afterwards render possible something more complete, I have preferred not to delay, but to give what I now can, *as* I now can. In truth, my object is to suggest our deficiencies, to point to them, and to prospect the quarters where valuable strata of information may be found. I shall say what I have to say in the most simple and least technical form—in a rough and unpolished way.

My philological acquirements are very deficient. As respects Southern India, Dr. Caldwell, by his comparative grammar, has made comparison easy. But there is no such synthetical account of the Northern languages. The character of each can only be separately learned. The Rev. Mr. Trump has done much for the languages of the extreme North West, but as respects the characteristics of Bengallee, Maratta, Guzeratee, &c. when compared to Hindee and Punjabee, I find no easy guide, and have not been able to acquire any adequate knowledge. —Cashmiree is still scarcely known at all. We very much want such an account of the languages of the North as Dr. Caldwell has given us for the South.

In the mere matter of nomenclature, it is surprising how much confusion arises, both from calling the same tribes by different names, and also from calling different tribes by the same name. The former error can only be met by explaining in detail the tribes variously known in various localities; but in respect to the latter, some general caution seems necessary. It often happens that the same term is applied both to a Tribe or Caste, and to the profession usually exercised by that caste, and that while in one sense the term is proper to the caste, whether exercising the same or any other profession, in another sense it is applied to all exercising the profession, whether of the same or of any other caste. For instance, in the greater part of the Punjaub, the great agricultural tribe is the Jat, and there the words 'Jat' and 'Zemeendar' have come to be used by the people as almost synonymous. A man who is asked of what caste he is, will reply 'a Zemeendar,' meaning a Jat. And, *vice versâ*, a Punjabee will sometimes call a man a Jat, meaning only that he is a Zemeendar. When I pressed some of the servants of the Maharajah of Cashmere regarding the Ethnology of the valley of the Upper Indus and other little known parts, I was at first much puzzled by finding them declare that the great mass of the people there are 'Jats,' but I presently discovered that they meant merely Zemeendars or cultivators, there being in fact no Jats within the Hills. In the West and South too, I believe that the terms 'Koonbee' and 'Wocal' are used both to designate certain agricultural tribes, and cultivators generally; so that while "the Wocals are by the Mahommedans called Koonbees," that circumstance gives no assurance that the tribes are the same. The term Bunneah or Banian is properly applied to the great trading caste, but it also means a trader, and is often so applied. Again in India *religious* denominations are often applied in a way which confounds them with proper tribal denominations. The character of the Hindoo religion is such that it is a pretty safe Ethnological guide, converts not being ordinarily received. Mahommedan and other proselytising religions, on the other hand, are no guide in Ethnology; on the contrary, the Mahommedan Laws of Marriage and Legitimacy are such as to tend very much to efface Ethnological demarcations. For our purposes therefore, Mahommedan denominations may be entirely put aside. But the mere fact, that people are Mahommedans, should not deter us from seeking their Tribal denominations in the back ground. Many Mahommedan tribes still retain their Hindoo caste names, some Hindoo laws, and something of caste exclusiveness.

Though not so pure or characteristic as their Hindoo brethren, many Mussulman Rajpoots and Jats are just as well known as such as the Hindoos; while many whole tribes have become Mahommedans without changing their tribal designations and occupations. Most of the modern Sikhs in no way separate from their tribes, and are known as 'Jat,' or 'Khatrie,' or 'Braman Sikhs,' one member of a family being frequently a 'Sing,' while others are not. Jains, I believe, are not ethnologically distinguished from Hindoos. Among the Bunneahs, it appears that some are Hindoos and some Jains, in the same tribes and sections of tribes. Very puzzling in the South is the term 'Lingaiyat' applied to those Ultra-Sivites who wear the Lingam, who seem *almost* to form a caste, and who are generally spoken of as such. So far, however, as I can gather, the term is really a mere religious denomination, and the Lingaiyats are of various castes, which should be distinguished.

In all inquiries then, great care is necessary in sifting out tribal, as distinguished from mere professional and religious denominations. When we arrive at proper tribal titles, it is farther desirable to inquire into the aliases or varieties of title often possessed by the tribes; for it may happen that while an obscure local title is in the most common use, another, less frequently used, will at once indicate identity with some well known and widely spread caste.

It is also very necessary to attend to the distinctions between great caste titles, and the sub-divisions of those castes. All the great castes have numerous gotes or sub-divisions; and when a man is asked to what caste he belongs, he will sometimes give the name of the general, and sometimes of the special caste or gote. Some of these sub-divisions really are or may be ethnological sub-divisions, others, from the peculiarity of Hindoo laws, are not so. On the principle which forbids the marriage of relations (carried by Hindoos to an extreme) men of the Rajpoot and other castes cannot marry in their own 'gotes,' but must seek their wives in other gotes. In blood therefore such castes really form but one race—so far at least as the intermarriages are carried—for there are many tribes claiming to be Rajpoots whom the higher tribes will not recognize. Of other castes, the primary sub-divisions keep altogether apart. I apprehend that under the general term 'Bunneah,' are to be found many separate tribes who would on no account eat together or intermarry. I think, however, that throughout all the great Hindoo castes, a strong ethnological resemblance exists. I do not propose in this sketch to attempt to notice the sub-divisions, except in any case in which they may suggest marked ethnological features.

The details of Rajpoot and Bramin heraldry and hierology have been amply given in several excellent works, and I shall touch on nothing of that kind.

A caution which seems to me to be necessary is, that the accounts of their origin given by many tribes, and especially by their Chiefs, must be received in a very guarded way, because there is a great tendency to invent origins illustrious in the eyes of men of the races and religions to which they belong. Among the Hindoos, the Rajpoot rule is so famous, that almost all tribes which have taken to soldiering or acquired power, pretend to a Rajpoot origin. At this day, some of the followers of Maratta Chiefs have the impudence to tell strangers that they are really Rajpoots, as if their origin was not matter of the most recent history; and almost all the aboriginal tribes who have risen to any power (or at least the chief families among them) affect a Rajpoot descent. As Colonel Dalton describes it, they are undergoing a gradual process of '*refining into Rajpoots*,' a process probably founded on a very small Rajpoot immigration and alliance, and a very large amount of invention. Even the Jats and other tribes who need hardly descend to such stories, frequently make themselves out to be Rajpoots who have been separated from the orthodox for some looseness of practice; but my impression is, that most of these stories are quite idle. Even acknowledged Rajpoots of the North-Western hills who are, in an Ethnological point of view, a much finer and purer race than any in the plains, assert that their ancestors came from Ajoodea or Oude. So in Cashmere, the Bramins there, whose mere features at once proclaim them to be one of the highest and purest races in the world, instead of adopting the more ancient and better traditions which would point to their country as the common origin of the Bramin races of India, prefer the story that when Kashyapa dried up the Lake (a geological fact patent even to Hindoos) detachments of all the most famous and most sacred of the different Bramin classes were brought into Cashmere, who, amalgamating, formed the present

Cashmeeree Bramins. The real cause of all these stories, I take to be this. The Hindoos, as Hindoos and from an orthodox Hindoo point of view, did not attain their highest religious, literary, and political development, till they were settled in the plains of India ; consequently the early Bramins of the valleys of the Himalayas are not considered nearly so orthodox, so sacred, or in the Hindoo scale so high, as the more famous Bramins of the plains. And the Rajpoots of the Punjab and the adjoining hills, are not so high in the scale of strict Rajpoot orthodoxy as the Solar and Lunar races of Ajoodea. Hence it is that the races, really earlier and purer, think it necessary to claim descent from those who, in our point of view, are really very inferior.

Again, most tribes which have been for many centuries converted to Mahommedanism, set up some origin founded on the traditions and literature of the dominant Mahommedan races. They are generally descended from Soleiman or Nooshervan, or something of that kind. Jewish names and traditions are particularly in vogue among the Mahommedans (Abraham, Jacob, Joseph, and many others known to us, are their most common names, in the form of Ibraheem, Yacoob, Yoosoof, &c. &c.) and it has been pointed out, that the Affghan assertion of Jewish descent loses most of its significance, when we find how many other tribes have stories of the same kind. I have not been able to ascertain whether the "Soleiman's Throne" met with in so many places is to be specially referred to the Jewish Solomon, or whether the term is merely the "Suleh-man" or wise man of the East. At any rate I believe that most of the pretended Mahommedan genealogies are in brief 'bosh.'

I do not mean that popular traditions are to be neglected, on the contrary, I think that they often lead us far towards the truth ; but I say that we must use caution and discrimination, to sift the wheat from the merest chaff.

I should add that I believe that the claim of aboriginal and other tribes to Rajpoot and such like origin, is not always without some foundation in fact. The Rajpoots seem, like the Normans, to have frequently found their way in small numbers among inferior races, and there amalgamating and intermarrying with them, to have acquired by force of character a leadership over them, and to have considerably raised the position of such tribes. There is, I think, a good deal to suggest that during the various invasions of Southern India by a succession of Northern 'Yavanas,' small tribes of these latter may have taken up their position in difficult parts of the country, and there, amalgamating with the aboriginal tribes, have formed half-breed races of much robber-like and semi-military energy.

Before going farther, I would suggest the following as especially deserving the attention of those who are willing to aid in a popular way in classing the various tribes and castes in India.

1. Physical appearance. The three main types, Caucasian, Mongolian, and Negro or Negritò, are well-known. In India we have, in the extreme North, the finest and purest Caucasian type, the handsomer and more open form of that which we know as the Jewish cast of countenance; fine head and features, high brow and nose, long beard, tall, lithe, powerful figure, colour generally light. Throughout India, we have this type modified and subdued by every variety of straight and snub nose and plebeian features, much as in Europe, and with a dark skin unknown in Europe. Sometimes the skin becomes very black, and the lips are thick and protuberant; *there* may be marked the infusion of blood of the Negrito type which probably modifies the higher phase of the Caucasian type, even when actual Negrito features cannot be traced.

This Negrito type we find in India not accompanied with the muscular form of many Africans, but in a small slight race. The principal points to be marked, in addition to colour, are the lips, already alluded to, shape of face, nose, and eyes, presence or absence of a considerable beard, character of the hair.

Among the Thibetans and Nipalese we have extreme examples of the type which I call generically Mongolian. The eyes particularly there is no mistaking. The hair is straight. The colour is yellowish, but never dark.

2. Language is liable to disturbances, and has been perhaps too much taken as a sure guide, but it is always of great assistance, and in 19 cases out of 20 tells a true tale. In practice I think that no considerable philological acquirements are necessary to enable an observer to make most useful observations of a language quite unknown to him, if he can only get the rudest interpreter. There are certain

words which may almost be taken as unfailing tests in classifying language; for instance, the first few numerals, the names for the commonest parts of the human body—as hand, foot, nose, eyes, mouth, head, &c.—the names of the commonest family relations—father, mother, brother, sister—sun and moon, fire and water—the personal pronouns, and one or two others. I shall try to add to this paper some of Mr. Hodgson's lists. I do not know that they are all the best selected words, but they are uniform lists of different languages in parallel columns, and will enable any observer to determine on the spot whether the savage he has caught, *primâ facie*, seems to belong to one or other of the classes represented in the columns. I shall also make a smaller list of English words, a translation of which I would recommend to be sent with each account of a tribe or race, speaking a language in any degree peculiar.

It should be observed that it may not unfrequently happen that men who seem to speak but a rough jargon of some well known language may, on close observation, be found to use peculiar terms for some of the most familiar objects, and that these latter may be invaluable as containing the remnants of their original language, all but absorbed in another which they have for the most part adopted. Especially will such words be valuable, if they can be in any degree identified with those in any of the Aboriginal Vocabularies.

Grammatical structure is somewhat more difficult of observation, and so far as I know, the general structural character of all the modern Indian languages is in a considerable degree similar. I mean that there is no such radical difference of formation as there is between Hindee and Arabic. But those who can give a little attention to the subject, might supply small grammars of declension, conjugation, and derivation, which would be eminently useful. And on the Eastern Frontier, the distinction between Indian and Indo-Chinese grammatical forms might probably be readily marked.

3. Religion. There is so much similarity in the religions of so many rude tribes, that there may be doubt whether such worship as that of the Sun, Moon, and the lord of Tigers represents a wide spread religion, or merely a coincidence of very obvious ideas repeated again and again; but it is worth noticing these ideas, in the hope that some

substantial inductions may be formed from putting together many observations.

And among the more civilised races, I think it not improbable that an accurate observation of the prevalence of Sivite and Vishnuite ideas respectively, among particular tribes and castes, may be found to have an ethnological significance. I cannot help thinking that these two forms of modern Hinduism may in fact represent entirely different religions derived from widely different sources, and that while the Vishnuite faith came from the north, the Sivite may have had some other origin, and may be the special property of races which of old peculiarly affected it. Sivite monuments certainly seem to be marks of a very old faith in the greater part of India, and the essential element of it, the reverence for and deification of the procreative power, seems to be the same idea of natural progression which is carried on by the Buddhist doctrine of gradual perfectibility (raising man almost to the rank of a god) in opposition to the Vishnuite or Vedic creed of a separate creation of gods and their occasional incarnation in the form of man. If then pure Sivites, Buddhists, and Jains are in some way connected, and they all prevail most in the West, who are those who brought their doctrines there? and whence did they come?

4. Laws. I believe that, laws are among the most persistent ethnological marks, and that, as such, they have been too much neglected. Caste, and Marriage as a sacrament strictly limited by caste, seem to be Arian institutions. Arian are strict rules of inheritance, resulting from that sacred form of marriage and subject to none of the caprices of Mahommedan and similar laws. Arian is the private property in land, as distinguished from the Tribal; the property first of the village—then of the family—then of the individual; and a consequence is, the attachment of the Arian to his native soil. Especially Arian is the form of what we call constitutional, as opposed to patriarchal and arbitrary government. The Indian village or Commune is a constitutional unit, common to all the Arians. A main distinction, as I think, between two great classes of Arians is to be traced in the constitution of these Communes—Aristocratic among the one—among the other democratic, and recognizing as equals al free citizens, to the exclusion of Helots only.

Among the non-Arians, on the other hand, the rule of the Chiefs seems to be patriarchal and arbitrary—property in the soil is tribal rather than individual. There is little local attachment to the soil. he aboriginal tribes of India move from place to place, abandoning one location and taking up another in a light way; they are even ready to give up their land, to become labourers, and to emigrate in a way to which the Arians are by no means prone. They seem to have among themselves no caste, they eat anything and every thing. Marriage is, I fancy, but a loose tie. On all these points, however, we want much information.

5. Manners and mental characteristics. Under this I must include so much that I cannot attempt to detail it. Suffice it to say, that any information regarding the temperament and bearing, the intelligence, the customs and habits, the amusements and the ceremonies of little known tribes, may be in many ways most useful.

It is patent in India to the most superficial observer that, owing to the peculiar institution of castes, mere vicinage (even lasting many hundred years) has not, as in Europe, led to the welding of different races and tribes into proper local nationalities: that, in fact, in the same locality many different races exist together without complete intermixture, while a single race may frequently be traced through many different provinces and countries, always retaining its own peculiarities under a great variety of circumstances and in contact with many varying races. On the other hand, language can never be exclusive, it must be the means of inter-communication between man and man, caste and caste, without distinctions of race or creed. Hence, however much by religion and race a tribe may be segregated, if it be politically and to a great extent socially united with other peoples, it almost always in the end adopts their language, or a common language is formed by intermixture. That is the ordinary state of Indian society. In the business of life, the different castes are united in one society; some are in the upper, some in the lower strata; one is the lord, another the priest, another the free cultivator, another the hewer of wood and drawer of water; but still they form one social whole. Farther, although the rules of caste and marriage may hinder the inter-communication of blood, it cannot but be that in the long course of time, during which different tribes live in the closest intercourse, there must be some irregular percolation from one to the other; in the course of thousands of years, something of the blood and features of one will be infiltrated into the other.

Thus it has happened that in India there is a sort of double classification of the people, similar to that which we sometimes see in rocks in which there is a double stratification, one line of strata running say horizontally, and another line crossing the same rock say vertically. When we trace a tribe or caste from one Province to another, we shall find that in some things it retains the class character, in others it varies according to provincial character, the latter chiefly prevailing in point of language.

I propose to trace, so far as I can, the different tribes and classes throughout India, irrespective of local nationalities, and to some extent irrespective of language. I had thought that I might afterwards, when that is completed, remark on the quasi-nationalities created by the use of special languages and the social specialities of particular provinces; but I find that our information is as yet so imperfect, that I prefer to leave this latter task to another day. I shall merely make some casual remarks on language and a few other national features, as they occur in the course of my narrative.

Till we have accomplished an Ethnological Geography, whether Tribal or National, I shall for the most part use the ordinary terms of our Modern Political Geography, and speak of the Punjab and Scinde, Bengal and Mysore. But for facility of reference, I must make one or two explanations. I shall speak of Hindustan and the Hindustanees as the terms are applied by the natives, to the whole of the great Central region of Northern India from the Punjab on one side to Bengal on the other, and from the Himalayas to the Southern declivities of the Satpoora Range running across India in about the parallel of 22° Lat. I include in Hindustan, Bahar, (confining the term of Bengal to Bengal Proper) as well as Oude, Rajpootana, and Malwa. South of Hindustan to the West is the Maratta country, which may be roughly indicated as bounded by a line drawn from Nagpore to Goa. And farther South are the Southern countries, sometimes called Dravidian, first the Telinga or Telugu country to the East, the Canarese to the West; beyond them again the Tamil country to the East, the Malabar or Malayala country to the West.

As respects the physical features of these countries, it will be remembered that the whole of Bengal proper, the N. W. Provinces and Oude, the Punjab and Scinde, with part of the adjoining desert country, form a great semi-circular plain in which there is no place of refuge (with little exception) for remains of aboriginal races; in all these countries the modern races live together as one social whole. But throughout Central and Peninsular India, while the most open plains and best cultivated parts of the country are similarly inhabited, there are scattered about, over every province, hills and jungles giving cover to aboriginal tribes which hold themselves aloof from the general population, and are very different in language, manners and other particulars.

It is well known that the great plain is bounded on the north by the line of the Himalayas, rising almost suddenly in great and rugged height, but yet habitable for a considerable distance inland before the snows are reached. That boundary is so uniform that more need not be said respecting it, except as regards the northern extremity of India. There the plain is not at once succeeded by the Himalaya. The range called the Salt Range runs across from Jhelum to Kala-Bagh on the Indus, and thence to the Affghan mountains, cutting off as it were and enclosing a sort of triangle, and supporting a somewhat elevated country something of the character of the Peninsular portion of India, and lying between this Salt Range and the Himalaya. The Salt Range, it will be presently seen, is an Ethnological boundary of some interest.

I now commence my survey according to Tribes and Castes.

First, I take as a great division the black aboriginal tribes of the interior hills and jungles. There can, I suppose, be no doubt that they are the remnants of the race which occupied India before the Hindus. I need not here go into any question, whether any portion of them had received any civilization from any other source. It is enough that all these tribes have many ethnological features in common. They are evidently the remains of an element, the greater portion of which has been absorbed by, and amalgamated with, the modern Indian race, and which, mixed in various degrees with the high-featured immigrants, has contributed to form the Hindoo of to-day. In the South their speech still forms the basis of the modern languages. If proof were wanting that the predominance of Caucasian features has been attained, in a great part of India, but gradually, and that it is within the historical period that these features have altogether preponderated, it is only necessary to look at the ancient sculptures of the South and West. Take for instance the caves of Elephanta near Bombay. Who, looking at the faces there cut in stone, and observing the universal thick lip and peculiar feature, can doubt that when those were cut, the non-Caucasian element was still large even among the higher classes?

My scheme, however, is not to separate any of the tribes or castes of modern Indian society, and to designate them as aboriginal. All those people who have been either completely or partially amalgamated into Hindoo society, whether as proper Hindoos or as Helots and outcasts, I regard as coming within the designations of 'Modern Indians.' I shall class as Aborigines only those tribes which still live apart, forming communities by themselves, under their own leaders, and often speaking their own peculiar languages.

As Modern Indians again I class together all the high-featured northern races, and all the various tribes, castes, and nationalities formed by them after absorbing so much of the aboriginal element as has been amalgamated with them, whether they are now Hindoos, Mahommedans, or of any other religion. Of course they are mainly Hindoos. I draw no wide ethnological line between the Northern and Southern countries of India, not recognising the separate Dravidian classification of the latter as properly ethnological. It seems to me that among all the Hindoo tribes the Arian element now prevails, and that the presence, more or less, of the aboriginal element is only a question of degree. As a question of degree, I do not think that there is, at any geographical parallel, any decided line. It is remarked by Max Muller that languages are seldom properly speaking mixed. Vocables may be mixed, but a single grammar and structure usually prevails. Therefore the change from one language to another must in so far be sudden. It is still, I believe, open to dispute whether the grammar of the present languages of Northern India is of Sanscrit or of Aboriginal origin; but at any rate this we know, that in the North the Arians gained so rapid and complete an ascendancy as to introduce their own radical words, numerals, &c., and to render the language essentially Arian, while in the South the Aborigines held out longer, the tide of Arian immigration was more gradual, and the Aboriginal grammar and radicals formed the mould which was only filled up by a large over-lay of Arian words. The change then of language takes place, where passing southwards we exchange the Maratta for Telugu and Canarese. But looking at the people, we see no radical change of feature or characteristics. The last of those who are more properly Arian in language, are not essentially superior to the first of those whose language is by its structure classed as Dravidian. The Marattas who are classed as Northerners (though they probably take their name and much of their blood from the aboriginal Mhars and such like tribes, whose features survive in their monuments) have no decided advantage over their Canarese neighbours; on the contrary, the Canarese of Belgaum and Dharwar are deemed superior to the Marattas of the adjoining districts. And to a traveller in Mysore and most of the Southern countries, the general features and appearance of the people is, I think, not very greatly less Arian than that of the lower classes of Hindustanees. The truth I take to be, not only that in a mixture of races there is a tendency of the higher, more marked, and more prominent type to predominate, but also that it may well be that, although the people speaking a Dravidian language in the South, may always by force of numbers have linguistically prevailed over each separate batch of immigrants, and so far annexed them, still by successive immigrations, notwithstanding a Dravidian form of speech, the Arian blood has come in reality greatly to prevail. The mere fact that they are recognised as Orthodox Hindoos, seems to imply the Northern origin of all the better castes in the South, and that is their own account of their origin. I have no doubt that the Southern Hindoos may be generally classed as Arians, and that the Southern society is in its structure, its manners, and its laws and institutions an Arian society. After all, in their main characteristics, the Southern people are very like those of the North.

Among some of the inferior tribes of the South, the remains of the thick lips, the very black skin, and other features may, as I have said, still be traced, but, colour perhaps excepted, the aboriginal features are probably gradually wearing away.

Notwithstanding the identity in the main of the North and the

South, it will be seen when I come to details, that the change of language very much puzzles and baffles me in the attempt to trace the tribes and castes from North to South, and in fact causes a substantial gap in the contiguity of my survey, which I trust that others will fill. To return to a geological metaphor, there is as it were a serious *fault* at the point where the change of languages takes place. A similar series of strata goes on upon the other side, but I can't exactly identify the particular veins and say which is which. The same series of classes with similar characteristics prevail in the South, and, knowing that they must have come from the North in a continuous stream, one feels sure that they must be identical with Northern congeners. It remains for those who have an intimate knowledge of the country on either side of the Fault to connect the broken links. Meantime, with the exception of the Bramins (who may be traced all through India), I must notice the people of the Southern countries separately.

Commonly as the term is used, it may be well to say a word in justification of the use of the term 'Arians' as applied to all the Northern people. Not only are they known by the Southerners as Aryas, (see Buchanan,) but in fact I believe the term to be the correct one. I am aware that some have set down the Jats and others as Scythians and Turanians. I have no intention of quarrelling with any one who chooses to call them Scythians, for that is a very wide and uncertain word, which may have been applied to Germans as well as to Jats. But if the word Turanian is applied to Punjabees, in the sense of expressing that branch of the human race which we call Mongolian, the squat, flat-faced, peculiar eyed, beardless people of Central, Northern, and Eastern Asia, then I say that the term is wholly inapplicable. Anything more unlike Mongols than the tall, handsome, high featured, long bearded Punjabees it is impossible to imagine. To say, on the strength of some obscure similarity of names, that any of these people are Mongols and Tartars, is not only as unfounded as the connection between Monmouth and Macedon, but is opposed to the most palpable physical facts. It would be about as reasonable to say that the people of Tamworth are really Negroes of Timbuctoo, because Tam and Tim are clearly the same word. An Englishman is not more unlike a Negro, than a Punjabee is unlike a Mongol.

Assuming then that the North-Indians are what we call Caucasian in feature, the only question would be whether they may be in any degree Semitic. This there seems to be no ground for supposing; there is no radical trace of Semitic language, and we nowhere trace any considerable immigration by land of Arabian or other Semitic tribes. That being so, I hope that I may properly call the North-Indians Arians, and extend the title to all those Indians in whom Arian features predominate, even where they have been softened down and otherwise qualified by intermixture.

Although I believe any division of the Northern tribes in India into Arian and Turanian to be quite out of place, I have long had an impression that the result of a thorough examination may be to divide the Indian Arians into two classes; the earlier Arians, the descendants of the most ancient Hindus, a people acute, literary, skilled in arts, but not very warlike, and rather aristocratic than democratic in their institutions; and the later Arians, warlike people—possibly once Scythians—democratic in their institutions, and rather energetic than refined and literary. War does not seem to have been one of the earliest arts; we are told that the earliest Egyptians have left little in their monuments which suggests that art, and it may be that the earliest Hindus had little occasion for it, meeting with but simple and peaceful savages. The later Arians appear, in my view, in their manners and institutions more nearly to resemble the German tribes, and perhaps to them might more properly be applied the term Indo-Germanic. The earliest Hindus appear to have had an intimate connection with the hills immediately adjoining India on the North-west, and there may well have been gradual immigration from the hills to the plains. But at a later period, when the people in possession of the North of India had acquired considerable power, it seems hardly possible that large bodies of conquering immigrants should have found their way to India by Cabul and the Khyber Pass. Those defiles are far too difficult to be forced by strangers in large bodies accompanied by women and children. The Affghans, and those who have ruled the Affghans, have had the command of the direct route; but if Rajpoots, Jats &c. came as immigrant peoples, they probably came by the route of the Bolan, occupying the high pastoral lands about Quettah, and thence descending into the plains below. We shall find accordingly that the Jats (whom on this theory we may suppose to have been the latest comers) occupy just the area which would tally with such a mode of immigration.

In physical appearance I would divide Indian Arians into two classes, as far as we can call that a division which is only a question of degree. The people of the extreme north, the pure Arians, large, fair, high-featured, I shall call "High-Arian" in type. The prominence and beauty of their features is remarkable. The brow is remarkably high and well shaped; the nose connected by a high bridge with the high brow is also well shaped, sometimes straight, more often slightly curved; the eyes are very fine, the lips thin, mouth of a good shape, the beard long and full. The type once seen cannot be mistaken. The prominence of the brow in adults somewhat conceals the eye, but in the children it is something marvellous. On the other hand, the more subdued features, more frequently approaching a low and snub-nosed type, and resembling those which are common among the lower classes in Europe, are in India generally accompanied by a shorter (but still pretty robust) form, a skin darker (but still more brown than black), and an appearance altogether inferior, but yet not aboriginal in its style. This I shall call the "Low-Arian" type.

In addition to the two main divisions, of aborigines, and modern Indians, I propose to put under a third division, those whom I shall generally describe as "Borderers," that is, the tribes on the borders, whose blood and manners show the influence of immigrants of races other than those already noticed. These meet and mix with the native populations, and form some marked classes. On the West Coast there has been a considerable immigration of Arabs and others; the same has been the case in Lower Sinde. Along the whole line of the Himalayas, and on the whole of the Eastern Frontier, Turanian races meet the Indians.

Thus then I have three main classes:—

1. Aborigines,
2. Modern Indians, and
3. Borderers.

The 2nd are of course by far the largest and most important class.

Besides making the distinction among modern Indians of high and low Arians, there are one or two other points which I would notice, before going into details.

I should like to class Hindus as High and Low Hindus. There is a full-blown style of Hindus (principally Hindustanees) who have adopted to the full all the modern Hindu superstitions and observances, who are very particular about their cooking and such matters, and in consequence generally eat but one large meal once a day, whose widows may not re-marry, and who are in a continual state of anxiety about the rules of their caste. These are high Hindus. There is another class of Hindus, much less particular, whose religion and religious observances sit very easy upon them, whose widows re-marry, and whose prejudices do not prevent their taking good wholesome meals as often as they can. Such are the Punjabees, some of the Hindustanees, and I believe a good many of the Southerners. These I would call low Hindus.

With respect to caste, whatever there may once have been, there is now no proper Military caste. The fighting and dominant tribes are, it may be said invariably, in the main Agricultural and are classed as such. Why the old Vaisyas are sometimes said to have been the Merchant class I do not understand. It is clear that they were the body of free people, whose duty it was to till the land, keep flocks, carry on trade, and many other things besides. The Soodras were the Helots, "whose duty is expressed in one word, viz., to serve the other three classes," evidently the conquered race. Now-a-days it seems to be considered that, except the Brahmins, almost all are Soodras, that is, all have more or less intermixed with the lower races and lost their purity of blood. Hindu Society then has lost its former great divisions, and has been split up into an infinite variety of decent castes of mixed parentage, who have absorbed the old Soodras, as well as the Vaisyas. Under them again new tribes of Helots are found, probably tribes more recently conquered.

The Agricultural tribes may, for the most part, be divided into three classes :—

1. Those whose proclivities were originally Pastoral, and generally somewhat predatory.

2. Agricultural tribes in the proper sense, that is, Farmers—men who both cultivate the soil on a large scale, and keep cattle and waggons when the country is favorable to that kind of Farming. These tribes are also most frequently those who have the greatest

Military vigor, and most democratic constitution, and generally occupy the dominant position in the country.

3. The gardening tribes, *i. e.*, those who do the smaller and finer farming and kitchen gardening. These are generally peaceable and unmartial people.

I shall not always exactly follow this order, but shall take first the tribes who are politically most important.

The Mercantile tribes I shall notice separately, and then the Writer tribes, where such tribes exist. When I speak of literate occupation, I mean exclusive of mercantile business, that being almost everywhere in the hands of mercantile castes. Next come the Artizans, and finally the Helots and inferior classes.

The Aborigines.

In giving any general description of the Aborigines, I must premise that it is by no means to be supposed that all or most of the individuals of the race will correspond to the description. The fact is that the Aboriginal tribes now remaining are but like scattered remnants of a substance floating here and there in a mass of water, into which they have been all but melted, and in which they are on the point of disappearing. By far the greater part of their substance has already commingled in the fluid around them, the remainder is saturated with it, and it is only in the very kernel and inner centre of the largest lumps, that something like the pure original substance is to be found. There is not in Peninsular India any very large tract of very high and difficult country; the Aboriginal tribes are for the most part not collected in any great masses supporting one another, but are found in small and detached tribes here and there, wherever a bunch of hills or an unhealthy jungle has given them a refuge. Even in these retreats, they are everywhere closely surrounded by, and to a considerable extent penetrated, or as I called it, saturated with an Arian element which modifies both their features and their language.

Another circumstance has perhaps almost as much contributed to modify many of these tribes. There seems to be no doubt that at points in Indian history, where one dominant race has given way and before another has been fully established, tribes of hardy aborigines from the hills, accustomed to the use of weapons in the chase and probably to a good deal of robbery, have come down on the enervated people of the plains and valleys, and have established a temporary dominion over considerable tracts of country. Just as on the departure of the Romans and before the establishment of Teutonic rule, the Picts and Scots came down on the cultivated portions of Britain, so it seems certain that, at periods long subsequent to the glories of the Solar and Lunar Rajpoots, Aboriginal Bhurs and Cheroos established considerable principalities in parts of Oude and of the Benares and Behar Provinces. So also Bheels, Mairs, and Kolees seem to have had at one time considerable power in Rajpootana and Goojerat. In comparatively modern times, the Bedas or Beders (whose name is I believe really identical with that of the Vedahs or Vedders) seem to have established considerable power in the South, and the Gonds in Central India acquired quite a wide dominion. Under such circumstances, the savage conquerors are generally themselves socially conquered, and the tribes so situated, while gaining some civilisation, lose much of their peculiarities of blood and feature, and more of their language.

By far the largest tract in which the Aboriginal tribes prevail, and may be said to form the mass of the inhabitants, is that extending through the hilly country from the western and southern borders of Bengal, Behar and Benares to the frontiers of the Hyderabad and Madras territories, and from the Eastern Ghats inland to the civilised portions of the Nagpore territory; but even in this tract it appears that there are evident monuments of old Hindoo civilisation, showing that Hindoos, or at any rate Sivites, had at one time a far greater hold on much of this country than they now have, and that probably after being partially civilised, it was gained back by the Aborigines. Even now this country is intersected by settled and cultivated tracts. Hindoos are scattered about it, and there is an admixture of Hindoo blood. Still, in all this part of the country, Aboriginal tribes muster very strong, and they preserve their language, their manners, and their peculiarities much better than elsewhere. It is, however, as I have said, only in the heart and kernel of the best preserved tribes, that we must look for the real original characteristics existing in a palpable and little-diluted form. In less pure specimens, they will be found less distinct. My impression is that, if we look carefully, they will seldom be altogether wanting. The *thick-lipped* expression of countenance lingers long. The Gond Raja of Nagpore is of a family for generations civilised and Mahommedan, doubtless of very far from pure Aboriginal blood, and rather fair-skinned, but even in him I noticed the thick lips as prominent as in an African. Major Tickell seems to describe the 'Hos,' who are identical with 'Lurka Coles' and closely allied to Moondahs and Sontals (one of the ugliest of races), as handsome; but everything is comparative, and I suspect that this beauty is of the same kind as that which enthusiastic African travellers are constantly discovering in Negro tribes. The Hos of the border land have probably much intermixed with Ooriahs, and are less ugly than their congeners are always described to be.

Setting aside then the numerous half-breeds, borderers, and people of imperfect type, I take it that the general physical type of all the purest Aboriginal tribes, is that which is commonly known as Negrito. They are small and slight, *very* black, face broad and flat, the thick lips already mentioned very prominent, noses broad and nostrils wide, beard scanty, hair very abundant and tangled, of a shock-headed appearance, sometimes curly or even woolly. The peculiar Mongolian or Chinese form of the eye is not conspicuous, and altogether the features and the face are rather what we best know as African than Mongolian. This description crops up everywhere in all the various descriptions of Aboriginal tribes. I have not collected all these testimonies, but I will give one or two on which I can lay my hands. Col. Dalton says, "The Jushpore Oraons are the ugliest of the race, with foreheads 'villainous low,' flat noses and projecting maxillaries, they approach the Negro in physiognomy." And again, "The Kaurs, next to the Jushpore Oraons, are the ugliest race I have seen, dark, coarse-featured, wide mouths and thick lips." In a note which he was good enough to send in answer to some inquiries which I made, he adds, "The Oraons have more of the African type of feature, and I have seen amongst them woolly heads." An isolated tribe on the East Coast, called 'Chenchwars,' are described in similar terms, and said to be "just what you might suppose to result from the crossing of the Malacca Aborigines with the common people of this country," the Malacca Aborigines being very marked Negritos. The Savage Gonds in the forests east of the Wyngunga seem to be of a similar type. So in the papers with which I have been favoured from Bombay, I find that Major Keatinge, describing the three tribes of Gonds, Koors, and Bheels who meet about Asseerghur, says, "All three tribes are very black, with a decidedly African expression when met in the centres of their country." And Capt. Probyn, speaking of the more civilised Gonds who are now, he says, finer and fairer, still adds, "with somewhat African features." Major Keatinge adds what illustrates that which I have already said, "On the outskirts of their country, their features are much modified, showing plainly that they do not succeed in keeping their blood pure. The Chiefs have generally made it a point to get women of other castes into their households, and I have consequently observed that none of them have the national features."

In the South, the Chermars of Malabar are described as "very diminutive, with a very black complexion, with not unfrequently woolly hair." And of some of the tribes of the Kodagherry hills it is said that "flattened noses, dark complexion and large white teeth filed into the form of a saw give them an African appearance." The Nagadees are said to be "in complexion invariably of the deepest black, their hair thick and curly, their features brutish, their forms diminutive." That the type which I have described prevailed among the Aborigines generally in ancient times, is evident from the Purans, where they are described in extremely uncomplimentary terms as 'vile monsters,' 'allied to monkeys,' 'as black as crows,' 'of flattened features and of dwarfish stature.' Their long thick matted hair is also particularly mentioned.

The ancient Greeks also describe the South-Indians as like Ethiopians, and it is difficult to assign any other country to the Oriental Ethiopians of Herodotus.

It may be stated, as a physical peculiarity of the Aboriginal tribes, that most of them seem to have a remarkable power of resisting malaria, and thrive in the most malarious jungles where no other human beings can live. This may, however, be the result of long habit; some tribes inhabiting healthy localities sicken easily enough elsewhere.

The languages of the Aborigines seem to have all this much in common, that they are of the structure described as Turanian. They are neither like the Monosyllabic Chinese on the one hand, nor on the other like those Arabian and African languages which seem to form their changes by variations in the body of the word. The Indian Aboriginal languages, in common with the Hindustanee, the Turkish, and some Arian tongues, seem to form declensions, conjugations, and derivations, and to supply the place of what we call 'prepositions' by *post-positions* and *post-inflections*. The verb or governing word comes at the end of the sentence, instead of at the beginning as in English, somewhat thus, our order being just reversed.

Rem	acu	tetigit
Cheez	sui-se	chuha
Thing	needle with	touched he.

The word 'Turanian,' as applied to an immense class of languages, does not, however, imply any immediate connection with Thibetans or Mongolians, from whom the Indian Aborigines are physically so world-wide asunder. It is used in that very wide sense which includes not only all the Mongolian races, but all the Polynesian races, and all the Negritoes of the Indian Archipelago, Australia, and Van Diemen's land. A few vocables are said to be found, common to the Dravidian tongues and to some other Turanian languages. But the greatest resemblance is said to be not to the nearer Mongolians, but to the most distant Finns, and it is at the same time admitted that there are at least as great indications of a special connection with the Australian Negritoes. It may then generally be said, that both in physique and in the structure of their language, the Aborigines present a type analogous to that of the Negritoes of the South Seas, Papuans, Tasmanians and others, as well as to the nearer Negritoes of Malacca and the Andamans.

That which I have already said of the general character of the laws and institutions of the Non-Arians as distinguished from the Arians, is all that I can give as common to all these tribes. On this and many other points, we require much more information.

One tribe only I must except, as quite without and beyond the general descriptions of the Aborigines which I have given, viz. the Todas of the upper plateau of the Neilgherry hills. They are not properly Hindoos, but no one who sees them, would for a moment suppose that they belong to the Negrito races. They are evidently Caucasians of a high type. In truth they are but a very small tribe; the common tradition and consent of the country makes it clear that they came as conquering immigrants to their present position at a comparatively recent period, and their pastoral habit renders their migration easy. Their language, so small a body may well have almost lost during their wanderings among Dravidians. They may be anything Caucasian, and from anywhere ; ordinary Aborigines they are not. It has been said, that in their speech some words have a resemblance to the Brahui dialect, but personally they do not seem to resemble Brahuis, they are rather like Greeks.

The points of structure which I have given, as common to all the Aboriginal languages, are, it will be observed, of the widest character. And this brings me to the fact that by the test of language the Aboriginal tribes may be divided into two great classes, having very few vocables in common. The first great division is that of the tribes speaking dialects radically allied to the civilised languages of the South, commonly called the Dravidian languages. These then I shall call the Dravidian Aborigines. There is no doubt that the wild tribes of the southern hills speak wild and primitive forms of the southern languages. The Carambers seem to be ancient Tamil speakers, the Maleasurs of the Western Ghats approach nearer to the Malayala. The Burghers and Kotahs speak a primitive Canarese, the Ramooses, a language which seems to be for the most part Telagoo.

The Gond language is as clearly Dravidian as Telagoo or Tamil, and the Gonds are so considerable a people that the Gondee might almost be added to the list of regular languages of the southern type. The name Khond is so like Gond that, next neighbours as they are, one would almost suppose the words to be the same. They are said to be different, but at any rate the Khonds also are shown by their language to be clearly Dravidian. More distant is the tongue of the Oraon tribe, to whose physical characteristics I have already alluded, and who are now found among tribes of the other division (to be presently noticed) in the Chota-Nagpore territory. But the radicals and main features of the Oraon language leave no doubt that they are of Dravidian stock—a circumstance which does not suprise us, as we learn that they are comparatively recent immigrants from the west into their present locations. East of them again, in the Rajmahal hills, we have the last of the Dravidian tribes (so far as has yet been ascertained), speaking a language akin to that of the Oraons. Those hills form a kind of knot at the extreme eastern point of the hill country of Central India. It was known that the people were entirely different from their neighbours the Santals. The latter cultivate the lower lands, and it may at first sight seem surprising that the higher grounds should be in the possession of more recent settlers of a distant southern stock. The fact, however, seems to be explained by the plundering habits of the Rajmahal hillmen. They seem to have occupied those hills as a kind of stronghold, from which they could conveniently plunder the plains around them.

The greater part of the Chota-Nagpore division and adjoining tracts is occupied by tribes whom I take as representative of the second or northern division of the Aborigines. There are 'Lurka Coles,' 'Hos,' 'Bhoomiz,' 'Moondahs,' and Santals, and wilder tribes of the border hills, all speaking dialects of a language very different from the Dravidian. In fact, so far as vocables go, no substantial connection can be traced. Max Müller speaks of these tongues as quite unconnected with any other. Still I venture to think that there seems to be some similarity of structure between them and the Dravidian languages. Major Tickell has published in the Journal of the Society a grammar of the Hos or Lurka Col language; and I note the following as a few of the peculiarities common to it and to the Dravidian tongues, as the latter are set forth by Dr. Caldwell.

First, there is the general coincidence of structure, which I have already noticed as common to all the Aboriginal tongues as well as to Hindustanee, Turkish, &c. In this respect, the northern Aborigines do not differ, and they similarly use postpositions, &c.

Further. In the Dravidian tongues there is no regular gender, all inanimate things are neuter, and the terms male and female are prefixed when necessary.

It seems to be the same in the northern aboriginal tongues.

Adjectives do not decline, nor are there degrees of comparison.

It is the same in the northern tongues.

There are two forms of the first person plural, one to include, and the other to exclude the person addressed.

This peculiarity also is found among the northern tribes, as well as in the Australian tongues.

Relative participles are used instead of relative pronouns in both classes of languages.

The northern tongues seem to be considered more highly inflected than the Dravidian, and they have a regular dual form which the others have not. The verbs have no passive voice.

It would seem to imply a higher organisation in the northern aboriginal languages, that the vocabularies show them to be more complete, and less to borrow from their neighbours all words beyond the very simplest. For instance, in the matter of numbers, while the Gonds do not go beyond ten, the Oraons beyond four, nor the Rajmahalees beyond two in Dravidian numbers, (borrowing all the rest from the Hindee,) the Coles and Santals count up to high numbers in their own tongue, only using scores instead of the decimal notation of hundreds, as do many Arian tribes. I have seen it stated that the Dravidian Khonds count by dozens.

Max Müller remarks that savage tribes, with no letters to fix their tongues, alter their speech much more rapidly than civilised nations; and it may be that, when we have two groups of people adjoining one another and with a general physical similarity, such a general structural resemblance of language as I have noticed may mark a remote common origin, even when the community of vocables can no longer be traced. But at any rate, the difference is now so wide as to establish, as I have said, two distinctly marked groups.

The generic name usually applied to the Aborigines of the hill country of Chota-Nagpore, Mirzapore and Rewah is 'Coles' or 'Koles.' Europeans apply the term to the Dravidian Oraons as well as to the others, but perhaps erroneously. It is difficult to say to which tribes the name is properly applied, for most of them have other distinctive names. But in the south of the Chota-Nagpore country, about Singbhoom, &c. it is certainly applied to the 'Lurka Coles,' and I can myself testify that on the Mirzapore-Jubbulpore road, the Aborigines are called by the natives Coles or Kolees, which they volunteered to explain to me to be the same word "which you call Coolee." On the Bombay side again a very numerous class of Aborigines are styled Kolees. In the Simla hills also, the inferior people are known as Kolees. Altogether I have myself little doubt that the ordinary word Coolee, as applied to a bearer of burdens or labourer, is the same word, and that in short it is the word generally applied by the Northern Indians to the Aboriginal tribes, most of whom they reduced to the condition of Helots.

There seems to be good reason to suppose that the original form of the word was 'Kola' or 'Kolar.' In fact, India seems to have been known to the ancients (who approached it coastwise from the West) as Colara or Coolee-land (Asiatic Researches, Vol. IX.) and the people as Colaurians. If Kolar be the original form of Kolee, it would seem not improbable that, as in the mouths of some tribes by dropping the '*r*' it became Kola or Kolee, so in the mouths of others, by dropping the '*l*' it would become Koar, Kaur, Koor, Khar or Khor, a form which would embrace a large number of those tribes as now designated. I propose then to call the northern tribes Kolarian or Coolee Aborigines.

One may see frequent allusion to Kolarees or Colleries in the south of India. It appears that the word there used is properly 'Kallar.' In the Canarese language, the word 'Kallar,' it seems, simply means a thief or robber, and hence some of the predatory Aborigines of the hills, are designated Kallars or robbers, just as the thieves of Central Asia are called 'Kazaks' or 'Cossacks.' The word is applied so differently from that of Coolee, that there may fairly be doubt of its being the same. But the subject is worthy of farther inquiry, and if it prove that in fact the two words are identical, the term Coolee or Kolarian must be applied to the Aboriginal tribes generally, not to one division of them. Meantime, however, I apply it to the Northern tribes only, but I confess I have misgivings whether the more general sense may not prove to be the true one.

Beyond the difference of language, I am unable to state with confidence any very marked features distinguishing the Dravidian and Kolarian groups of tribes (each taken as a whole) from one another. But a marked difference in habits, manners, and national characteristics, has been found to exist where the two classes are in the closest contiguity. The Santals and Rajmahalees are known to present a marked contrast, and on the Chota-Nagpore plateau I am told that "the difference is so great, that they appeared to be quite another nation," and "their customs, appearance, even manners, are very different." Of these differences we have not the details, but I hope that they may be furnished in Col. Dalton's promised paper on the Coles.

The Kolarian Santals are a very ugly race, and I gather that their neighbours, the Dravidian Rajmahalees, have rather the advantage of them in this respect, but these latter have probably kidnapped a good many Arian women from the plains. I have fancied that I have noticed in some of the 'Dhangar' labourers in and about Calcutta, a peculiar little 'pique' 'retroussé' sort of nose, as distinguished from the flat broad-nosed features of the Santals, but this scarcely amounts to an observation. It may be noticed that in the passages which I have quoted in regard to the general type of the Aborigines, the African style was more especially attributed to Dravidian Oraons, Gonds and Chenchwars, &c. The Kolarians, Kaurs, Khairwars and Koors, are also represented as only one degree less ill-favoured; so, on the whole, I imagine that in point of personal appearance there is not much to choose between the two groups. Ethnographers seem to distinguish the Negritoes of the Southern Seas into two groups, a woolly or curly-haired group, and a straight-haired group; perhaps there may be found to have been some such division in India.

The Santals and most of their immediate congeners, are certainly a more simple, mild, and industrious race than the Rajmahalees, Gonds, Khonds, and Southern Kallar tribes; but again the Lurka Coles seem to be warlike, and the hill Khorewahs are described as wild savages, armed with battle axes and bows and arrows. On the whole, I should rather imagine that the Kolarians are more frequently good Coolees, and the Dravidians oftener troublesome Kallars.

The descriptions of the Aborigines as a good-natured people, ever dancing and singing (in a way that reminds one of the pleasanter descriptions of the Negroes,) I find to be applied to the Kolarians,—Santals, Moondahs, Khorewahs, &c.—more than to the Dravidian tribes.

As respects religion, although the indications are too slight for any confident generalisation, the accounts of the Kolarian creed seem pleasanter than those of the Dravidian beliefs and rites. The latter seem to deal in demonology, fetishism, frantic dances, bloody and even human sacrifices, in a way which reminds us of the worst African types; while several different accounts of Northern Aborigines, in widely different parts of the country, represent them as reverencing in an inoffensive way the sun, moon, and Lord of tigers, and mild and innocent Bhoots or household spirits. The superstitious belief in tigers' claws as a charm, is shared with the Aborigines by all the Hindustanees. Another practice of the Aborigines the latter also have in hilly tracts, the heaping up cairns of stones at particular points, and tying bits of rag to a particular tree as votive offerings. This last may be seen anywhere, and these practices are probably very widely spread.

If there really be such a distinction between the Dravidian and Kolarian religions as that at which I have hinted, it is very like a similar distinction in Africa. In a work on South Africa by the Rev. Mr. Grout, we are told that the gods of the Hottentots are above, the sun, moon, &c. while those of the Kaffirs and more warlike Negroes south of the line are *below*, demons and evil spirits. Among some of the latter too are seen the horrid rites and bloody sacrifices. It strikes me that there is some resemblance in appearance between Hottentots and Santals.

A curious testimony to the ancient rights of the Indian '*Boomeas*' or people of the soil, is the practice in many parts of Central India where Hindu chiefs are dominant, that a new chief on his accession receives the *teka* or investiture from the blood of an Aboriginal Kole, Gond or Bheel.

I proceed to mention the various tribes in detail, so far as my imperfect knowledge of them permits.

The Aboriginal tribes now living apart from the general population in the South of India, appear to be very small and scattered. They are there for the most part absorbed in the general social system. Pariahs and others, as is well known, merely form a lower social grade. The robber tribes, Beders and such like, seem for the most part to have robbed themselves into a respectable and even aristocratical position. The Beders in some parts of Mysore now form a considerable portion of the population, and they have many Polygarships. There seems to be some doubt whether the Badagtas and Kotas of the lower Neilgherry hills are properly Aborigines, they being, it appears, immigrants in those parts, and the Carambers the true Aborigines. I have not been able to meet with any very connected or detailed account of the thoroughly Aboriginal tribes of the hills and forests of the Neilgherries, Pulneys, and Western Ghats. The word *Maleasur* seems to mean simply a hillman, and the more proper tribal designations appear to be Carambers, Irulars, Puliars, and Veders. These seem to be tribes in the very lowest stage of savageness, with in fact scarcely any agriculture, mere men of the woods. They are represented as of very diminutive stature, with thickly matted locks and supple limbs, living under trees in caverns or in the rudest wigwams, keeping sheep or collecting forest produce, very stupid but also very mild and inoffensive, except that they have a great reputation as sorcerers, and themselves believing in a religion of demons and witchcraft, are by their neighbours believed to be highly gifted that way. Altogether they seem to be very inferior to the simple but sturdy and industrious Coolees of the north.

The Chenchwars, already mentioned, and several very petty and isolated tribes exist in the Eastern Ghats about and north of Madras. I can only give the names of "Chendaurs" and "Yende" as near the Kistna and Pulicat Lake. Allusions seem to be made to the existence of Aboriginal or quasi-Aboriginal tribes at different points in the Western Ghats and Coasts; the name of "Chermars" and "Neade" are mentioned in Travancore and Cochin, but they are no doubt the same as Chermars and Nagadees, the slaves of Malabar. The Dhers and Ramooses of the centre and west of the Peninsula seem to be mixed with the general population. On all these points more precise information is much required.

It is not till we cross the Godavery to the north, that we come to the country really held by the Aborigines.

In the highlands between the Godavery and the Mahanaddee, the savage Khonds, notorious for their human sacrifices, are to the East, the barbarous and less known tribes of Gonds to the West and more in the interior.

The Khonds appear to be in contact with Hindus and to have some of that race among them. Their blood is probably somewhat mixed, and they are not described as so ugly and ultra-Aboriginal as some other tribes.

Of the Gonds of the forests of Bustar and thence running up towards the Wyngunga we know very little, except that they are extreme savages, black, ugly, barbarous and dangerous. The name "Marees" seems to be there applied to them, and they appear to be nearly independent, owning a scant allegiance to chiefs whose blood is for the most part Gond. From thence the Gonds extend a long way North, and occupy a broad tract east and west wherever the country is jungly or hilly, but becoming more and more civilised and more dominant over others as we go northwards. The valley of Sumbhulpore may be taken as for the most part marking the division between the Gond country on one side, and that of the Aborigines of northern stock on the other.

On the east the Gonds, under the name of Gours, extend into the borders of the Chota-Nagpore agency in Oodeypore and Sirgoojah, but they are there much Hinduised and have lost their language. The Raja of Sirgoojah, though pretending to be a Rajpoot, is suspected to be a Gour; at any rate the Gours are there the dominant tribe. Thence westward along the line of the Sautpoora hills, through all the hilly country of the districts of Mandla, Jubbulpore, Seonee, Chandwara, Baitool and Hoshangabad, in fact in some degree to the neighbourhood of Asseerghur, the Gonds predominate. In the wilder parts, they speak their own Aboriginal language, and seem there to be a simple and not intractable people, following both pastoral and agricultural pursuits. In the older maps, the name Gondwana is given to a wider tract of country in this part of Central India, being that which was in modern times rather politically than ethnologically Gond. The Gonds (in a somewhat civilised form) were in fact for some time masters of all this part of the country, including the open and cultivated tracts about Nagpore, Raepore, Jubbulpore, &c. and perhaps as far as Ellichpore on the one hand, and on the other to the south of the Godavery, where some of them are found among the ordinary Telinga population. Deogurh in the Sautpooras was the chief seat of their power. They immediately preceded the Marattas. These latter ousted them from the open and valuable tracts, and they do not now form any considerable part of the population of the plain country, but they maintained a feudal dominion in much of the hilly country; and to this day not only the chiefs and large zemindars of the Sautpoora range, but most of the men of considerable position in parts of Saugor and other districts north of the Nerbudda are, I understand, Gonds, diluted or improved Gonds as the case may be, (most of them wish to become Rajpoots, and others have become Mussulmans), but still Gonds.

Following up the Dravidian tribes, we next come to the Oraons, now located in the midst of Kolarian tribes and much mixed up with them. The Gonds or Gours have been mentioned as found in a not very pure form in the west of Oodeypore, and Sirgoojah of the Chota-Nagpore division. In the highlands to the east of those states and of Jushpore, the Oraons are found. Col. Dalton mentions them as forming the greater part of the population of a considerable portion of the Jushpore highlands, and it is these whom he describes as the ugliest of the race. Thence eastwards the Oraons have pushed themselves into the proper country of the Moondahs (of Kolarian race) in the plateau of the Chota-Nagpore district and adjoining country. They must have been strong, to effect an ingress to a country not originally their own, but I do not understand that they are now at all dominant over the others. In fact they seem to have very much adopted the habits of the Kolarians, among whom or in contact with whom they live, are industrious and laborious, and as much as the others contribute to the supply of the labour market of Bengal. I understand that they form a considerable proportion of the Calcutta *Dhangars*; that last term being one the proper meaning of which I cannot ascertain, but which, so far as I can learn, is applied generically to the aboriginal labourers in Calcutta.

Separated from the Oraons by a considerable space (principally of lower but still more or less hilly country, occupied by mixed tribes of Kolarians, Hindustanees, and Bengalees), are the Dravidian Rajmahalees, whose proper tribal name, I have not ascertained. They are sometimes called Maler, but that is merely the Dravidian form for mountaineers, the word applied to so many of these tribes.

These are the men who are well known in connection with Mr. Cleveland's endeavours to tame and reform them. They seem to have been in those days terrible depredators. That all the parts of India adjoining the Central hills, both at this point and throughout a considerably wider range, were in times of anarchy dreadfully subject to injury from the hill-men, is still attested by the numerous and extensive 'ghatwallee' tenures held all along the foot of the hills and about the Ghats and passes. They are particularly numerous in the Bhaugulpore and Beerbhoom districts, adjoining the Rajmahal hills on either side. Such estates pay little or no revenue, but are held on the condition of guarding the passes against hill robbers, murderers, and cattle-lifters. The hill-men have been successfully reclaimed,

I believe that they cultivate quietly, and there appears to be now little complaint against them. Organised and serious raids on the plains are, I understand, unknown. The Rajmahal men are those who were enlisted into the British military service to form the local corps known as the Bhaugulpore Hill Rangers; but when the usually quiet Santals were impelled by a sense of wrong to a headlong sort of rebellion, the other (and it was supposed more military) race forming the Rangers, when opposed to them, by no means distinguished themselves, and they have since, I think, been disbanded.

I now pass to the Kolarian tribes. The more civilised and numerous tribes of this race, occupying an extensive country about 150 miles west from Calcutta, and known as Moondahs, Bhoomiz, Hos, and Santals, speak languages so nearly identical, that they may all be regarded as Sub-divisions of one people. They are in fact very like one another in many ways. They occupy most of the British districts of Chota-Nagpore, Singbhoom, Maunbhoom, and the hilly part of Bhaugulpore (Rajmahal hills excepted) now known as the Santal Pergunnahs; also parts of West Burdwan, Midnapore and Cuttack. They are a simple industrious people, and are reputed to be remarkably honest and truthful. Their country is healthy and, unlike most aboriginal tribes in most parts of the world, they seem by no means to be dying out, but multiply and supply the labour market. Partly on account of the cheapness of labour in their country, partly on account of their tractable disposition and freedom from all caste and food prejudices, and more especially, I think, because of that want of attachment to the soil which distinguishes the Aboriginal from the Arian, they are much sought after and highly prized as labourers. Many of them are settled in the service of Bengal Indigo-planters; they are very well known as labourers on the Railways, roads, and other works of Western Bengal; and they are now, I believe, the favourite material for emigration to Assam. Unfortunately, however, coming from a healthy high and dry country, they have not that capacity for resisting malaria for which the wilder tribes are remarkable, and seem to die very rapidly.

In the Chota-Nagpore country, the 'Moondahs' seem to have so far adopted Arian manners, as to live together in considerable villages, instead of apart in detached houses or isolated hamlets, according to the common practice of these tribes; but I am told that so great is their instability and want of attachment to any particular spot, that not unfrequently, on some petty quarrel with their zemindar, a whole village will abandon their houses and seek other locations, or put themselves under the guidance of a Coolee recruiting-agent. The Hos and Bhoomiz* of the lower parts of Singbhoom and Maunbhoom, seem to be tolerably civilised. The Santals, though geographically near the plains, seem to be among the most shy and socially-isolated of the race. They cultivate the lower lands of their country, but seem to have kept very much to themselves, and to prefer locations surrounded by jungle and segregated from the world. They too, however, have now taken much to labour for hire, and they must have become intimate with Europeans. In the case of these people is to be found practical illustration of a truth of wider application in India, viz. that in a mere pecuniary and commercial point of view, tact and scrupulous fairness in dealing with the natives are more effectual than all other means, and go farther than any laws and any administration. I believe that certain of the Railway Engineers, who have gained the special confidence of the Santals and allied tribes, construct the railway mile for mile infinitely cheaper than any others.

On the borders of the hills, a set of half-breeds seem to be not only by profession Ghatwals, but to constitute a sort of caste under that name.

I have alluded to the language of these Kolarian tribes. One would hope or expect here to find the origin of the non-Arian elements of the Hindee and other northern languages. This, however, has not yet been so. It is difficult to distinguish between words borrowed by the Aborigines from the modern Hindustanee or Bengalee and those of a common origin. A few of the words in Hodgson's lists are like Hindee, but most of them seem to be Arian words. Some words seem to be used throughout India as 'Donga,' a boat, and some are words of much wider use as 'Ka' 'Kahee' or 'Kova,' a crow and 'Pussi,' a cat. It is then no doubt the case that the very brief and imperfect vocabularies of the Kolarian tongues yet published, have not shown an immediate connection with any other known language. More

* Bhoomiz, I believe merely means 'people of the soil' from *Bhoomi*, being nearly the same word as the Persian 'Zemindar.' What the Hindoo tribes are to the Mahommedans, the aborigines are to the Hindoos.

minute inquiry would be very desirable. Besides a more exact and full grammar, I think it would be well to separate out from the Hindee a list of non-Sanscrit words of common use, (and which are not also common to the greater part of the world, such as "*kowa*," a crow, and some of the universal Turanian words), and having thus got what I may call a *Hindee proper* vocabulary, to compare it carefully with the dialects of the Santals, &c.

In addition to the semi-civilised tribes which I have mentioned, nearly the same language is spoken by the wilder Lurka Coles of the hills to the West of the Singbhoom district. North of these latter again, in the highest hills to the North of Jushpore, and in those between Sirgoojah and Palamow, Col. Dalton mentions a considerable tribe called Khorewahs, who speak much the same language, whose manners and habits are the same, and who are evidently of the same stock, though much less civilised; some, he says, utterly savage and almost Nomadic. They are said to be of small stature, but better looking and lighter than their neighbours, the Dravidian Oraons, with shaggy heads of hair and some beard.

Mention is made of some other very wild tribes scattered about the Chota-Nagpore division, Kherrias (who are a mystery even to Col. Dalton), Bendkurrs and Birhores in the south of the division, and Bhuhars or Boyars (not to be confounded with very different Bhuyas to be subsequently noticed) in the north; but the languages and affinities of these tribes have not been ascertained sufficiently to place them. They are described as "regularly wild inhabitants of the hills and jungles, who have no fixed villages, but move about from place to place, burning down the jungles, sowing in the ashes, and after reaping what is produced, going elsewhere."

On the Sumbulpore borders, the Coles, intermixed among the Gonds, are said to be known as "Kirkees."

Mr. Samuells mentioned a wild tribe in the jungles of Cuttack, whom he calls 'Janguas,' perfect savages, small, slender, nearly naked, and horrid in appearance. They speak a strange language, and he gives a few words, some of which seem like the language of the Santals, &c., as 'Minnah,' one, and 'Bana,' two.

The Aboriginal tribes near Cuttack strike a bargain by breaking a straw.

In some places the word 'Soor' or 'Sourah' seems to be used, as if the same as 'Santal;' and Mr. Stirling, in an article on Cuttack, (in the Asiatic Researches) enumerates 'Santals' and 'Soors' separately among the tribes of Coles. It would seem then as if Soors or Sourahs were a tribe of Santals on the borders of the Cuttack division. But the Soors under the hills north of the Mahanaddee, while described as small, mean, and very black, and like the Santals naturally harmless, peaceable and industrious, are also said to be without moral sense and ready to cut firewood or other men's throats indifferently, an accusation not, I think, brought against the Santals.

Again, Macpherson tells us, that the hill tribes *south* of the Khonds, and running up to near the Godavery, are *Sourahs*. That is quite a different location, and I have not found any farther account of these Sourahs. Caldwell says that the Tamil people were anciently called 'Sorahs,' but as they are the most Dravidian of all the southern people, they can hardly be allied to the Kolarian Santals, and the word must be different. The whole subject requires a good deal of fresh light.

Passing north, I have till now reserved, for separate notice, the tribes chiefly prevailing in the district of Palamow, the hilly country of Mirzapore and Rewah, and the borders of Benares and Behar. These are the Aboriginal tribes most directly in contact with the modern Hindustanees, and there is this difficulty about classifying them, that I have not been able to ascertain their original language. They now generally speak some sort of dialect of the Hindee, and are more mixed with the Hindustanees, perhaps I may say generally more civilised, than the tribes located farther in the interior of the hills. The principal tribe of these parts are called 'Kharwars' or 'Kharawars.' There is also a widely spread tribe of 'Rajwars.' A division of the Kharwars are called 'Bhogtahs.' The Kharwars seem to be altogether the dominant tribe of Palamow and Singrowlee (the Mirzapore hill country). Both Kharwars and Rajwars are also found in considerable numbers westward, in parts of Sirgoojah and Jushpore, while to the north-east, in the parts of the plains adjoining the hills, they are numerous. In the Gya district, near the hills, the Rajwars are the chief labouring class. They live in the villages as a kind of serfs and bearers of burdens, carry palanquins, and when out of employ, are apt to be thieves and robbers. A little farther west, the Kharwars seem to perform the same functions; they are mentioned by Buchanan as in the outskirts of the Patna and Arrah Districts. On the road from Mirzapore to Jubbulpore, where it passes through Rewah, &c., the palanquin bearers and coolies are Aborigines. When I passed that way some time ago, not having then gone into the subject, I did not ask the particular tribe, nor have I since been able to ascertain it, but in all probability they are Kharwars.

All these people have in their faces unmistakeable marks of their aboriginal origin. But they speak Hindee. This then brings us to the difficulty about language. Col. Dalton is not aware of any Aboriginal language spoken by the Kharwars. I have had the impression that in the Mirzapore district they spoke their own language; and Capt. Blunt, who in the last century made a remarkable journey from Chunar right through the hills to the Godavery (see Asiatic Researches, Vol. 7), almost at the outset of his journey mentions the Kharawars of the Singrowlee hills as very savage, and speaking a separate and quite unintelligible language. But the Rev. R. C. Mather of Mirzapore, who has been good enough to write for me a note on the subject (of which I have already made use), and who refers to a tour made by the Rev. Mr. Jones, is unable to say that any aboriginal language exists in these parts. He says that both the Kharwars and another similar tribe, locally called 'Majhwars,' speak the Hindee, or at least understand it when spoken. It would be very interesting to ascertain if the remains of an original language exists among these people, for with them more especially we should expect to find the non-Aryan Hindee roots. If aboriginal tribes so situated have no separate language of their own, it may arise from either of two causes; either they may have abandoned their own language and adopted that of the people who are flooding over and as it were submerging them; or the fact may be that, in its most radical parts, the language of these latter having been the same as their own, an influx of vocables on this common basis may altogether obliterate the landmarks by which languages are distinguished. Till however, this is cleared up, I think that we must on other grounds class the Kharwars, &c. with Kolarians rather than with Dravidians. Mr. Mather, quoting Mr. Jones, says that, passing on from the Kharwars, he came to the 'Oraons,' in whom he found "the difference from the Mirzapore Hill people to be so great, that they appeared to be quite another nation." In fact, the Oraons are now a good deal interposed between the Kharwars and Kolarian Moondahs, but Col. Dalton also says that the Kharwars and Oraons, though in contact, are very unlike one another in language, appearance, manners and customs. The Kharwars, he says, are not quite so African looking as the Oraons, but some of them seem to be not much better favoured. A long connection with the plains would best account for the adoptions of the language and some of the manners of the plains-people by the Kharawars and Rajwars. And here the question has suggested itself to me, whether they may not perhaps be identified with the Cheroos and Bhurs, those aboriginal tribes whose dominion in the plain country to the north of these hills is matter of history, who seem certainly to have come from and to have gone to the country now inhabited by these tribes, and who from this point of their history almost or wholly disappear. Buchanan seems to speak ambiguously, sometimes classing Kharawars and Cheroos together, sometimes treating of them as separate. While mentioning the Cheroos as nearly extinct in the plains, he speaks of them as still existing in numbers in the high country within the hills. In the accounts of the latter country, on the other hand, I find no mention of either Cheroos or Bhurs under those names. Farther inquiry seems necessary. Our use of Roman letters applied to native names is very uncertain, and if we could suppose the C in Cheroo to be pronounced hard as in Cole, Cheroo would become Kheroo, and Kheroo would be not very different from the Khara of Kharawar (the 'war' is a mere termination), while Khara might again be connected with the name of the Kolarian Khorewahs already mentioned, and with the *Koors*, equally Kolarian, to be subsequently noticed. Again, the Bhurs are more commonly known as 'Rajbhurs;' may not Rajhbur have been corrupted into 'Rajwar?'

The present dominant position of the Kharwars in a considerable country would seem much to tally with the idea of their representing the tribes once so famous. Both the Rajas of Singrowlee and Jushpore are Kharwars, however they may claim an origin from Rajpoot foundlings, and they are the people who most affect what Col. Dalton calls 'refining into Rajpoots.' Although many of them may have achieved a good deal of improvement in their blood and appearance, they are not originally a handsome race, for Col. Dalton expressly tells us that in the more remote parts, the Kharwars of Palamow, and especially the Bhogtahs, are very ugly and ill-favoured. Like the other aborigines, they have no proper caste and eat anything.

I leave, for separate notice, a very numerous tribe all along the borders of Bengal, Orissa, and part of Bahar, called Bhuyas, whose connection with the races above described is not clear.

In this region of India, it only remains to mention one more Aboriginal tribe, called Kaurs, found in the extreme west of the Chota-Nagpore Agency about Korea, Oodeypore, and the adjoining parts of the territory of Nagpore proper, the Pergunnah of Korbah of Chatteesgurh. They are described as a very industrious thriving people, considerably advanced in civilisation. They now affect Hindoo traditions, pretend to be descended from the defeated remnants of the Kooroos who fought the Pandavas, worship Siva and speak Hindee, but in appearance they are ultra-aboriginal, very black, with broad noses and thick lips, and eat fowls, &c., bury most of their dead, and contemn Bramins; so that their Hindooism is scarcely skin-deep.

From the last mentioned point westward, through a broad tract of country, the plains are occupied by the ordinary Indian Arians, the hills and forests by the Gonds (who here in the centre of India meet the Hindustanees on the North, the Telingas on the South, and the Marattas on the West); and we do not again come to Kolarian Aborigines, till we get in fact to the West of India. There is then a hiatus, as respects the Kolarians, of four or five degrees of longitude, where by the advance of the conquering Gonds they have probably been split asunder. It somewhat singularly happens that the first people of this race whom we come to in the West, bear as nearly as possible the same name as the last we left in the East. The latter were called 'Kaurs.' In the Western Sautpooras, in the hills about Gawalghur near Ellichpore, and thence towards Indore, is a tribe called '*Coour*' or Koor Koos. These people speak an undoubtedly Kolarian language. The name is sufficiently near to *Gour* to cause them to have been sometimes confounded with their neighbours, the Gonds, but the difference is clear. In the notes with which I have been favoured from Bombay, Major Keatinge mentions them as "a tribe of Gonds calling themselves Koor Koos," but he goes on to distinguish them from the Gonds, mentioning the geographical location of each, and adding that the two tribes keep themselves separate, do not intermix, and that each has a separate language of its own. He does not give particulars of the language, and it is from a paper on which I stumbled in an old number of the Society's Journal, and which does not appear to have been previously much noticed, that I have been able to identify this tribe with precision. Dr. Voysey, writing at Ellichpore so long ago as 1821, also at first calls them Gonds, but he goes on to say that they are also called 'Coours,' and that the Gonds consider themselves a distinct tribe from the Coours and neither eat nor intermarry with them. He then gives a small list of Coour words. This was taken long before Hodgson's vocabularies were published, and the two seem never to have been compared. I have compared Dr. Voysey's list with Hodgson's lists of words of the Kolarian tribes of Lurka Coles, Santals, &c. and find a remarkable coincidence. For instance, take the numerals.

	Coour.	Hodgson's Coles, &c.
1.	Mea,	Mi.
2.	Bariah,	Barria.
3.	Aphe,	Apia.
4.	Aphoon,	Apunia.
5.	Munea,	Monaya.
6.	Turrume,	Turia.
7.	Aya,	Iya.
8.	Ilhar,	Irlia.
9.	Arhe,	Area.
10.	Gyl,	Gel.

And again.

	Coour.	Hodgson.
Man,	Hoko,	Ho.
Water,	Da,	Dah.
Fire,	Singhel,	Sengel.
Tree,	Darao,	Daru.

House,	Oah,	Oa.
Mouth,	Ah,	Á.
Eye,	Meht,	Met.

In fact, of the first nine of Voysey's words which are also given by Hodgson, seven are identical, a circumstance very remarkable, seeing how far these illiterate tribes are separated from one another. None of the words correspond with the Dravidian synonyms, so there can be no doubt that we have traced the Kolarians so far.

Immediately beyond the Koors, from Asseerghur westwards, we are in the Bombay Presidency.

As I cannot ascertain that Mhars and Mangs and Ramooses now live as entirely separate tribes, I may at once say that, so far as my information goes, the Bombay Aborigines are (for my present purpose) all comprised in the two tribes of Koolees and Bheels. These tribes are scattered over a great portion of the Presidency, and in some parts, the Koolees especially, seem to live as a part of the general population. But the Koolees in part, and the Bheels more generally, are still found in portions of their original seats as distinct tribes, and they both seem to be numerous. Their name, position, and character seem to mark the Koolees as Kolarians. But beyond this, the more precise test of language is unfortunately wanting. I have not been able to find that these tribes have now any aboriginal languages of their own. They are generally said to speak dialects of the civilised languages of the neighbouring countries. In one or two places allusion is made to the existence or supposed existence of a Bheel language in remote jungles, but I have not found any precise indication respecting it.

I was at first inclined to conjecture that the separation into two tribes of Koolee and Bheels, and perhaps the more predatory character of the latter, might point to a division of race; that the Bheels might be Dravidians. I find, however, that the general opinion of those qualified to judge seems to tend to the belief that there is no essential difference between the two tribes. Forbes in his Ras Mala says: "Koolees or Bheels, for though the former would resent the classification, the distinctions between them need not be here noticed." Capt. Probyn says, "I think there is no actual difference between Koolees and Bheels. Their religion is the same." Mr. Ashburner:

"There is no real difference between Bheels and Koolees; their habits, physiognomy and mode of life are the same, modified by local circumstances." And the Rev. Mr. Dunlop Moore says, "Koolees frequently marry Bheel wives." Other authorities, however, say that they do not intermarry. They both seem to claim a northern and not a southern origin, pointing to the hills of Rajpootana and the north of Goozerat. The Bheels say that they were originally called Kaiyos; Sir John Malcolm says that they are related to the Meenas of Rajpootana, and once ruled in the Jeypore country. Forbes again tells us that the Koolees were originally called Mairs; while in Rajpootana, Col. Tod speaks of Mairs or Meenas as one race.

The Rev. Mr. Dunlop says that, though these tribes speak the same languages as their neighbours, "certain words are universally recognised as peculiar to Koolees as well as Bheels." He only instances one word written in a character which I can read, and that is 'Bhoroo' or 'Bhooroo,' the *head*. As I write, I have turned up the word *head* in Hodgson's vocabularies, and find that the Kols, Santals, Bhumiz and Moondas use the word 'Bu,' 'Buho' or 'Bohu' which seems to be the same word. The Dravidian words for head are entirely different.

It would be in many ways very interesting and important to rescue any remains of aboriginal words or aboriginal dialects of these tribes, and especially to find whether among them can be traced any non-Aryan radicals of the Goozerattee, Maratta, and the Hindee dialects of Rajpootana.

Though probably in the main of the same class and similar origin, the Koolees and Bheels are now quite distinct tribes, and there is this considerable difference that the Koolees have come much more into contact with Aryan blood and civilisation, are in appearance generally much more Hindooised than the others, and consider themselves altogether a higher class. As has been said, both tribes are now much scattered over many parts of the Presidency and in places a good deal intermixed, but their proper locale seems to be as follows. The Koolees are the Aborigines of Goozerat (where they now live in considerable number), and of the hills adjoining that Province. The hills east of Goozerat are called 'Kolwan' and seem to be the property of Koolee tribes, just as in the Chota-Nagpore territory the country of the Lurka Coles is called "Kolhan." The Bheels are the proper possessors of the hills farther in the interior and east of the Koolees, there occupying both the Sautpoora and the Vyndia ranges, and extending into Rajpootana. In the latter direction and about the Vyndians some of the tribes claim to be crossed with Rajpoots, and these are called Beelalahs. The Bheels are numerous in Candeish, and are found in some parts of the adjoining Deccan. They sometimes find their way to the Coast where they are stated to be known as 'Dooblas' or the "Kala Pooruj" or 'black men.' The Koolees seem to be scattered down the Coast country nearly as far as Goa, and north again into the 'Thurr' and the neighbourhood of Scinde. While the wilder Koolees of the hills are like the Bheels, the mass of more civilised Koolees are said to be not only fairer and more Caucasian in feature, but also more sly and cunning and less truthful. A large proportion of both races have been much diluted in point of 'aboriginality' of feature by intermixture, but the Bheels less than the others. Many of the Koolees live in villages and adopt some Hindoo practices. They are stated to average about 5 feet 3 inches in height. Though most of them are now quiet agriculturists and labourers, they were not always so. The wilder tribes of the race are still predatory, and Forbes mentions the Koolees as by far the most numerous of the arm-bearing castes who in former days, living in the hills between Goozerat and Rajpootana, disturbed the country. He describes them as of diminutive stature, with eyes which bore an expression of liveliness and cunning, clothes few, arms bow and arrows, habits swift and active, bold in assault, but rapid in flying to the jungles, independent in spirit, robbers, averse to industry, addicted to drunkenness, and quarrelsome when intoxicated; formidable in anarchy, but incapable of uniting among themselves. This description seems exceedingly well to apply to the wild Bheels of modern days, whom indeed Forbes classes with the Koolees.

Many of the Bheels are so independent and so much apart in their own hills and jungles, that it seems very strange that they should have no language of their own; I think that the search for such a language, or the remains of it, should not be abandoned without very careful inquiry.

I have not been able to ascertain whether there are any of these aboriginal tribes in the Kattywar hills, or who are the aborigines of Kattywar. I have not met with any precise mention of them. Lassen in his map places Koolees (Kolas he calls them) in the centre of Kattywar. He had probably some authority for doing so, but more precise information on the point would be desirable.

North of the Bombay country, in the Aravallee range running towards Ajmere, is the country of the Mairs or Mhairs, with whom I have said that the Koolees claim kindred, and whose name also suggests the question whether they may be related to the Maratta Mhars. Tod says that Mhair means Mountaineer, from 'Meru' mountain. The modern Mhairs are probably a very mixed race. Col. Dixon, who is avowedly enthusiastic in their favour, makes them out to be rather good-looking, and tells the usual story (as told by the chiefs to him) of their descent from Rajpoots. They admit to have taken a few Bheel and Meena women. It is probably the case, as Col. Dixon says, that for hundreds of years they have been recruited by Hindustanee refugees and rascals of all sorts. Though now out of the way, it must be remembered that Ajmere was, under the emperors, one of the chief seats of Mahommedan power.

The Meenas constitute a large portion of the population of Rajpootana, especially in the Jeypore country between Ajmere and Dehli. I have said that they are supposed to be related to the Mhairs, and they are called the aborigines of the country, but I doubt if they are so in the sense in which I am now dealing with separate aboriginal tribes. In Upper India, out of their own country, these Meenas are principally known as dacoits; and of those that I have seen in that capacity, my impression is, that they were not small and aboriginal-looking, but fine powerful men. I suspect that if originally a half-breed derived from aborigines, the Meenas are now members of the ordinary Indian society, and that Aryan features predominate in them. Farther information, however, is required.

I am not aware of any aboriginal tribes in Bundlecund. In a recent Archæological paper read at a meeting of the Society, mention was incidentally made of "the wild Sherrias" found about the southern sources of the Nerbudda, and I also find mention of a tribe called 'Naikras' in the hills of Oodeypore, said to be like the Bheels, but somewhat lower in the scale of humanity. I do not know whether these are really sub-divisions of the Bheels or separate tribes. In fact there may be many remnants of tribes in the jungles of Central India yet undescribed. I have now, however, noticed all the aboriginal tribes of the hilly portions of the Indian Peninsula known to me, with the exception only of the Bhooyas of the borders of Bengal.

In the plains, of course, we do not look to find separate aboriginal tribes, and those now classed as 'castes' will be afterwards noticed; but before leaving the subject of Koolees or Kolaries I may mention an assertion of Col. Tod that all the weaver caste throughout Hindustan are of this class, though they now call themselves 'Julahas' or Julahees. I do not know what is the ground for this assertion, but the weavers who have not turned Mahommedans are certainly sometimes or generally known as 'Korees' and considered to be low in the social scale.

There are no aboriginal tribes, of the character which I have been describing, in the Himalayas. The Kolees of the Simla hills and Domes of Kumaon are merely inferior castes living among the general population. Both in Kumaon and Nepal, there seems to be a sort of tradition or popular belief of the existence in some remote forests of a 'Ban-manush' or wild man of the woods, but I cannot find that any one has ever seen one of these creatures, or that his existence is really in any way authenticated. One can hardly say whether the story points to the recent disappearance of the last remnants of an ancient race, or whether it is merely a nursery tale.

It is not then in the Himalayas, but in the forests at their foot, that we must look for some aboriginal tribes. And here I must observe that I think the use of the term Sub-Himalayan by Hodgson, and (following him) by most other authorities, leads to a good deal of misapprehension, from an Indian point of view at least. We are in the habit of considering the Simla hills, Kumaon, and Nepal to be part of the Himalayas (and with good reason too I think), but Hodgson calls everything below the Snowy Range "Sub-Himalayan," and classes as 'Sub-Himalayan' people who live higher than the highest mountaineers in Europe, in the most precipitous mountains, 8,000 or 10,000 feet high; while the people really living under the hills are usually put in another class. I am now about to notice tribes who have nothing whatever to do with the hills, but live in the forests and what is called the 'Terai,' at the foot. No two climates and locations can be more dissimilar than those of the hills and the Terai, and no races are more distinct in their habits, manners, and aptitudes than the people of the hills and those of the jungle belt below.

It may be generally said that there is no Terai or forest belt northwest of the Seharunpore district and the Dehra Dhoon; but thence eastward this belt stretches along the foot of the hills through Rohilcund, Oude, and the Bengal Frontier, up to Assam. A great part of it belongs to the Nepalese. A very interesting paper by Dr. Stewart on the Boksas, a forest tribe found in western Rohilcund and in part of the forests or Sewalik hills of Dehra Dhoon, was published in the Society's Journal last year. They are entirely confined to the forest tracts, where they enjoy a wonderful immunity from the effects of malaria. They never (says Dr. Stewart) settle more than two years on one spot, but after getting a little out of the soil, move to fresh locations. They are of short stature and spare habit, and in feature certainly Turanian of some sort, with broad faces, depressed noses, prognathous jaws, thick lips, and very scanty beard and moustaches, but in colour apparently not darker than the ordinary Hindoos of the country. They are fond of game and pigs, eat almost anything, have no caste, and are reputed to be very skilful in witchcraft. They have no separate language. They are simple, inoffensive, and good-humoured, but very ignorant and indolent. Their cultivation is very scanty and rude, but they also collect forest produce and wash for gold. They are supposed to be dying out.

I have seen mention of another small and savage tribe in the Rohilcund Terai called "Rawats" or "Rajis;" and passing westward we come to a very important tribe, the 'Tharoos,' who in fact occupy all the Terai from eastern Rohilcund all along the frontiers of Oude and into Goruckpore. They are in many respects very like the Boksas—in physical appearance and manners I should say extremely like—but they are much more industrious, and altogether a larger, more settled, and, one may say, less savage tribe. They, like the Boksas, keep exclusively to the Terai and forest, living where no one else can live. They are shy and timid, but frank and truthful, when you get hold of them, and are very good cultivators in their own simple way. They are not particularly dark, and, in addition to the ordinary breadth and flatness of face, have a good deal of the Chinese-looking form of eye; so that it is difficult from appearance to say, whether they really belong to the Negrito, or to the Indo-Chinese stock. The fact is that though no two races can be more unlike one another than the slim, black, tangled-haired Negrito, and the stout, fair, lank haired Thibetan, yet when we come to half-breeds, the difference may not be so great. When the colour is softened or heightened, and the size increased or decreased to that of the ordinary Hindoo, and the hair reduced to civilised limits, there is the same appearance of breadth and flatness of face, and these latter characteristics are more apparent at a glance than any distinction between prognathous and pyramidal skulls. It would seem too that the Chinese peculiarity of eye is caused by the broad cheek bone common to both races, and perhaps it may be that while the eye being sunk deeper in the Negro and Negrito, and more covered by a more fleshy form of face its form is not so apparent, in the half-breed it is brought out, and the skin tightened by the high cheek-bone shows the Chinese-looking form of eye. I have noticed some of the Ghatwals on the borders of Bengal and Behar, who looked not unlike Goorkas. Thus then it becomes difficult to distinguish those tribes, on the northern and eastern frontiers, whose blood may be supposed to have become a good deal mixed by long contact with other races, and whose colour may have been softened by the cool, moist and shady climate of the Northern Terai.

I must also say that I think Hodgson has somewhat contributed to mix up the two races in our ideas, for in his enthusiasm to establish a connection between his Tamulians and the eastern races, he scarcely attempts to distinguish them, and classes as Tamulians, Bodos, Dhimals, &c. of whose connection with the Aborigines of the South of India there does not seem to be the slightest evidence in language, and who in appearance are as different as can be.

To return to the 'Tharoos;' as I said their appearance might leave doubt of their origin, and unfortunately they are not known to have any language of their own. Those with whom we have come more immediately in contact (including all those in eastern Rohilcund) certainly now speak Hindee, but the tribe is so large and important, that it would be, I think, desirable not to give up without farther inquiry the attempt to find a Tharoo language, though it will be more difficult now that, by the transfer of the Oude Terai, the great mass of them, and all those least mixed with Hindustanees, are Nepal subjects.

In other respects the habits and manners of the Boksas and Tharoos certainly point rather to an Indian than a Thibetan origin. I saw something of the Tharoos before they were annexed to Nepal; and their general style suggests a good deal of resemblance to the Santals for instance. Mr. Robert Drummond, who has served both in Pillebheet and in Central India, and who knew the Tharoos well, tells me that in many ways they remind him very much of the Aboriginal tribes of the Central hills. They have the same simple ways and the same religion of Bhoots and familiar spirits. He also mentions a singular circumstance, that on looking over a map of the hill country of Bhaugulpore (now called the Santal Pergunnahs), he was struck by the occurrence of many names which he had supposed to be peculiar to the Tharoos.

The claim of the Boksas to Rajpoot origin is of course ridiculous, but it is clear that all their traditions point to the south and south-west as the country of their origin, not to the northern hills. These tribes have in fact little intercourse with and no known congeners in the hills. The Boksas and Western Tharoos are separated from the Thibetan tribes by a great tract of very difficult country occupied by Arians; and though the Eastern Tharoos are nearer to Nepalese races who show Thibetan blood, it seems hardly probable that inhabitants of the hills should be driven out into the Forest below (of which the hill-men have a great horror); while, that Aboriginal Indians should be driven from the plains to the neighbouring jungles, would be probable enough. I am inclined to think that the Tharoos and Boksas are probably not Thibetan, farther than the accession of refugees and others from Nepal may have introduced a little of that blood. Dr. Stewart suggests the possibility that they may be akin to the Indo-Chinese races who occupy the lowlands near the Berhampooter; but though that may be possible, it seems to be a long way for emigrant tribes to find their way up to the Dehra Dhoon in countries where, for so many hundred miles, there is no trace of their congeners. On the whole, it seems more probable that they are Aboriginal Indians a good deal diluted. I have not heard of the Tharoos serving as labourers, but if they are akin to the Dhangar Coolees now so much sought after, seeing their immunity against malaria, they would be very valuable to any one who could induce them to emigrate. As yet, however, they are very shy.

From Goruckpore eastward in the Nepal Terai and along the Frontiers of Bengal, I cannot learn that there are any Aboriginal tribes till we come to the neighbourhood of Sikkim and Kooch Behar. Those whom I have asked knew of none, and it is probable that if there were any, Hodgson would have mentioned them. Dr. Campbell of Darjeeling speaks generally of the population of the Nepal Terai as composed of a most varied assemblage of bastard Hindus.

The Kooch Behar people have become so Hinduised, that their original character cannot be distinguished with certainty. They call themselves "Rajbansees," as I think do several Hinduised Aboriginal tribes.

About this parallel we come upon the Meches or Mechis who form the chief population of the forests and Doars at the foot of the Sikkim and Bhootan hills, and a few of whom have recently settled in the extreme eastern portion of the Nepal Terai. I understand that these people are the same as the Bodos of Hodgson, who are of an Indo-Chinese family. I shall rank them and other similar tribes as 'Borderers,' and now only notice them for the purpose of comparison. They are described as very Mongolian or Indo-Chinese in feature, fairer than the Hindus and of a yellow tinge, taller and larger than the Nepalese cultivators, addicted to spirits and to smoking opium. They make small and temporary clearances in the forest and are proof against malaria. In an industrial point of view they are evidently much inferior to the Tharoos.

Dr. Campbell incidentally mentions among the lowland neighbours of the Mechis a tribe inhabiting similar tracts called '*Thawas*' whom I have not seen mentioned elsewhere. They seem (so far as one can gather from the slightest notices) to be more industrious and settled than the Mechis. Dr. Campbell seems to speak of them as a different race. It would be interesting to know whether these Thawas may not possibly be related to the Tharoos.

Also among the neighbours of the Mechis are the Garrows, whose main habitat is the hill country just within the bend of the Berhampooter as it sweeps round from Assam into Bengal, the extreme western portion of the range which separates Sylhet, &c. from Assam. More to the east are the Cossya hills, to the west those of the Garrows. While all the tribes of the eastern hills are Indo-Chinese, I am inclined to suspect that the Garrows alone are Indian Aborigines, more or less mixed it may be. They seem to be quite distinct and different from the other tribes of the neighbourhood, and several officers, to whom I have talked, agree in thinking them more in the style of Coles and Bheels than of Indo-Chinese. I have not found any very exact description of them, but gather that they are small and dark, savage and troublesome. That they should belong to the Aboriginal races of India, is *primâ facie* by no means improbable, seeing that their hill country is, as the crow flies, scarcely more than 150 miles distant from that of the Santals and Rajmehalees, as may be seen by a glance at any map. There is a kind of straight between the eastern and western hills through which the Ganges and Berhampooter run before expanding in the broader Delta of Southern Bengal.

The little that is known of the language of the Garrows has not sufficed to connect them with any of the Aboriginal tribes mentioned by me, but it also seems to show that it is radically different from the surrounding Indo-Chinese dialects. It seems especially desirable to know something more of the Garrows and their language.

I have kept to the last the Bhooyas or Bhooians, because they seem to belong to both sides of Bengal, to West Bengal and Orissa on one side, and to Assam on the other. I have not met with any detailed account of their position in Assam, but I imagine that there can be no better authority than Col. Dalton who intimately knows both Provinces, and he, while describing them in the western hills, distinctly states that they were once the dominant race in Assam. It is always necessary to be cautious in dealing with names of this sound, since, as I have already mentioned, 'Bhoomea' means 'man of the soil,' and I believe that the word earth or soil also takes the form Bui. The Bhooyas have no immediate connection (that is looking only to the name) with either the Bhumiz or the Boyars. But Col. Dalton no doubt looks farther than this; and indeed he goes on to notice a considerable connection between Assam and the west both in races and in language. The Bhooyas in the west seem to be numerous. They appear to be the original occupants of much of the lower country to the south of the Chota-Nagpore plateau, great part of Singbhoom and Bonai, and the borders of Orissa. From a portion of their country they have been partly driven and partly they are dominated over by Coles, themselves probably impelled south and east by pressure from the north and west. They are still very numerous in all the districts and petty states hereabouts, and are found more or less all the way across the lower hill-country to the borders of Behar. Col. Dalton calls them a dark complexioned race, with rather high cheekbones, but not otherwise peculiar. They have no language of their own, but speak Oorya on the Ooriah borders, Bengalee on the borders of Bengal, and Hindee farther north. They are now somewhat Hinduised, but have still priests of their own and traces of an old religion, which seems even down to recent times to have included human sacrifices. Major Tickell speaks of the Aboriginal Bhooians who preceded the Coles in lower Singbhoom as "an inoffensive simple race, but rich in cattle and industrious cultivators." The descriptions of Col. Dalton and Major Tickell seem to suggest a resemblance in appearance to the Ooryahs, among whom high cheek bones seem to prevail with good features and straight hair. The Bhooyas whom I have seen in the hills towards the Bahar border seemed to have a larger dash of the black Aboriginal type. Seeing how far these Bhooyas are spread to the west, I was curious to know whether they might be related to the Buis, a tribe of Telengana and Central India who serve all over the centre, south, and west as palanquin bearers and domestic servants, and from whose name is, I believe, the most authentic derivation of the widespread word '*Boy*' as applied to a dark servant. Travelling from Nagpore towards Jubbulpore I observed that I changed the Buis of Central India for the Kahars of Hindoostan. Col. Dalton did not know whether there was any connection between Bhooyas and Buis. But quite recently, making a trip through a part of the Chota-Nagpore country, I found that the palanquin was carried by Bhooyas there and below the hill country till I got close to Gya, and I ascertained that they had no connection with the Hindoostanee Kahars by whom they were then relieved, but were considered to be a wholly different race. I cannot help thinking that the Bhooya palanquin bearers of Chota-Nagpore may be the same as the Buis of Nagpore Proper. At any rate it might be worth inquiring. These Bhooyas or Bhooians have been reputed to be the Aborigines of Bengal, and if that be so, it would quite account for their being found both in Orissa in the west and in Assam on the east. The difficulty is that there seem to be no such people now in Bengal, nor have I been able to identify them with any caste under another name. If, however, one travels in a palanquin from the Chota-Nagpore country into Bengal or Orissa, the bearers will be relieved not by Kahars as in Hindoostan, but by Gwallas or cow-keepers. These Gwallas do the work of palanquin-bearing and domestic service in Bengal, functions not performed by Gwallas so far as I know in any other part of India. An Aheer or up-country Gwala would never dream of such work. In fact the Gwallas in Bengal take the place of the Buis or Boys of the centre and south of India. They are now the most numerous Hindoo caste in Bengal and especially in Orissa. As I said, Major Tickell describes the original Bhooians as rich in cattle. May not the Hindoos have adopted them and turned them into Gwallas? I should also however mention that the lowest or sweeper class are called I understand in Bengal "Buimals," but I have not been able to ascertain the derivation of that word.

The Bengalees are certainly in many respects different from any other people of India, and if the Bhooyas are the Aboriginals of a great part of Bengal, we may the more readily believe that they are in fact different from the Coolees and Dravidians who have gone to compose the Hindoostanees and Southerners respectively. Who they are, and where they came from, are questions which open out a wide field of inquiry. Can any Aboriginal language or words spoken by them be traced? may they have any dash of more eastern blood? Is the mode of carrying palanquins rather a Chinese than an Arian fashion?

If we knew something more of the Garrows and the Garrow language, they might possibly supply a link in the history of Bengal.

Another race mentioned by Col. Dalton, as found both in the West and in Assam, are the Kolitas, whose name might suggest some relation to Coolees; but they seem to be now considered rather high caste and good looking Hindoos, so the name is probably not the same. Is every direction, however, there is room for inquiry.

One word regarding a people in another quarter who have been classed with the Indian Aborigines, the Brahuis of the higher parts of Belochistan near Khelat, &c. These people are set down as allied to the Dravidians upon, I think, the slightest possible evidence, but it is one of those things that, having once got into print, is in the absence of farther information repeated again and again, till it seems an established fact. Dr. Caldwell, in his amiable enthusiasm for his beloved Dravidians, and seeking to establish for them an aristocratic pedigree, without acknowledging obligation to the northern Hindoos, seizes upon the Brahuis as the link to connect them with the more northern nations and goes somewhat into the matter.

The Brahuis are described as a stout, squat, somewhat flat-faced people, fair, with hair and beards often brown if not red. That they have indications of some Turanian element both in feature and speech, may be at once admitted, using the word Turanian in its widest sense; but for the rest anything in greater contrast to the slim black Dravidian Aborigines, it is impossible to imagine. They are very remote from any Dravidian tribe, the nearest being the Gonds. Their language is not supposed to show any affinity to the Kolarians.

On the other hand, in one direction we have not far to seek for an explanation of the Turanian element in the features of the Brahuis. The Hazarehs of the hill country near Ghuznee and Candahar have it in a more marked degree, and are without doubt of Mongolian blood. They seem to be in many ways like the Brahuis, and we are told that at one time they possessed the country on the Khelat side of Candahar, and were nearer than they now are to the Brahuis. That the latter have some of their blood, or may even be a branch of them driven to the hills by Belochees or Hindoos, would seem *primâ facie* the most probable thing in the world. It is then only by the test of language that any Dravidian connection can be assigned to the Brahuis, and in the case of people otherwise so dissimilar and so distant, the linguistic evidence ought to be very strong, to satisfy us. I have been unable to find a paper giving a list of Brahui words said to have been published by this Society, but Dr. Caldwell seems to sum up all the evidence on the subject. He admits that "the Brahui language, considered as a whole, is derived from the same source as the Punjabee and Scindee" (in which no one ever suspected a Dravidian connection), but he goes on to show that the Brahui has also a Dravidian element in it. Now there are scarcely any two languages in which here and there words of similar meaning and similar sound may not be found, but so far as the vocabulary goes, Dr. Caldwell's list seems to show that he must have been very hard put to it. '*Khaff*,' the ear, and '*pid*,' the belly, seem to me at least as near to the Hindoostanee '*kan*' and '*pet*' as to the Dravidian '*kadu*' and '*pir*' or '*bir*.' '*Kat*,' a bedstead is, I think, distinctly a Hindee or Punjabee word. '*Dir*,' water, seems to me as near to the Kolarian '*dah*' as to the Dravidian '*nir*.' '*Ae*' or '*ayi*,' a mother or nurse, and '*pussie*,' a cat, are words of world-wide use.

So also the pronoun '*ni*' or '*nim*,' thou or you, appears in some shape in every dialect not purely Arian, from Australia to northern Siberia and from Japan to Finland. I really cannot find above 6 or 8 words which Dr. Caldwell shows to be especially like Dravidian words, and to make out these, he picks and chooses from every one of the different Dravidian dialects and accepts some rather distant resemblances as '*pak*' to go, Tamil '*pogu*.' This much seems to me to prove nothing whatever.

Again, take his grammatical resemblances. Some seem to be too wide, applying to many other languages, and others too minute. The use of postpositions and the want of comparatives and superlatives in adjectives is equally a coincidence with Hindoostanee and many other languages, neighbours of the Brahui on one side. The expression of gender by separate words and of plurals by postfixes denoting plurality is equally common to many other languages, including the neighbour of the Brahui on the other side, the Persian, *e. g.* '*nar-gow*' a '*male cow*,' and *Aspahan* '*horses*.' The genitive in '*na*' seems just as like to the Hindoostanee and Punjabee '*ka*' or '*da*' as to the Tamilian '*ma*.' The dative-accusative in '*e*' is a familiar Hindoostanee or Punjabee form, thus instead of '*Mujh-ko do*' Give me, it is constantly '*Mujhe do*,' and '*Use maro*' beat him, especially with the Punjabees. So also '*ten*,' said by Dr. Caldwell to mean 'self' in Brahui, seems very like the same syllable used to give precision in Hindoostanee as "*Use-ten do*," which I should translate '*give to him himself*.' At any rate '*ten*' is found nearer at hand than the Dravidian '*tan*.'

The copulative '*u*' 'and,' most people would think palpable Persian, and not go all the way to the Canarese for it.

It comes then in my view to this that the only real appearance of analogy to the Dravidian class of languages in particular (as distinguished from the body of Turanian languages in general) is reduced to two numerals. In Brahui neither 'one' nor 'four' and upwards in the least correspond with Dravidian numerals, but the two numbers 'two' and 'three' as given by Dr. Caldwell do seem similar. He gives the Brahui two, '*irat*' and three, '*musit*' or '*muoit*' which bear comparison with the Dravidian two, '*eradu*,' '*irandu*,' '*randu*,' '*ranu*' and three, '*muru*' '*mudu*,' '*mundu*,' '*munnar*,' '*munu*.'

The Brahui one '*asit*' seems very like the Pehlevi '*achat*,' and the Brahui *irat* may come from the Pehlevi '*tarein*' two, the Caucasian '*ieru*' and the Georgian '*ori*.' If so the 'three' would be the only tie to the Dravidians left, and that is not very close. The ground of induction seems insufficient to connect such dissimilar people. My impression is, that if, instead of saying that the Brahui language is mainly Punjabee with a Dravidian element, Dr. Caldwell had said that it is mainly Arian (Indo-Persic) with a Turanian element, that would have been more correct. At any rate in so important a matter fuller inquiry is necessary.

THE MODERN INDIANS.

I commence with the Bramins.

It is well-known that the Bramins as Priests are a necessary part of every Hindu society, and as Priests they are to be found wherever there are Hindus. In that character then it would be unnecessary to my purpose more particularly to trace them, for with their religious sects and tenets I do not deal. I shall only trace them for Ethnological purposes through the countries in which they form an important part of the general secular population. In fact, far from being restricted to the character of Priests, they are one of the most numerous castes in India, and probably that which follows the greatest variety of avocations. On the whole I should say that they are less prejudiced than any other of those whom I call full-blown or High Hindus. At any rate, whether it be that their character as keepers and expounders of the Law gives them greater licence, or that their intellect is more varied and their necessities greater, they do in various places and under various circumstances turn their hands to very many odd jobs as it were. Throughout Hindustan they have almost entirely lost that function of Clerks and Bureaucrats of the community which they still retain to a great extent in other parts of India; and it will be as members of the ordinary agricultural populations that I shall most deal with them.

Beginning from the north, we first meet with the Bramins in that quarter to which all their traditions point, within the hills north of the Punjab. The first Indians encountered by a traveller from Central Asia would be these Bramins of this extreme North-West corner, occupying both the valley of Kashmir and the hills immediately to the west and south-west of it.

Kashmir is a Bramin country. The lower classes have long been converted to Mahommedanism, but they seem to be ethnologically identical with the Bramins, and tradition also asserts that they are of the same race. At the present day no other Hindu caste save the Bramin is known, nor is there any trace (so far as I could find) that there ever was any other in the country. The Bramin population is numerous, but it would seem as if, while the illiterate multitude adopted the religion of the ruling power, the better educated and superior class maintained their own tenets; and at this day the Bramins (or Pandits, as they are usually called) form quite a sort of aristocracy. They are almost all educated and exceedingly clever, and so, being to a great degree above manual labour, they are an excessive and somewhat oppressive Bureaucracy, which not only has ruled Kashmir under every successive government, but sends out colonies to seek a livelihood throughout Northern India. The Kashmir Bramins are quite High-Arian in the type of their features, very fair and handsome, with high chiselled features, and no trace of intermixture of the blood of any lower race. It may be partly race and partly occupation, but they have certainly a greater refinement and regularity of feature than the Affghans and others of a rougher type; with, however, a less manly-looking physique and a colour less ruddy and more inclining to a somewhat sallow fairness. The high nose, slightly aquiline, but by no means what we call Jewish or Nut-cracker, is a common type. Raise a little the brow of a Greek statue, and give the nose a small turn at the bony point in front of the bridge (so as to break the straightness of line), you have then the model type of this part of India, to be found both in the living men and in the statues dug up in the Peshawar valley. There are also a good many straight noses, and some varieties as in all places, but much less departure from an ordinary handsome standard than in most countries. The figure of the ordinary working Kashmeeree is strong and athletic. But none of them are martial, and the Bramins are in this respect no exception. They rule by the brain and the pen, and not by the sword. It is this character that has gained them the favour of so many rulers of a different faith. Kashmere long belonged to the Cabul kingdom, but it was never in any degree colonised by Affghans, and is singularly free from any modern intermixture of foreign races. The fact seems to be that the valley never belonged to the Affghan nation, but was always retained as a Crown Appanage of the kings, who were very jealous of admitting into it subjects whom they might find it difficult to turn out again, and much preferred to govern through the Pandits. Others have to a great extent followed the same policy.

From a Hindu point of view, the Kashmir Bramins do not rank well. As they are Priests to no one but themselves, they are necessarily much more secular than Bramins who among other Hindus claim to be a priestly class, while they eat meat and are altogether loose in their observances, to an extent which makes them very far short of the modern Hindu standard. They are in fact not recognised among the modern Divisions of Indian Bramins, belonging neither to the 5 Gours nor to the 5 Dravidas, but forming a class apart. I have alluded to their attempt to claim the blood of all the Bramins higher in the sacerdotal scale, and suggested that it is more probable that the latter have sprung from and (in their sense) improved upon the Kashmeerees. In fact, the founder of the latter (Kashiyupa who drained the lake, colonised the valley, gave his name to Kashgar and Kashmere and to the people originally called Kashas or Kassias,) is still recognised by the Bramins and Hindus as the first of the seven Rishis, and even far away down on the west coast of India, the Bramins in general still trace their descent to Kashiyupa. I shall afterwards notice the name Kash as Khas occurring again and again in other parts of India, in a way which requires explanation.

The Kashmeeree Pandits are known all over Northern India as a very clever and energetic race of office-seekers. As a body they excel in acuteness the same number of any other race with whom they come in contact. Probably they are in no respect inferior to the Maratta Bramins, but they have not in Hindustan the same advantage as the latter have had in their own country among inferior races. The Kashmeerees, as foreigners among energetic races, have a much harder struggle, and though they get a good share of good things, they are nowhere dominant, nor have they usually risen to such high stations as many Maratta Bramins. The most conspicuous man whom I recollect was Raja Denonath, Ranjeet Sing's Financier and in some respects Chief Minister. Although the Kashmeerees seldom find their way as far as Calcutta, it is somewhat singular that in Bengal the first native to attain very high office is a man of this race, viz., Shamboonath Pandit, Judge of the High Court. Almost all the secular Pandits use the Persian character freely; they are perfectly versatile, and, serving abroad, will mount a horse, gird on a sword, and assume at a push a semi-military air.

The Kashmir language is separate and distinct, and the dress, manners, and fashions of the Kashmeerees mark them as in every way a distinct people. Of the language we only know that it contains a very large proportion of Sanscrit. The Institutions of the people have nothing of the democratic character.

In the hills also, between Kashmir and the Punjab, Bramins occupy the van (or perhaps we should call it the rear) of the Indian race to the west, though they have abandoned their Hindoo religion and become partly Mahommedans and partly Sikhs. They are in habits, language, and manners quite different from the Kashmeerees, and seem now to belong to a different nation. Their language is a dialect of the Punjabee (a very Pracrit tongue and certainly not borrowed from any Mahommedan race), while they are good soldiers and altogether more Punjabees than Kashmeerees. Beyond the Jhelum, the hill frontier is occupied by a tribe called Bambas, now Mahommedans, but originally Bramins; while on this side the Jhelum the hills are shared with other races by a numerous tribe of Bramin-Sikhs. The position of these men is curious. They became Sikhs long before the extension of Sikh power to those regions, and in a much more complete sense than most modern Sikhs, abandoning all pretence of Hindoo religion and adopting to the full the Sikh reformer's tenets. Indeed they were converted during Mahommedan rule, and when 'Sikh' was really a religious rather than a political name. The fact probably is, that they found the country too hot for Bramins, but did not care to become Mahommedans, so adopted the alternative of becoming Sikhs, and so free from the trammels of caste. These men are very useful soldiers and servants, especially under Sikh rule. A good many of them have been introduced into Kashmir as a sort of military colonists, partly by a Hindu governor under the Affghans, and partly by the Sikh rulers; but they remain quite apart from the Kashmir Bramins. One of the best native officers in the Punjab force, who is himself of this class, told me that the *Bambas* are without doubt Bramins under a corrupted name. He says that to this day the Sikh Bramins and Bambas exchange cakes on the occasion of certain ceremonies (births, funerals, &c. I think), and that there is no doubt that they are of the same stock. I believe that it certainly is so. It seems to be a common practice in India to give to tribes who have departed from the faith or mixed the blood of their ancestors, names derived from their original tribal names. Thus half-civilised Bheels are called '*Bheelalahs;*' Mahommedan Rajpoots are called "Rangars;" a tribe of bastard Bramins to be afterwards noticed (in Benares and Bahar) 'Bamuns' or 'Babhans.'

The Bramins of the frontier hills are, I think, even handsomer than the Kashmeerees. To my view, the people in general of those hills are the handsomest of the human race.

Descending from the Himalayas, there are some Bramins near the foot of the hills. Except a few priests, I do not think that they are found beyond the Indus, but they are, I understand, pretty numerous in part of the Rawal Pindee district. South of the Salt Range, in the plains, they are well nigh overwhelmed by the strong flow of Rajpoots and Jats (advancing, as I believe, at a later period and from another direction). The Bramins either never occupied the plains of the Punjab to the south-west, or they have been driven from that country. Even nearer the hills they are not exceedingly numerous. But still in that fertile and pleasant strip under the hills we have, among other races, villages of agricultural Bramins in the districts of Sealkot,

Goordaspore &c., in the valleys of the broken country between Hosheearpore and Kangra, and in parts of Umballa district and the adjoining Simla hills; and thus we, as it were, mark the trail of the Bramin race in its progress southwards from the hills of Kashmir to the banks of the sacred Saroostee or Saraswatee and the famous field of the Gulcheter at Tanessur close to the Grand Trunk Road, some thirty miles south of Umballa.

Here also the Bramin population in the country is not specially numerous. Other races have swept over the scene. But lower down the course of the Saraswatee, where it may be traced through the now somewhat desolate countries of Marwar and Jessulmere, the Bramins are still numerous. Where the low and comparatively moist tracts, in which the river once ran, still admit of cultivation, the Saraswatee Bramins are found very industrious and good cultivators, who claim to have occupied the country before Jats and Rajpoots became dominant. *There* is found (at Pokhar) the only temple in India still dedicated to the worship of Brama the Father. The town of 'Palli' seems to be a Bramin centre, and thence come a race of mercantile Bramins called 'Palliwals.'

Sir John Malcolm also mentions the Marwarree or Saraswatee Bramins as forming a considerable proportion of the most industrious cultivators in Malwa. And following the Saraswatee down to the Indus, we find that (some southern immigrants excepted) they are also the Bramins of Scinde, but said to be much looked down on by more orthodox southerners as eaters of meat and altogether little advanced Bramins.

The settlement on the banks of the Saraswatee is a well-known stage of Hindu history. Here the Bramins came in contact with other races, castes were recognised, and early Hinduism became literary and historical. But the extreme caste and religious system, the full-blown High-Hinduism of the Gangetic Bramins, was not yet. The descendants of those who continued to dwell on the Saraswatee seem to have much kept to the tenets of their forefathers. They are separate from the Kashmeerees and have a place among the recognised divisions of Indian Bramins, but their more advanced brethren give them the lowest place in the orthodox scale, and in their native country they chiefly shine by those simple and agricultural virtues in which their remote ancestors also probably excelled.

It is a curious problem, that lost river, the Saraswatee. The evident river-traces all the way down to the Indus, ancient Hindu history, and the universal traditions of the people of those regions, all go to make it as certain as any historical fact can be, that the Saraswatee was once a fine river, and that the countries through which it flowed (now for the most part desert and barren) were once well-watered and green. No mere diminution in the amount of rainfall, caused by denudations or the like, could have occasioned such as change. The outer range of the Himalaya runs all the way from the Sutlej to the Jumna without a break, and the tributaries of the Saraswatee receive but the outer drainage of the slope a few miles wide. No doubling or trebling of the rainfall could make any of these considerable perennial streams; nothing in fact short of a change of elevation of the ridges to the extent of several thousand feet would render possible any outlet in this quarter of the drainage of the interior of the Himalayas. The Saraswatee itself is now not a stream at all, but an absolutely dry bed, which is only filled by surface flooding in the height of the rains. The high embankments on the present Grand Trunk Road, on the Umballa side of Thanessur or Peeplee, mark the levels, and show the hollow where a great river once flowed. I have long had a theory that, in truth, the stream now called the Jumna once flowed in this channel. The present channel of the Saraswatee points upwards to the point where the Jumna issues from the hills, and ends in a confused drainage within 2 or 3 miles of that almost natural channel in which the Western Jumna Canal (running more like a river than a canal) carries the Jumna water in a course which eventually leads it lower down into the very bed of the Saraswatee. The Jumna at its first issue from the hills runs in a course which points directly towards the Saraswatee and the lower Indus, and the moment you cross, to the west, the high bank (which is accumulated along the course of most rivers), the whole of the drainage of the country is to the Saraswatee and not to the Jumna. In fact the bed of the Jumna is higher than that of the Saraswatee. Sir P. Cautley was anxious, by a change of the Jumna Canal, to carry it directly into the Saraswatee channel, and I believe that to divert the whole river would be a work within easy reach of modern engineering. May it not then be that nature caused a change the other way, that the stream now called the Jumna then belonged to the Saraswatee, but that those hill torrents from the Sewalik, bringing down masses of sand and earth, raised between them and the main stream a sort of James and Mary which eventually caused the latter to break away to the south-east? If the stream moved, most of the Hindus would probably move forward too and find themselves in the Gangetic valley.

The Saraswatee Bramins are also called (in the south at least) "Kashastalee" a name which seems still to mark the time when they were considered to be of Kashmeeree or Kasha origin. In fact there seem to be several stages in the history of Braminism. The oldest of the race may be the people of the upper hills who date from a time altogether prior to Hinduism. The Kashmeerees were a civilised and literary Braminical people not yet fully Hindu. The Saraswatee Bramins (those Kasha settlers in the plains of India) were the earliest and most simple and pure Hindus of Vedic faith, that faith being now worked out and developed; those of the Ganges and the rest of India are in various phases the types of modern Hinduism.

From the Gulcheter down to Dehli and in the country about Dehli, Bramin villages are scattered about, but the Bramins cannot be said to constitute a very large proportion of the agricultural population. Wherever they are found in this country, they are capital cultivators, quiet, industrious, intelligent; there is no better population, and the women work as well as the men. It was remarked by the fugitives from Dehli at the time of the mutiny, that whenever they came to a Goojar village, they were always plundered; whenever they came to a Bramin village, they were always kindly treated; while at any other village their treatment was uncertain. These Bramins too are, I should think, descendants of the Saraswatee Bramins. Some of the less pure agricultural Bramins of these parts are called 'Tugas' or 'Gour Tugas.' South of Dehli, in the Jyepore country, Bramins seem to be numerous, but I have not been able to ascertain if they are of the same branch. In the Seharunpore district too there are a good many Bramins of secular occupations, besides the priests of Hardwar.

Sir H. Elliott has remarked on the difficulty of accounting for the fact that all the Dehli country is occupied by 'Gour' Bramins. They can hardly, he thinks, have come from Gour in Bengal, from which they are separated by great tribes of Kanoujeas and others, and their own traditions point to Harriana as their original country. I would suggest the following explanation. The principal tributary of the Saraswatee is the 'Guggur' or 'Ghargar' which now gives its name to the main channel where it passes through the Harriana district. May not the name of 'Gour,' borne by these Bramins of Harriana, be a mere abbreviation of 'Guggur' or Ghargar? May not the Gour Bramins be simply Bramins of the Guggur or Lower Saraswatee?

Generally speaking I think it may be said that in the western parts of the present N. W. Provinces, in the Rohilcund, Meerut and Agra Divisions and in Western Oude, the Bramin population is not specially numerous. They are scattered about everywhere here and there, both as cultivators and in other capacities, but I know no large body of them. I don't know that they follow much any profession involving manual labour, except cultivation and almost any kind of service; unskilled labour as Coolees or spade labourers, they may undertake when pressed, but I do not think that they are artisans. There are a few considerable Bramin bankers in Hindustan, or at least one great house, but that trade is not generally in their hands.

Farther east, in the Lower Doab, Eastern Oude, and the adjoining districts, is the great country of the modern Hindustanee Bramins. Kanouj, the ancient head-quarters of the race, is on the old Ganges 50 or 60 miles above Cawnpore. It is now an insignificant place, and the mass of the Bramin population lies to the east of it. In the districts of Cawnpore and Futtehpore I believe that the Bramin cultivators far exceed in number any other class; in Cawnpore alone there are some 250,000 of them. It is much the same immediately on the other side of the Ganges, in the adjoining parts of Oude. The country of which this is the centre may then more than any other be considered especially that in which the Bramins are now settled as a people. And in the far distant country in which also they are very numerous, the Western Coast of Southern India, the Bramins claim to be colonists from the same region, saying that Paras Ram led them from Calpee (the great Ferry of the Jumna opposite Cawnpore) and causing the sea to recede, settled them under the Western Ghats. The Lower Doab is well-known all over Central and Southern India as the "Unter-bed."

Whether from the example of the Rajpoots, or for other reasons, these Bramins of the Unterbed and Oude have taken largely to the profession of arms, not usually much followed by them in other parts of the country; and beyond their own boundaries in their Military character they are reputed the most overbearing and disagreeable of their race. Yet I fancy that it is rather their profession than their natural character, which has attached to them this bad name. Numerous as they were in the Sepoy Army and foully as that Army behaved, I cannot find that the Bramins were really by any means worse than others; some of the most Bramin Regiments stood the best. And at home they seem to be quiet and peaceable enough. The Bramin district of Cawnpore pays, I think, a higher revenue rate than any other in India, except the peculiar Delta of the Cauvery about Tanjore. Numerous as the Bramins are in this part of the country and apt as soldiers, they have not been the dominant race. I do not know much of the history of the Cawnpore district, but I have never heard of Bramin rule; and certainly over the river, in Oude, the rule is with the Rajpoots, not with the Bramins. All the really old Talookdars are Rajpoots, as are the Rajas of Bundlecund and Baghelcund beyond the Jumna.

I am not sure what is the extent of the Bramin population in Bundlecund. In the Banda District I think that they are common, and certainly in 'Baghelcund,' or Rewah, they are very numerous; but whether the same martial race, I do not know, for there they condescend to very menial services and groom most of the horses on the Jubbulpore road.

In the proper Bramin country, I think that some of them affect the Rajpoot prejudice against actually holding the plough, but even there they perform every other agricultural labour. Agricultural and military as they are, they rejoice in the classic names of Dobee, Tewaree, and Choubee, that is men of two Veds, of three Veds, of four Veds, and are considered to be very high caste. Between the Ganges and the Gogra, as we recede from the Ganges, the population becomes more Rajpoot than Bramin, but there are many Bramins about 'Ajoodia,' the old 'Oadh.' Beyond the Gogra again is a numerous Bramin population of a different tribe from the martial Bramins of the Ganges, humbler, and not soldiers. Thence to the north of the Gogra and Ganges all the way into Tirhoot there are, I believe, many Bramins. South of the Gogra and thence across the Ganges, into the Arrah District (Bojpore), runs the Rajpoot dominions. But about Benares, and still more in the greater part of Bahar, the dominion is held by a numerous class of bastard Bramins called 'Bamans' or 'Bhabans,' to which belong both the Raja of Benares and almost all the great landholders of Bahar. There seems to be no doubt that this class is formed by an intermixture of Bramins with some inferior caste. They live in strong and pugnacious brotherhoods, and are in character much more like Rajpoots than Bramins. The main country of the Bramins may then be described to be that part of Hindustan (between the Vyndyas on one side and the Himalayas on the other), from the longitude of Kanouj and Lucknow to near the frontiers of Bengal, with a large segment of more especially Rajpoot country (stretching from Lucknow to Bojpore) cut out of the centre of this tract.

The Hindustanee Bramins are all strict Hindus of the modern type. They are generally good sized and on the whole well-looking men, not I think particularly fair among the higher castes, but seldom so dark as the lower. Their features are good, but by no means generally of the peculiar High-Arian and sub-aquiline type. In fact the breed has here lost some of the purity of its blood, and the features are very much as in Europe. I think I have noticed among many of the Hindustanee Bramins a good deal of the open, blunt, bullet-headed, and as it were anti-aquiline style of countenance; not so handsome as more High-Arian features, but still pleasant enough. I do not think that in appearance they have any decided superiority over the higher castes of Hindustanees in general, though the higher castes have some general advantages over the inferior castes. By far the greater number of them are quite illiterate and have nothing of the clerkly character about them. The priests and Pandits are learned enough in their way, but they have never taken to the use of the Persian character. I doubt whether Hindustanee Bramins are as a body much more clever that several other classes; if they had been, they would have held their own better in spite of Mahommedan rule, as they have done in several other parts of India. As it is, they have scarcely any share of high office and very little literate service.

Besides serving as soldiers, they may be found among the lower hangers-on of courts, jails, &c., as process servers, guards over prisoners, and so on, but little in anything higher. As I have said, they turn their hands to many miscellaneous occupations not peculiar to any one else, and of course occasionally rise.

Sir H. Elliott calls the bastard Bramins of Benares and Bahar '*Bhoonhars*' and seems to consider them a branch of the Sarwarea or Transgogra Bramins. Again he speaks of them (quoting from the 'Harivansa') as Military Bramins descendants of *Kasya Princes*, and here he seems to connect the term *Kasya* with *Kashee*, the Hindoo name for Benares. I do not know the derivation of Kashee, or whether it is connected with Kashupya.

Bramins are numerous in Kumaon and Gurwhal. The great tribe of those Provinces are however "Khassias" who now claim to be Rajpoots, but whose title to that character is more than doubtful. Education is, I think, more general here than in the plains, and the Nagaree or ordinary Sanscrit character is always used. Again the Goorkhas, the dominant tribe in Nepal, are properly called 'Khas,' whence Gor-khas. They are certainly for the most part of Arian and Hindoo origin, and pretend to be Rajpoots; but, according to Mr. Hodgson, they are really bastard Bramins, the offspring of a cross between Bramin immigrants and the people of the hills. Both the Khassias of Kumaon and the Khas of Nepal assert that they are comparatively recent immigrants from the plains, but this is probably in a great degree connected with their claim to the blue blood of the Rajpoots of the plains. The latter by no means acknowledge the connection. The circumstance that a bastard Bramin race is dominant in the plains immediately under the Central parts of Nepal gives much colour to Mr. Hodgson's account of a similar race in the hills. May it not be that the Rajpoots have never got so far east in the hills, and that the hill country was occupied by pre-Rajpoot Bramins? May it be that the names Kashee, Khassia, and Khas, point to a time when the Bramins were known as Khasas or Kashmeerees, just as English colonists are known as Anglo-Saxons?

Mr. B. Colvin, long Deputy Commissioner of Almorah, tells me a curious circumstance, viz. that in Kumaon, although the hill dialect is in the main Hindee, it has some curious grammatical affinities to the Bengalee, both in some of the popular terminations, in the verb 'to be,' and in other particulars. I had before learned that there was a peculiarity of this kind in the Hindee spoken in the high country immediately south of Bahar, but there I supposed it to be a mere intermixture of the not distant Bengalee. The existence, however, of Bengalee affinities in the patois of Kumaon would seem to suggest the question whether these are not the remains of a form of Arian speech older that the modern Hindee, spoken perhaps before Rajpoots and Jats came on the scene, and then driven forward to Bengal in one direction, into the hills in another. I have not myself any acquaintance with Bengalee, but it would be interesting to enquire if it has any affinities with the older forms of speech in Kashmir and the north-western hills, or again with the Maratta and western dialects.

To get an idea of the Bengalee formation, I asked a friend the other day a single word, the pronoun 'he' and the genitive 'of him,' which he gave me '*Se*' and '*Taha*' or '*Tah.*' At this present writing, by way of experiment, I have just turned up these same words in Mr. Edgeworth's small Kashmir Grammar and find 'he,' '*Su*;' 'of him' '*Teh.*' The '*Se*' is a very old Arian form, found in the Kaffir hills, which disappears in Hindee and reappears in Bengalee; but the genitive '*Teh*' in Cashmiree, '*Tah*' in Bengalee, seems a singular and hardly accidental coincidence.

To return, this brings me to the Bengalee Bramins. They all assert a northern origin as a historical fact, and I believe that there is no doubt of it. Still their nationality is altogether Bengalee, and as the Bengalees differ from all other Indians, these Bramins also differ much in language, dress, habits, and general style from the Hindustanee Bramins.

In appearance they are certainly fairer, larger, and altogether Aryans of a higher type than the mass of the Bengalees. There is much more difference, I think, between Bramins and the mass in Bengal than in Hindustan. Some of them are fine looking men both in size and feature. They regain here too, some (though not all) of the aristocratic and bureaucratic position which they have lost in Hindustan. They have little competition from Rajpoots and rough northern tribes, and might have it pretty much their own way, were it not that they are hard-pushed by the clerkly caste of Kaits who also are numerous in Bengal. As it is, the Bramins have a large share of the landed property, the public offices, the educated professions, and some mercantile and banking business. They are very numerous. In the entire absence of statistics and detailed information in Bengal, the only source of ethnological information which I can find is in the jail statistics. These show that about 9 per cent. of the total number of Hindu prisoners are Bramins. We may suppose that the Bramins of Bengal proper come to jail less frequently than the inferior classes, and this return certainly seems to prove that the Bramin population must be very large. I do not understand that anywhere in Bengal they form the mass of the population, or that they are often found in the lowest ranks of agriculturists and labourers. They are rather more or less an aristocratic class, and though following a variety of callings and to some extent cultivating the land, will not ordinarily put their hand to the plough, and affect as far as possible the position of superiors. They are altogether unwarlike and somewhat effeminate in their habits.

In Eastern Bengal Mahommedans prevail, and some Bramins are supposed not to like to cross the Berhampooter, hence in that quarter they seem not to be very numerous. In Orissa I believe they are very many, and I see it stated in the Gazetteer of Southern India that in the Oorya portion of the Ganjam District many of the Oorya Bramins both obtain their livelihood as cultivators and traders, and follow the occupations of brickmakers, bricklayers, &c.

The result of education shows the Bramins of Bengal to be most acute and intellectually capable. But they do not appear to have the practical energy of the mercantile and some other classes, nor the political and administrative success of Maratta and Kashmeeree Bramins. In native times I do not remember to have heard of Bengalee Bramins in great places, unless we except Nandcomar who attained so unfortunate an eminence. In these days I believe that intellectual eminence is often combined with much high principle among the educated Bengalees, and I hope that both may bear practical fruit.

Going to the other side of India, in Goozerat the Bramins appear to be numerous, but I have not yet visited that Province, and have not exactly ascertained their position and avocations. Forbes does not seem to speak of them as forming any large portion of the cultivating classes. They trace their descent from Kashyupa, and are divided into a large number of tribes and sub-divisions. In a secular capacity they seem to have a good share of office (although there also they encounter an energetic writer-caste) and also to trade. The Jains of Western India have Bramins among them, and these would seem to be for the most part Goozerat men.

Next to Goozerat comes the Maratta country, extending from Damaun to the neighbourhood of Goa, and from Bombay to Nagpore and the Wyuganga. The Maratta Bramins are the most famous and successful of their race. That their fortune is due to their talent and energy, is shown by their success beyond their own bounds, in fact throughout Southern and Central India. But in their own country and among their own people, they are also favoured by circumstances. The lower caste men of the pen, who have ousted the Bramins in some countries of the north and more than rivalled them in others, are not found in the Maratta social system (those now found in the Bombay country are Goozerattees, and Bombay itself is in a mercantile sense very much a Goozerattee city). The mass of the Maratta people are of a comparatively humble class, without the pride and jealousy of Bramins shown by Rajpoots and Jats. Hence wherever there is a Maratta people or Maratta rule, Maratta Bramins are the brains and directing power. At first they contented themselves with the highest administrative offices under Maratta rulers, but later, as is well known, the Peshwa and other Bramins usurped the supreme power itself, assumed the command of armies, and openly ruled the confederacy. In truth, so miscellaneous, and so loosely held together by any other tie, were Maratta confederacies and armies, that these Bramins may be considered to be the real source of the power and fame of the Marattas as rulers in India. They were the heads of a body of which others were but the hands guided by them. Even to the present day in many States and places beyond their own limits, they have the chief power.

In fact perhaps no race, certainly no Indian race, has ever shown greater administrative talent and acuteness. The native country of the Maratta Bramins is chiefly to the west, and especially the Concan, south of Bombay, the hilly strip near the Western Coast.

It might be conjectured that centuries of Mahommedan rule might have caused the retreat of the Bramins from the more open plains to these regions; but I do not know that there is historical ground for this supposition, and think it more likely that under any rule they would hold their own and circumvent even foreign rulers. Their personal appearance would lead one rather to suppose that they came from the North-West. Many of them are very fair, and I think that there is among them a much greater tendency to the common occurrence of a somewhat aquiline, or what I call sub-aquiline type of feature than among Hindustanee Bramins. A very marked feature, not uncommonly met with, seems to be a light greyish kind of eye. Altogether, I cannot suppose these Bramins to be a branch of the race which, after occupying Hindustan, extended southwards. I cannot imagine how they could in the south, as it were, in some degree have returned towards an earlier type, instead of step by step becoming darker and more Indian-like. It is undoubtedly the case and is a subject of common remark, that all along the West Coast of India the people are much fairer than in the interior, even though most of the interior country above the Ghats is considerably elevated. Some have accounted for this by saying that colour does not altogether depend on the thermometer, that the inhabitants of the more umbrageous Coast are less exposed to an unclouded sun and dry atmosphere than the people of the bare and treeless plains of the Deccan, and that thus the difference of colour is to be accounted for. I will not say that this cause is wholly without effect, but I think it quite insufficient to account for the whole difference. The Bengalees in a moist atmosphere and amid a luxurious vegetation are generally dark. The blackest of the Aboriginal tribes live in the densest forest country in a moist malarious climate. Even on this very Western Coast I find the Aboriginal Helots of Malabar described as being "of the deepest black.". We must look then to some other cause modifying the complexion of many tribes on the West Coast, and that I take to be immigration by sea. That there has been much such immigration, is not only probable, but a historical fact. All along the southern portion of the West Coast, a large part of the population is notoriously to a great degree of foreign blood. The Moplahs are to a great extent Arabs, the 'Teers' or 'Teermen' are also said to be immigrants (as their very name indicates), and there are many Jews and Christians, though the latter I believe have not much trace of Western blood. All along the Bombay Coast also, from Goa to Kurrachee, are the descendants of Persian, Arab, Portuguese, and other Western immigrants. Hence I did not think it by any means absurd when an educated Bramin of Poonah suggested to me as a theory, that the Bramins owed the light eyes and light complexion noticed among them to an intermixture of Western blood. The Bramins would be less liable, however, to casual and recent intermixture than other races, and I incline rather to the theory that these Bramins of this part of the Coast may have more directly come from the original seats of the race by the route of the Saraswatee and the Indus, and thence perhaps by sea, without passing through Hindustan and Central India and there suffering any infiltration of Aboriginal blood. I have already traced the Bramins down the Saraswatee. Is it not probable enough that in very early days, when they were pressed by Rajpoots and Jats, they may have colonised the Konkan, reduced to subjection the rude Aborigines, and transmitted to descendants features preserved from great deterioration by caste rules, and forms only somewhat deteriorated in size and robustness by a southern climate and the absence of manual labour? If such an immigration took place so early as I suppose, it might well happen that, in long contact with southern elements and southern creeds, the colonists in the Maratta country would separate themselves from the old Saraswatee Bramins and become a separate division.

I have seen some allusions to Konkan Bramins as distinguished from Maratta Bramins, but have not been able to make out the exact distinction. Certainly Maratta Bramins are altogether the dominant race in great part of the Konkan. But it appears that there is a strip to the south, extending beyond the district usually known as the Konkan to some way beyond Goa, in which a mixed language called Konkanee is spoken. In this Konkan there are some Bramins still called 'Kashastala or Saraswatee' and from the Konkan some of them have penetrated into the north-western part of the Mysore country, where they are traders and in public employment, and described as very clever but greatly looked down upon by southern Bramins who profess to be much more rigid in their rules. In the towns of the North Canarese Coast, the Hindu traders are said to be chiefly "Konkanee Bramins who trade and keep shops."

In the Maratta Konkan the Bramins are at the head of the agricultural community. Most of the '*Kotes*' or village zemindars who rule over and claim the proprietary right in each village are of this caste. I have not been able to ascertain what proportion of the actual cultivators are of the same class. For the rest, office of every kind, including the village and pergunnah accountantships all over the country, and every service of the head and the pen, seem to be their great resources. They are not military, nor generally in any way men of the sword, though, as I have said, they have in their prosperity taken the command of Maratta Armies. Nor do they seem to have any great commercial proclivities. Among the various races who push to so great a point mercantile enterprise in Bombay I cannot find that the Bramins have any great share. Under our Government they have almost a monopoly of office in Western India.

Adjoining the Maratta country on the east is the Telinga or Telagoo country, very little of which I have visited and of the castes and population of which I have been able to learn less than of any other part of India. This at least, however, I find that here also the Bramins, though not so famous nor, I apprehend, so clever as those of Maharashtra, are numerous and powerful. The Telinga people are described as generally illiterate and as (unlike their Tamil neighbours) leaving literature and science to the Bramins; so that the latter would seem in Telingana, free from the competition of a writer caste, to have in their hands all the secular business of a clerkly character and a good deal more besides. I have not ascertained what proportion of the population they there form, and whether many of them are actual cultivators; but in more than one place I find it stated that many of the Zemindars are Bramins, and in Rajamundry the more respectable inhabitants of the Town are said to be chiefly Bramins.

I can only trust that this meagre account of the Telagoo Bramins will be supplemented by some one better qualified to describe them. Towards Madras I gather that there are some learned Gwallas called Yadavas and Telagoo Chetties (perhaps a merchant class, but I am not sure), who must a good deal interfere with the Bramins. They do not seem to be very conspicuous in Madras itself, which, though in the Tamil country, is not far from the Telagoo frontier.

In the Canarese country (comprising Canara, Mysore and parts of the Bombay Southern Districts and adjoining Nizam's country) the Bramins are not rivalled by a specific writer class, and have a large share of literate office, very generally (it appears) occupying that of Shanbogue or village accountant, besides many higher offices. But a very large proportion of the Canarese people are of the ultra-Sivite or Lingayet sect, who altogether ignore Bramins in their sacerdotal character; and there are energetic mercantile and other classes. The rule of the Marattas in one quarter, and of the Mahommedans in another was also unfavorable to the power of the Canarese Bramins, and thus they are by no means dominant. Maratta Bramins, Mahommedans, East Indians and others have a large share of the higher offices and occupations.

In the North Western part of the Canarese country, in the district of North Canara, in the high and hilly country above and about the ghats, and the adjoining parts of Mysore, there is a large population of Bramin cultivators who are on all hands represented as exceedingly industrious, thriving, and in every way good. Most of these people are called 'Haiga' Bramins, and they seem to be of pure race and of no bastard or doubtful caste. They especially affect the cultivation of the betel-nut, and both own and cultivate the land over a large extent of country. In the Canara District they constitute one of the most numerous castes, being given by a census taken some years ago as 147,924, to 146,309 Banters (corresponding to Nairs), and 151,491 of the inferior class called Billawars. In the Nagar district of Mysore they are also numerous, and they are there described as "very fair, with large eyes and aquiline noses," a description which would seem to imply for them a derivation from an uncorrupted and little intermixed northern source. They are stated not to be very literary or highly educated, being more devoted to agriculture.

In South Canara and what is called the Talava country, there are again many Bramins who do much cultivation, and on the whole West Coast, down to the extreme South of India, the country is said to have been extensively colonised by the Bramin colony led from Calpee by Parasram, who caused the sea to retire for their convenience.

In the centre of this tract, in Malabar, the Bramins, owing to political circumstances and hostile rule, have been to a great extent driven away, but they are very numerous in Travancore and Cochin; and in the Palghaut valley (a little inland, where the break takes place in the line of the ghats) the Bramins seem to be very numerous as cultivators, and are industrious and good in that capacity. The principal class of Bramins on the South Coast are called Namberees, and they have some very peculiar customs. They affect, however, much of the sacerdotal character, and seem to be very influential in Travancore and Cochin. Throughout the South Western Coast, however, wherever the Nairs and allied tribes are or have been politically dominant or are now numerous, the Bramins have by no means a monopoly of office, even among Hindus; for the Nairs themselves are frequently educated and hold very many public offices.

The Namberee Bramins are described as very like the Nairs and general Hindu population of the South Coast, but as not unfrequently fairer.

It remains to notice the Tamil country. There also the Bramins are numerous, but it appears that throughout the extreme South, they again lose that literary predominance, or almost monopoly, which they enjoy in the Maratta and other countries in the middle zone of India as well as in the extreme North. I have mentioned that the Nairs of the Malayala and Talava country by no means resign the pen to the Bramins; and so also it appears that throughout the Tamil country offshoots of the dominant tribes, under the names of Modelliars, Pillays, &c., do much of the clerkly work, and the Bramins have not generally the office of village accountant and collector—the possession of which is the greatest test of predominance in that respect. I gather that the Lingamite sect is less numerous in the Tamil than in the Canarese country, and consequently the Bramins are in a sacerdotal point of view more important. They also push their fortunes in many secular ways. They rent much land, but will not hold the plough, and are extensively employed in the public offices as hurkaras (messengers or process servers) and in such like capacities, also as keepers of choultrees and in many other occupations. With reference to what I have said of them as renters rather than cultivators, I should add that, though the Palghat country is included in Malabar, it appears that most of the cultivating Bramins there are of Tamil extraction. Many of them condescend to officiate as astrologers and religious guides to the very lowest and scarcely Hindu castes of Southern India.

Briefly I would thus recapitulate the position of the Bramins in the principal Provinces of India.

In Kashmir, they are altogether dominant by the brain and pen, but are not military.

In the Punjab, Scinde, and countries about the Saraswatee, Bramins are superseded by other races, and are only found here and there in the eastern part of this tract as industrious cultivators claiming to be the ancient occupants of the country.

In Hindustan, Bramins have altogether lost literate predominance (with the exception of some immigrant Cashmeerees), and also political predominance, except something retained by quasi-Bramins of mixed caste in the extreme east of this country. But they constitute a large section of the population of Hindustan, especially of the eastern half, and a large proportion of the cultivators, soldiers, &c.

In Bengal and Orissa, Bramins form a large portion of the Hindu population, occupy to a great extent an aristocratic position, and have a large share in the superior rights in land, in offices, and in the literate professions; but are at the same time quite rivalled by Kaists.

In the Maratta country, Bramins are altogether dominant in literate work, and have the largest share of political power.

In the Telinga country, Bramins are in possession of most of the literate work, and apparently of a good deal of office, land, &c., but my information is very imperfect.

In the South of India, Bramins have but a moderate share of the literate work; but on the West Coast, they have a large share of the land and form a large proportion of the best cultivating population; while in the east of this country they seem to be not dominant and are rivalled by several other tribes, though here also they are numerous and employed in many capacities, secular as well as sacerdotal.

The Jats.

On the general scheme of tracing the Arian races from the North-West, I take the Jats before the Rajpoots. These Jats are in fact by far the most perfect specimen of the democratic and more properly Indo-Germanic races, whom I believe to have appeared in India later than the early Braminical Hindus, and who, while Hindu in much of their speech, laws, and manners, have also some peculiarities and institutions, and perhaps some grammatical forms of speech not to be traced in the earlier Braminical writings. These tribes, now constituting over a great part of India an upper and dominant stratum of society, have given to a great degree their own tone and colour to many Provinces. In great part of Jat-land the Jats are not only the upper stratum, but the great body and mass of the free people; and hence we have among them their original institutions in the greatest purity, little modified by modern Braminical Laws, or by those necessities of Military and Feudal organisation which so much alter the institutions of a free people, when they become dominant conquerors over other races greatly superior in number.

There is some variation in the pronunciation of the word 'Jat,' it being sometimes (chiefly in the west country) pronounced so short that it may be written 'Jut;' sometimes (in much of the Punjab) variably used, and sometimes (chiefly in the east) pronounced very long as 'Jāt' and even occasionally written by early English authors 'Jaut.' And the present religion, dress, &c. of the race also differing in different regions (they are Mussulmans in the west, Sikhs in great part of the Punjab, and in some sense Hindus in the east), some people have supposed Mahommedan Jats of Scinde to be radically different from Hindu Jauts of Bhurtpore, and the wide extent and populousness of this great race is not very generally known. In fact, however, any apparent differences in the extreme of the type disappear, when we trace them as one great continuous population throughout the whole tract, and find that the one extreme gradually and imperceptibly merges into the other.

To prevent future doubts, I will, however, add that there may possibly be small local western tribes of similar name, distinct from the great Jat nation. It seems that on some parts of the frontier Jats are known as a somewhat pastoral and light-fingered tribe; and Burton in his 'Scinde' speaks of a tribe of Beloochis bearing the name; also says that it is the name of a wandering tribe found about Candahar, Herat, Meshed, &c., and that in all the Western parts of Central Asia, the term is used as synonymous with thief and scoundrel. These gentry may be offshoots of our Jats thrown by circumstances on the resources of their mother-wit, or they may be some other tribe; but at any rate they are in no way a type of the great agricultural nation whose habitat I am about to describe, and about whose oneness and complete ethnological nationality there can be, I think, no doubt whatever.

In all the east of Beloochistan, about the routes by which the most open and constant communications between India and the countries to the west are maintained, in the Provinces marked in the maps as 'Sewestan' and 'Cutch Gandava,' Jats form a large, probably the largest portion of the agricultural population, and claim to be the original owners of the soil. In fact the Beloochis are there but a later wave and upper stratum. The Persian Tajiks are the original agricultural class of all the west of Affghanistan and Beloochistan; then there is a tribe apparently somewhat mixed, called 'Dehwars,' found about Candahar and thereabouts. The Jats are not found in Affghanistan, but in Beloochistan they succeed the Tajiks and Dehwars, as we go east by the Bolan and routes thereabouts. Here then they are not confined to the plains, but occupy the hilly country.

Descending into the plains, we find the Jats spread to the right and left along the Indus and its tributaries, occupying upper Scinde on one side and the Punjab on the other. But it is particularly to be remarked that in the Punjab they are not found in any numbers above the Salt Range, and they are wholly unknown in the Himalaya. In fact, to the north they are altogether excluded from the hilly country, a circumstance which seems to me conclusively to show that they did not enter India by that extreme northern route. The hills to the north seem on the contrary to be a barrier by which the flood of Jats was checked.

In all Upper Scinde the Jats are still the prevailing population, and their language is the language of the country. It is moreover matter of history that they were once the aristocracy of that land, though latterly other races have dominated and the higher classes among the Jats have lost somewhat of their position. In the south and west of the Punjab too they have long been subject to Mahommedan rulers, but latterly as Sikhs they became rulers of the whole Punjab and of the country beyond as far as the upper Jumna, in all which territories they are still in every way the dominant population. Over great tracts of this country, I should say that three villages out of four are Jat, and that in each Jat village the Jats constitute perhaps two-thirds of the entire population, the remainder being low caste Helots, with a few traders, artisans, &c.

The Juts of the Indus seem on the map to be separated from the Jauts of Bhurtpore and Agra by the whole breadth of Rajpootana, but the fact is that the ordinary geographical nomenclature gives rise to much misconception on the subject. By far the greater part of what we call Rajpootana is, ethnologically speaking, much more a Jat than a Rajpoot country. The great seat of Rajpoot population and ancient power and glory is on the Ganges, and it is said that since the Mahommedans conquered them there, the chief Rajpoot houses have as it were doubled back on the comparatively unfruitful countries which now bear their name, but where, notwithstanding, the most numerous section of the population is Jat. Col. Tod expressly tells us that northern Rajpootana was partitioned into small Jat republics, before the Rajpoots were driven back from Ajoodea and the Ganges. It is clear then that the Jats extend continuously east from the Indus over Rajpootana. They do not seem to have occupied (or at least do not now occupy) lower Scinde, nor are they found in Goozerat, although in the history of the latter country mention is made of incursions of Jat horsemen on the frontier in conjunction with Katties. Their line of settlement lies farther north. They may have arrived on the Saraswatee, before its banks lost their moisture, and if so, their passage to the east would be comparatively easy. Throughout the more open parts of Rajpootana they share the soil with the Aboriginal or semi-Aboriginal Meenas, the remains of the Bramin population, and the dominant Rajpoots; the Jats having, I gather, the largest share of the cultivation. The southern and more hilly parts of Rajpootana (where Mhairs, Meenas, and Bheels so much hold their own,) are not Jat, but in Malwa again they are numerous, and seem to share that Province with Rajpoots and Koonbees.

To the north, in the north-eastern Punjab and Cis-Sutlej districts, as we get near the hills, I think there are evident indications that the Jat population has been advancing on what has once been a proper Rajpoot country, after having perhaps been, before that, a Bramin country. It is not clear whether the Bhattees of Bhatteana were originally Rajpoots or really are Yuti or Jats. But from Bhatteana northwards, Rajpoot villages are scattered about in considerable numbers among the Jats, and there are traces of more extensive Rajpoot possessions. The Rajpoots seem to be here undergoing gradual submersion. But in the extreme north of the Baree and adjoining Doabs of the Punjab (the Baree is that Doab in which Lahore and Umritsir are situated) there is still a strip immediately under the hills, which may be classed with the adjoining hill country as still mainly Rajpoot. To the west, advancing through Rajpootana, we come to the Jats of Bhurtpore and Dholpore, famous in history. Gwalior was a Jat fortress belonging, I think, to the Dholpore Chief. They do not go much further south in this direction. From this point they may be said to occupy the banks of the Jumna all the way north to the hills. The Dehli territory is principally a Jat country, and from Agra upwards the flood of that race has passed the river in considerable numbers, and forms a large part of the population of the Upper Doab in the districts of Allighur, Meerut, and Mozuffernugger. They are just known over the Ganges in the Moradabad district, but they cannot be said to have crossed that river in any numbers.

To define then the Jat country; take as a basis the country on both sides of the Indus from Lat. 26° or 27° up to the Salt Range; from the extremities of this base draw two lines nearly at right angles to the river and inclining south, so as to reach Lat. 23° or 24° in Malwa, and Lat. 30° on the Jumna, thus including Upper Scinde, Marwar, and part of Malwa on one side, and Lahore, Umritsir, and Umballa on the other; then connect the two eastern points by a line which shall include Dholpore, Agra, Allighur, and Meerut. Within all that ambit the Jat race ethnologically predominates, excepting only the hills of Mewar and the neighbourhood, still held by Aboriginal tribes.

The Jats of Beloochistan are described, from an Affghan or Candahar point of view, as fine athletic men with handsome features, but rather dark.

In Upper Scinde, up the course of the Indus, and in the south-western Punjab, they are now for the most part Mahommedans, and in that character seem to be somewhat inferior to their unconverted and perhaps purer brethren; the more so as they have been long subject to foreign rule. The language spoken along the line of the Indus and throughout Upper Scinde is there known as the "Jatee Gul" or Jat language, but is in fact identical with that which we call Punjabee. The Punjabee may, in fact, properly be called the Jat language; to the Jats the dialect seems especially to belong, and by them chiefly it is spoken. Advancing eastwards into the Punjab and Rajpootana, we find Hindu and Mahommedan Jats much mixed; it often happens that one-half of a village or one branch of a family is Mahommedan, and the other Hindu. Further east, Mahommedan Jats become rarer and rarer, and both about Lahore and all that part of the Punjab and along the line of the Upper Sutlej and Jumna the great mass remain unconverted. In the Punjab they all take the name of 'Sing,' and dress somewhat differently from ordinary Hindu Jats, but for the most part they only become formally Sikhs, when they take service, and that change makes little difference in their laws and social relations. The Jats of Dehli, Bhurtpore, &c. are a very fine race. They still bear the old Hindu names of 'Mull' and such like, and are not all 'Sings.' In Rajpootana the Jats are probably a good deal intermixed by contact with Meenas, &c., and they have now been long subject to an alien rule. One does not there hear much of them otherwise than as quiet and submissive cultivators.

The Jat Sings of the Punjab and the Upper Sutlej may probably be taken as the best representative type of the race. They are a remarkably five variety of man—tall, large, well-featured, with very plentiful and long beards, fine teeth, and a very pleasant open expression of countenance. I am told that in the Punjab Regiments, which select from several of the finest races in the world, the Sikhs are upon the whole the largest men, although they are not so stout-limbed or in certain respects quite so robust as the Affghan Pathans. Perhaps the larger population to choose from may have something to do with the superior size, but I should say that on an average they are taller than Pathans, with the upper part of the body especially well developed. In pluck and Military qualities they excel the fairer and in some degree more beautiful non-Pathan races of the northern hills. Altogether then they are not excelled by any race in Asia.

There is among them a large proportion of High-Arian feature, but there is much more variety and not so universal a high-nosed type as among the men of the frontier hills. Compared to northern races they are dark, but in every other respect they are, take them all in all, a very remarkably fine handsome people.

They are as energetic in the arts of peace as in those of war. There are no better cultivators; hard-working and thrifty, they let little land lie waste, and pay their revenue punctually. They have this great advantage too that among them a woman is almost as good as a man, works as well and makes herself as generally useful. They are not literary, they leave that, with proper mercantile business, to the Khatrees (to be afterwards noticed). But many men and some women can read and write in their own rough way, and as waggoners they not unfrequently carry their grain and other goods to distant markets on their own account.

They have an excessive craving after fixed ownership in the soil, and are essentially agriculturists. They seldom undertake a gardening style of cultivation, and prefer broad high lands to more cramped though moister locations. Where the country is more fitted for cattle, they breed them largely, and both ordinary carts and large mercantile waggons are generally plentiful in the Jat countries. Camels too they sometimes breed. But still, in India the Jats have never anything of the pastoral, roving, Gypsy-like character.

I have alluded to the democratic institutions of the Jats, institutions to which we do not find allusions in the books of the Bramins. Yet it is certain that such institutions prevailed in the North of India as early as the time of Alexander the Great. The Greek accounts are distinct on the point. They represent the institutions as in fact extremely democratic, and add that the Indians ascribed their free constitution to Bacchus, by whom they were led into the country. I mentioned Col. Tod's testimony to the former existence of Jat republics in great part of what is now Rajpootana. I know of only one recognised republican State which came down to our day, that of 'Phool' or 'Maraj,' from which sprung the chiefs who founded the States of Patteealah, Nabah, Jheend, &c. The old territory of the Phoolkeean race was recognised, and treated, among the Protected Sikh States, as a regular republic. But I fear that, with many less creditable institutions, it has now been brought under the general rule of British dominion.

However, States apart, every Jat village is on a small scale a democratic republic. As respects property, there is neither that common tribal right which we find among the wilder Arabs, Turcomans, and New Zealanders, nor that complete joint family which figures so largely in the Hindu Law of the Braminical sages. Every man has his share of the cultivated land, separate and divided. It may be that a father and sons cultivate in common, but entire commensality seldom goes farther. The union in a joint village community is rather the political union of the Commune, so well known in Europe, than a common enjoyment of property. The village site, the waste lands and grazing grounds, and it may be one or two other things belong to the commune, and the members of the commune have in these rights of common. For all the purposes of cultivation, the remainder of the land is in every way separate individual property. And the government of the commune is no patriarched rule, but simply representative government. A Communal Council or Punchayet rules by right of representation. For the rest, the laws of these people are of Arian, Indo-Germanic, and to some extent of the more liberal Hindu type. Marriage is a sacred and irrevocable bond, though remarriage of widows is permitted; and alliances are restricted by the bonds of caste. The hereditary succession and general hereditary character of everything, which usually attends this system of caste and exclusive marriage, prevails among the Jats. Property is equally divided among sons. Daughters get nothing but that which may be given to them at the time of marriage. All the Jats are divided into many Gentes and Tribes, after the universal fashion of the peoples of this stock, and the usual fashion is to marry into another Gens.

In that portion of the Protected Sikh Territories which Sikhs from the Lahore country had occupied as conquerors, there was a perfect feudal system. The chief of a tribe, as General, had a large appanage; smaller chiefs owed him allegiance and service for their smaller domains, and under-holders under them again (all holding on a permanent hereditary tenure), till we come to the tenure of a single horseman. These latter again have come to be divided under the operation of the rules of inheritance. But this system, it will be observed, is only adopted abroad for purposes of foreign domination.

Beyond the caste system common to them with most Indo-Germans, the Jats have very little of the ceremonial strictness of Hindu caste. In Punjabee Regiments, they mess freely like Europeans, and have their comfortable two or three meals a day.

The Jats sometimes claim to have been originally Rajpoots, and it is so stated in some of the written accounts; but that is only one of the many stories of the kind prompted by a desire to stand high in the Hindu scale, and its futility is illustrated by a counter-story told by some of the Mahommedan Jats, viz. that they are descended from one of the companions of the prophet. That the Jats and Rajpoots and their congeners are branches of one great stock, I have no doubt. It may be possible that the Rajpoots are Jats who have advanced farther into Hindustan, have there more intermingled with Hindu races, have become more high and strict Hindus, and achieved earlier power and glory. But that the Jats are Rajpoots who have receded from a higher Hindu position, is a theory for which there is not the least support, and which is contradicted by every feature in the present position of the now rapidly progressing Jats.

The suggestion that Rajpoots may be Jats more highly developed in a Hindu point of view, would make the latter the earliest and most primitive, though at the same time perhaps the purest of the race; just as I have supposed the Bramins of Cashmere and the Frontier hills to be Hindus of an earlier stage of Braminical development. But I am more inclined to suppose the Jats to be later immigrants from Central or Western Asia. The character of the northern hills is such that immigration from thence could only gradually filtrate into the plains; but by the passes of the Bolan, great immigrations are possible. Looking at the area of Jat occupation, it is just that which we might suppose to be covered by the steady flow of a large flood of population issuing from the Bolan, about Lat. 28° or 30°, as from a funnel, and thence spreading over the plains and pushing away before it other populations. The Rajpoots, again, when I come to treat of them, will be found to be ranged in a kind of horse shoe form round the outer edge of the Jat area, the mass of them occupying the richer valley of the Ganges. My conjecture is that the Rajpoots are an earlier wave from the same source, and who came in by the same route, who have farther advanced and have been more completely Hinduised, while the Jats have come in behind them.

The Jat or Punjabee language is but a dialect, bearing somewhat the same relation to the Hindee of the Rajpoots and other Hindustanees that Lowland Scotch bears to English. In its main grammatical and essential features it is not widely different. There are certainly in it many words which sound strange to a European only superficially acquainted with the common Hindustanee, and it would be very interesting to examine all these words and ascertain whether any and what foreign elements can be found. But I may state broadly that by far the greater number of these words are really of plain Sanscrit origin, and very many of them are quite familiar to those well acquainted with the purer Hindee dialects. I have been surprised to find how Sanscrit are most of the words which (little linguist that I am) I had supposed to be peculiarly Punjabee. Indeed the Rev. Mr. Trump broadly states the Jat language to be one of the most Pracrit of Indian Vernaculars, and so it clearly is. There remains the old question which concerns it equally with the Hindee, whether the grammar can be derived from the Sanscrit. It seems very improbable that so great a mass of people as the Jats should have lost all traces of a separate language, if they ever had one. If so, it may surely be recognised in some Punjabee words. For the rest, the only doubt seems to be whether the Jats and Rajpoots, speaking an Indo-Germanic tongue allied to the Sanscrit, may have brought with them the grammar which now distinguishes the Punjabee and Hindee; or whether the Bramins, when they spread wide over Hindustan and mixed among a large Aboriginal population, adopted some Aboriginal grammar, and fitted into it their own vocabulary, making a language which Jats and Rajpoots also have received in India; or whether in fact all these tribes have derived a common tongue by direct Pracrit descent from the Sanscrit.

The Rajpoots.

I have already made so many allusions to the Rajpoots, that I have half anticipated my description of them. The best proof that they are not a part of the original Hindu system, but rather something engrafted upon it, is (I think) to be found in the difficulty of defining what is and what is not a Rajpoot. I have already shown, in noticing many tribes, that it is almost impossible to say where the Rajpoots begin and where they end. I shall now, however, confine myself as far as possible to the tribes who are generally acknowledged to be real Rajpoots of blue blood.

They can scarcely be said to have any broad general tribal name like that of the Jats. It is hardly contended that they are really the old Kshatryas of the early Braminical accounts; and though, in a military point of view, they have occupied and more than occupied the place assigned to the Kshatryas, still their numbers, their position and the existence among them of the institutions shared with them by the Jats and unknown to the old Hindoo Shasters (in them we find no trace of democracy) would all go to show that the Rajpoots are another race. In fact the days of the Kshatryas were those of the earliest Hindu annals, many hundred years before Christ, while the Rajpoots may be considered to have been the immediate predecessors of the Mahommedans in the rule of Hindustan. Except then in an affected way and with direct reference to the old Sanscrit Nomenclature, the Rajpoots are not usually called 'Kshatryas,' while the name Rajpoot also is by no means universal among them, and merely means 'Son of a Raja' or 'Royal.' In some parts of the country, they usually call themselves 'Thakoors,' a word which also means Chiefs or Nobles.

They are more frequently known by the names of their tribes as 'Chouhans,' 'Soorujbansees,' 'Bais,' 'Rahtores,' 'Baghels' (or Waghels') or the like, but the practice of marrying into another tribe makes all these high-caste tribes identical for ethnological purposes. I shall continue, then, to call them Rajpoots.

They are chiefly known to Europeans in their military character and as feudal conquerors. But in reality, in their own villages in the plains of the Ganges, they are simple agriculturalists of a constitution very much like that of the Jats, only less pure and complete. The fact is that the Rajpoots have had their day, and are now a down-going race. Partly the furnishing of armies and feudal hosts has exhausted the material and corrupted the simplicity of their original villages; partly infanticide and other causes tend to diminish their numbers; the result of all which is, that over great tracts of country we find them rather a minority trying to maintain a failing rule over a scarcely subject majority, than forming full democratic bodies of free Rajpoots. Still, in some parts of the country the agricultural Rajpoot villages are strong and numerous; the land is divided among them, every Rajpoot is free and equal, and the commune is administered on democratic principles. Wherever this is so, their institutions are like those of the Jats. Although they have never cared much for Bramins, they have, unlike the Jats, the ceremonies and superstitions of Hindu caste. They cook once a day with great fuss and form, almost every man for himself after the most approved Hindustanee fashion, and are very particular about caste-marks, &c. &c. Their widows may not remarry, and it is their excessive point of honour to marry their daughters to none but men of the best tribes (a feeling allied to our chivalry no doubt) that renders the daughters such a burden to them, and makes female infanticide unfortunately so common among them. Their wives again are shut up after the Mahommedan fashion, and are lost for agricultural labour. Altogether Rajpoot females are a very unsatisfactory institution, and this goes far to weigh down and give a comparatively bad name to men who who are often industrious enough.

Like the Jats, the Rajpoots are not found in any numbers to the North of the Salt Range, nor are they in any of the hill country west of the Jhelum.* If they ever occupied the Western Punjab, they have been driven forward by the Jats, and they are now only found about the Salt Range itself, where a small tribe called *Jhanjhooas'* (now Mahommedans) represents a Rajpoot race that seems to have been once great in those parts. But in the North-Eastern Punjab near the hills, the Rajpoot population is (as I have already noticed) more numerous, and the Himalayas of the Jummoo and Kangra districts are occupied by Hindu Rajpoots who are there altogether the dominant race. I do not know if the highest Rajpoots to the south east

* It was somewhere suggested that the Gadoons or Jadoons just over the Indus, where that river issues from the Himalayas near Torbela, are Rajpoots, but that seems to be a mere conjecture, founded on a fancied resemblance to the name of a Rajpoot tribe. There is not the least doubt that the Gadoons are pure Pushtoo-speaking Pathans.

would admit the equality, but the Kangra and Jummoo Rajas and their clans affect among themselves to be of very blue blood indeed, and they are certainly very fine handsome men. The Kangra Rajpoots in particular are very fair and handsome and High-Arian looking. I fancy that in all these hills, for a considerable distance to the east, there is a great deal of Kashmeeree or rather old Kasha blood. The women of the hills are in deserved repute and much sought after in the plains. The Kangra Rajas have endless genealogies, but I think that their clansmen are somewhat effeminate looking and not very first rate soldiers. The men of the Jummoo country, the immediate clansmen and subjects of the Maharaja of Cashmere, (and who also occupy the west of the Kangra district), commonly called Dogras, are not spoken of with so much Hindoo respect, and are not so pretty and be-jewelled looking as the Kangra men, but they are much more robust and brave. In the Punjab force, no men are preferred to them as soldiers; they are quiet, staunch, steady and reliable, without the disagreeable Hindustanee airs of the old Sepoy Rajpoots. The Rajpoot population of these hills must be very considerable. East of the Sutlej, in the Simla hills, many of the Rajas and their followers are Rajpoots, but most of the agriculturalists are of another caste called Kanaits.

A large proportion of the Rajpoots scattered about the Eastern Punjab, Cis-Sutlej territory, and Dehli districts are now Mahommedans, as are occasional Rajpoot villages all over Hindustan and a good many Rajpoot Rajas, this being no doubt the result of the favour shown to the Rajpoots by the Mogul Emperors; but east of Dehli conversion is quite the exception, by far the greater number are staunch Hindus.

In the Gangetic valley the body of the Rajpoot population may be said to lie next to the Jats to the east, in the middle Doab, Rohilcund, and Oude; and still farther east the country is shared with a Bramin population. Before Rohilcund (given as a jagheer to Rohillas) acquired its present name, it was known as the Rajpoot Province of Katerh, and to the present day in all lower Rohilcund the Rajpoot communities, (they are there called Thakoors) are strong and numerous. They are also numerous in Western Oude, but for what reason I know not, neither the Rohilcund men nor those of

Western Oude entered the Sepoy Army in large numbers. In the Central Doab, in the districts of Mynpooree, Futtehgurh, Etawah, &c. Rajpoots are numerous, and a good many of them served in the army. The Raja of Mynpooree is, I think, one of the highest of the famous Chouhan clan. The lower Doab is, as I have before noticed, more a Bramin country; but Eastern Oude, especially most of the broad tract between the Gogra and the Ganges, is the home of the great Rajpoot population which supplied so large a proportion of the Sepoy Army. At home these Rajpoots are by no means a loose military class, but a purely agricultural population. The prejudice against the particular act of holding the plough which so many of them affect, is reduced to the narrowest possible limits, and many ex-Sepoys may now be seen grubbing up weeds, raising water by manual labour, and performing all the lowest agricultural functions. Baiswara, the country of the Bais Rajpoots, lying almost parallel to the Bramin country of the lower Doab, is a famous nursery of Sepoys. In all this part of the country, so far as there still subsist ancient superior rights in the land, they belong to the heads of Rajpoot clans.

Some of the inferior clansmen hold subordinate tenures and village proprietorships, but the great mass of the Rajpoots of Oude are now reduced to the position of mere ryots, in which capacity they are much intermixed with Bramins. Many of the superior rights have passed away to modern men.

Passing to the east of Oude, Rajpoots are pretty numerous in Azimghur and Ghazeepore, but, as I have already mentioned, in the surrounding districts and those farther to east, the chief Rajas and landholders are the bastard Bramins or 'Bhamuns' whose clansmen abound in Behar. In the Arrah district only (in the east) in the small Doab between the Soane and the Ganges, the Rajpoots are strong and numerous. Their leader was the famous rebel landholder, Koer Sing, and they supplied to the Native Army the numerous class known as '*Bhojpore*' Sepoys.

This is almost the limit of Rajpoot ethnological occupation to the east, but turning round to the south-west, the Raja of Rewah is chief of the Baghel Rajpoots (whence his country is called Baghelcund), and has no doubt a numerous following of his clansmen, though Aborigines on one side and Bramins on another are also numerous in his territory. The Boondeelas of Bundlecund are not, I believe, considered to be very pure Rajpoots; they have probably suffered some intermixture, but they are notoriously bold and martial, form a dominant aristocracy, and used to be very troublesome to us. I do not know the proportion of Rajpoot population in Scindia's territories to the west, but believe that it is numerous. In Malwa, Rajpoots of the Rahtore, Chouhan, Sesodya and other clans form a large proportion of the population, and all the surrounding hilly country which is not held by pure Aborigines seems to have been from very old times in the possession of Rajpoot or semi-Rajpoot chiefs. The Mewar or Oodeypore Rajpoots, occupying a strong and elevated country in the west, claim to be the most ancient of the race; and I have seen it stated that some of the western Rajpoots are comparatively fair, with light or grey eyes. If so, that would seem to indicate that they reached their present location by a direct route from the west, and not by doubling back from the Ganges, as is supposed to have been the case in northern Rajpootana.

In the history of Guzerat the Rajpoots are very famous, and many of them seem to have been of the same high-caste tribes whose blood is reputed the best in the east, the Waghels, for instance, being (it appears) the same as the Baghels. They are evidently still numerous, but I have not been able to ascertain what proportion of the population they form, and to what extent they take part in the actual cultivation. Forbes does not speak of them as if they were among the most numerous cultivators.

In Kathywar, Rajpoots seem to be numerous, and from the practice of infanticide we may suppose that they consider themselves high-caste, but I cannot exactly make out whether the Kathis are counted as Rajpoots, or whether the many petty chiefs of Kathywar are principally Kathis or proper Rajpoots. The Kathis seem to have been undoubtedly immigrants from the west and at one time neighbours and allies of Jats.

In Lower Scinde there are undoubted traces of ancient Rajpoot rule, and the Summa Rajpoots ruled more recently under the Mahommedan emperors. Farther west, in Beloochistan, there seem to be traces of Hindu rule of a character more orthodox than that of the Jats, but whether the Rajpoots ever had dominion there, I am unable to say.

Looking back, it will be seen that (as I before said would be the case) I have traced the Rajpoots all round the edge of the more compact mass of the Jat population;—from the Salt Range through the Northern Punjab and adjoining hills to Rohilcund, Oude and the Centre Doab; thence by Bundlecund through Scindia's territory, Malwa, Mewar, Guzerat and Kattywar into Lower Scinde.

There remains in the centre of this circuit the greater part of Rajpootana which I have described as ethnologically more Jat than Rajpoot, though the Rajpoots now rule, after doubling back from the Ganges. They form a numerous and dominant aristocracy, organised on the feudal principles necessary to domination.

Though a full and complete Rajpoot village mainly inhabited by Rajpoots is democratic in its constitution, I have never heard of a Rajpoot Republic on a larger scale; and whether it be from long habits of domination by means of a feudal system, from the imbibing of a Hindu spirit, or from their original genius, they seem to be more than the Jats given to suffer the rule of Rajas and Chiefs. In Rajpootana, however, the chief seems generally to be but a chief, and not a despotic ruler. Numerous fiefs are held by subordinate chiefs, who are again surrounded by Military followers holding many petty jagheers and grants of land on a hereditary service tenure. It may well be supposed that under such circumstances, when the British peace-preserving power is at all relaxed, the authority of the chiefs is very apt to collapse. They never could hold their own against the Marattas. But still, as a quasi-chivalrous aristocracy, with their bards, and genealogies, and military get-up, and contests about the possession of high-caste young ladies, they make a very pretty picture.

The normal Rajpoot, however, to my view is, as I have said, the cultivator of the Gangetic valley, where, at the eastern extremity of the horse-shoe which I have described, they spread out in a broad region into a large population. Physically I do not know any striking features which broadly distinguish the Gangetic Rajpoot from his neighbour the Gangetic Bramin. In a Sepoy Regiment, setting aside caste marks, &c., I doubt whether they could be distinguished. They are both in fact the type of the higher class of the modern Hindustanee population. Both are tall men, though in the native army Commanding Officers went in too much for height, and many of the unpadded recruits looked at first rather lanky. The modern Rajpoots are quite as Hindu as, and a good deal more prejudiced than, the Bramins. In their own villages they are pleasant good fellows enough, but as Sepoys they were a disagreeable overbearing set, and, so far as I can gather, were upon the whole about the worst class in the mutiny.

As agriculturalists their style of cultivation, &c., is much the same as that of the Jats, although very greatly inferior. They are very fond of land, and do not affect the finer garden cultivation but the broad farming style of agriculture. They also keep cattle when the country is fitted for it, and are very fond of laying their hands on other people's cattle when they have the chance,—a weakness from which the Jats also are not altogether free.

They are as a rule wholly un-literary, and very much confine themselves to the two professions of agriculture and arms.

The Rajpoots everywhere speak dialects of the ordinary Hindee. I am not aware that any traces of any other language have ever been found among them.

The Koonbees or Koormees.

To the south of the Rajpoots and Jats, the country is mainly occupied by the class above mentioned. In all the central and eastern parts of the N. W. Provinces, or in fact of Hindustan generally, the Koormees are scattered abont in considerable numbers as a well-known and very industrious class of quiet cultivators. They own villages of their own, and are also more widely spread in detached families or groups of families. They affect the finer garden style of cultivation much more than Jats and Rajpoots, and like the Jats are assisted by industrious women.

As I shall afterwards notice, the Koonbees seem to be nearly connected with the Mallies, whose name we apply to the whole profession of gardeners.

The name is variously written, Koormee or Coormee, Kunabi, Kunbee or Koonbee, and there is no doubt that the terms are synonymous.

In Hindustan the Koormees do not go much beyond their own agricultural calling, but they are not absolutely unknown as Sepoys, and they have occasionally, though rarely, risen to higher posts, especially one somewhat notorious family in Oude. In fact, in the Gangetic valley the Koormees, though much appreciated as cultivators, are somewhat looked down upon by the higher castes as mere humble tillers of the soil. If we proceed south from the Lower Doab, towards the Jubbulpore and Saugor territories, Koormees become more numerous, and there are hereabouts a good many 'Lodhas,' a tribe apparently cognate to Koormees, and who are also pretty well known in the North West Provinces. They seem in this part of the Central Provinces to have at one time occupied a very considerable position. Thence westwards, on both sides of the Nerbudda, and still farther west to the north of the Nerbudda in parts of Malwa, that is in fact throughout the southern borders of Hindustan, Hindee-speaking Koormees are very numerous. In most of this country they are the chief cultivating class. In Malwa they meet the Jats and share with them the character of the most respectable and industrious cultivators. In Rajpootana there is a cultivating class called 'Pittuls' who are supposed to be Koormees under another name.

Farther west in Guzerat the Koonbees form the main body of the best cultivating population. They seem to be in the main the owners of the land, and though quiet and unpretending, are said to be still sturdy and independent and altogether a fine agricultural people.

Throughout the whole of the Marâtta country, the Koonbees are the main agricultural and landholding tribe. Here also they generally are quiet simple agriculturalists, but the Maratta Koonbees do not seem to be so energetic and good in this way as their northern congeners. They have lived long under much oppression and subject to great disadvantages. In the Nagpore country, Berar and Candeish, however, they are now a sufficiently industrious and easily managed population. To the south, where they meet the Canarese in the Deccan, every one is agreed that the latter are decidedly superior in industry and agricultural energy.

I have seen an allusion to Telinga Koonbees in the north-eastern portion of the Nizam's territory, in the country down the Godavery below the limits of the Maratta tongue, but whether these are really Telingas of this caste, or whether the word is only used to express Telinga cultivators, I am not sure.

In Hindustan the Koormees, as a lower class, are on an average darker and less good looking than Bramins and Rajpoots, but still they are quite Arian in their features, institutions, and manners. So they are in the Maratta country; indeed the Marattas are still known to the people of the south as 'Aryas,' but they have probably towards the south a larger intermixture of Aboriginal blood, and it is notorious that the Marattas are small men compared to the northern tribes.

The constitution of the Koonbees seems to be less democratic than that of Jats and Rajpoots. In the Maratta country (and indeed in the countries to the north of that also) the villages are for the most part ruled by hereditary patels or headmen without much trace of representation, so far as I could learn, and individual property in land has been in many parts subject to many changes and vicissitudes.

Nothing puzzled me more than this, viz. to understand whence came the great Maratta Military element. In the Punjab one can easily understand the sources of Sikh power; every peasant looks fit to be a soldier. But the great mass of the Maratta Koonbees look like nothing of the kind, and are the quietest and most obedient of humble and unwarlike cultivators. On inquiry I gathered that in fact throughout by far the greater part of the Maratta-speaking country, all through Nagpore, Berar, and the Northern Bombay districts, the agricultural Koonbees furnish very few soldiers, nor ever did furnish many. Although the Koonbee element was the foundation of the Maratta power, though Sevajee and some of his chiefs were Koonbees, it appears that these people came almost exclusively from a comparatively small district near Sattara, a hilly region where, as I judge, the Koonbees are very much mixed with numerous aboriginal and semi-aboriginal tribes of Mhars and others, and where, losing with the intermixture many of their agricultural virtues, they acquired more of the qualities of predatory soldiers. It is notorious that Sevajee relied principally on his '*Mawallees*' of the Western Ghats, who were apparently little better than non-descript predatory tribes. In their best days, it does not appear that the Marattas were ever Koonbees to the same extent and in the same sense that the Sikhs were Jats. In fact the Maratta confederacy was more a political than a personal union. Many of the oldest chiefs were not Koonbees. Holkar was of the shepherd, and the Guickwar was of the cow-herd caste. All these as well as the Koonbees were quite illiterate, and would have done little without the directing power of the Bramins. When they were farther advanced, the Maratta forces seem to have been mere mercenary armies, a congregation of every loose fortune-seeker of every race and class, Mahommedans included, with a nucleus of the population of Sattara and Poonah, from which the proper Maratta chiefs had sprung.

Take them all in all, I think that the Koonbees must be considered one of the most important as well as one of the most useful and most easily governed tribes in India. A great territory is in the main theirs, extending from about 23° or 24° to about 16° Lat., and from the western frontiers of Guzerat to the countries watered by the Wyngunga and the Middle Godavery, and the upper streams of the Nerbudda.

Other Agricultural Tribes.

I have traced the Jats, Rajpoots, and Koonbees as the three chief territorial tribes peculiar to Northern India. I must now go back to notice other landowning tribes intermixed with them.

I shall take first the farming tribes, apt in the use of arms and of a constitution similar to the Jats and Rajpoots; these are principally found in the Punjab. Second, the tribes more or less pastoral in their proclivities, though now almost universally settled in agricultural communities. Third, the fine-farming or gardening tribes.

I have noticed how much the Salt Range seems to be the northern limit of both Jats and Rajpoots. The people north of this range are a great puzzle. They are those who seem to me the finest and handsomest in India, perhaps in the world. They are all now Mahommedans, but are wholly Indian in their language, habits, manners, and constitutions. There can, I think, be no doubt of that; the line between them and their Pathan neighbours is very distinctly drawn, the languages especially being totally different. Knowing the Pathans so well, any relationship with them is never suggested; a Pathan is with them a Pathan, and a man of another tribe is not a Pathan. But they have fanciful Mussulman genealogies, the Dhoonds and Tanaolees from the Caliph Abbas, the Kurrals from Alexander the Great, the Awans from Roostam and the Gukkurs from some other Persian hero.

There are a large number of petty tribes, very like one another, but known by their own tribal names only; they have no common appellation. On the one hand much in their features, &c. would seem to show that they have kindred with the Kashmeerees or with the pre-Hindu congeners of the earlier Indians found in the hills farther west; on the other hand, their language and character, dress, and the architecture of their houses would indicate that they are nearly allied to the Punjabees. The language is altogether Punjabee. In these respects they wholly differ from Kashmeerees. Jats and Rajpoots are so well known that one would think that if they belonged to those tribes, they would say so. As it is, the only tribe which admits a Hindustanee origin, is that which seems to have the least claim to it, the Dilazaks, the predecessors of the present Pathan tribes in the Peshawar valley, and who seem to have themselves so considerable an infusion of Pathan blood that it has been doubted whether they are not earlier Pathans.

The Swattees too, the people driven out of Swat by the Euzofzyes, though in the main of the blood which supplied the early Indians, must be considered pre-Hindus, and have now a considerable Pathan intermixture.

The Gukkurs were the rulers of the Rawal Pindee district in comparatively modern times. They might possibly be foreign conquerors, but if so, it would seem singular that they should have completely lost their language, and so entirely assimilated to those around them. In appearance I do not think Gukkurs could be distinguished from Awans. Both are very large fine men, but not exceedingly fair, inhabiting as they do a dry, bare, rather low country, hot in summer. The Awans are the most numerous of these frontier tribes, and the best; there is no finer people in India. They are settled in large agricultural communities in the 'Chuch' plain, immediately facing the Peshawur valley on this side the Indus, and are also found in smaller bodies somewhat to the east, in the Jhelum, Guzerat, and Sealkot districts. They are good soldiers as well as good cultivators, and might be taken for the best class of Jats.

The Dhoonds and Tanaolees are to the north in the outer range of the Himalaya and about the Indus near Torbela. I have not been in the Tanaolee country, but the Dhoonds seemed to me to be the handsomest among handsome tribes. It is to be remarked, however, that in the country far towards the frontier in this direction, the people who are the fairest and handsomest, are not considered the most plucky and trustworthy; the blood of Cashmere and Swat does not seem altogether to tend to these latter qualities. I cannot attempt to trace the minor tribes of Alpials, &c. &c. &c. Both the Awans of the lower lands and the Dhoonds, &c. of the higher lands seem to have democratic village constitutions.

Till we know something of the language of the tribes of the hills west of Cashmere, it would not be safe to speculate on the origin of the people of this corner of India. If the language of the hills is nearly allied to the Hindee and the Punjabee, we may suppose that these are Indianised tribes from the same source. If on the other hand the hill tribes speak a tongue of an earlier Arian form, then we must look to people of the blood of the Jats and Rajpoots for the introduction of the Hindee form of speech both here and in the rest of Hindustan. Looking to the want of any proper tribal name of the Rajpoots, it might be that before they became famous in Hindu story, some of them occupying the Punjab surmounted the Salt Range and mixing with some aboriginal Caucasians, formed the present tribes. Nowhere is there room for more interesting inquiry than in this direction.

Passing farther down in the Punjab I only remember one class of the character that I am now describing, the Doghurs, a Mahommedan tribe found near the Sutlej, fine, good-looking, high-featured men, but not very reliable and rather given to cattle-lifting. I do not know their origin.

Beyond the Sutlej again I have mentioned the Bhattees of Bhateeana, whose origin is also obscure. But they are certainly one of the very finest and handsomest tribes in India.

In the Simla hills, most of the land is held by a local tribe called Kanaits. They are inferior in position to Rajpoots, more perhaps of the level of Koormees and Lodhas, but they are often educated, and men of this class are generally ministers to the Rajpoot chiefs. In certain places there is a partial and local practice of polyandry among them, but it is not the general custom of the tribe. All those who are not (in the upper hills) in contact with Tartars are quite Arian, though not very large; the women *very* nice-looking.

It will also, I think, be proper to mention the Indian Pathans, before I leave my present class of Fighting-Farmers.

I do not now touch on the proper Pushtoo-speaking Pathans. I do not reckon them as Indian, and all the Pathans beyond the Indus, as well as a few on this side (in the north of the Hazareh District and west of that of Rawal Pindee), are Pushtoo-speakers. The Pathans are the only Central-Asiatic people who have in comparatively modern times colonised to a considerable extent in India. They have never come in large bodies, nor occupied any large tracts at any one spot, but Affghanistan has always been as it were the base of operations of all the successive Mahommedan Empires in India; and from that base Pathans have immigrated in the service or under the protection of Mahommedan rulers, and have settled themselves here and there at many places throughout Northern India and even in some places in Southern India. They are not nearly so much mere Urban fortune-seekers as other Mahommedans, but are generally settled in villages, in many of which they own and cultivate the soil, and in some of which they form large brotherhoods, approaching those of Jats and Rajpoots. Their constitution and modes of government also seem to me to be in these villages very similar. They have been generally a favoured class who have had in places a good deal of jagheer and rent-free land, and still look a good deal to service, but many of them pay their rent or revenue by honest cultivation like any one else. Indian society is a wonderful solvent and absorbent; every one who long lives in it, becomes Indianised; and so all the Pathan colonists, even those whose immigrations are matter of recent history, are essentially Indian, not Affghan. Among Indians, they have very marked characteristics, but their nationality is changed, and the Pathans from the Frontier, who came down in the mutiny times, utterly refused to acknowledge the proudest Indian Pathans as having anything in common with themselves, and chopped off their heads with the utmost non-chalance. In many respects, however, the Indian Pathans are a very great improvement on the wilder Pathans of the Frontier. They are very much more civilised and educated. In India, in fact, the Pathans are quite an aristocratic class. Notwithstanding the wide door to corruption of blood opened by the Mahommedan laws of marriage, they are still a very handsome people;

a large proportion of them are in a respectable well-to-do position, and many of them are very well educated. After all a well-educated Mahommedan has much more in common with us than most Hindus, and comes much nearer our idea of a gentleman. It may be, too, that these Pathans retain some little trace of that non-Indian character which makes us readily become familiar with Affghans. Altogether I have no hesitation in saying that (putting the Punjab apart), among Hindustanees, the Pathans are by far the best class with whom we come in contact. They have always been very numerous in our Irregular Cavalry and also had a large share in our Civil Service. I shall be sorry, if, partly on account of the more insinuating and it may be in some respects sharper character of subservient Hindus, and partly from the difficulty of imposing our education on those who have already an education of their own, these and other Mahommedans are gradually extruded from the public service.

Pathan settlements are dotted here and there about the Punjab, but they are not very numerous. In Hindustan they are more so. They are found about Dehli, and are very numerous in the Upper Doab and Rohilcund, though it must not be supposed that the latter is really a Rohilla country; it is only a Rohilla jagheer, and the Pathans, though positively numerous, are relatively but a small minority of the population. It may be mentioned that the term 'Rohilla' does not signify any particular tribe, but is applied in India to Pathans generally, meaning apparently "mountaineer." The Rohilcund and Dehli Provinces are the chief nurseries of Pathan soldiers, &c., but all over Hindustan, and indeed all over India, Pathan Principalities and Jagheers, Pathan settlements, and Pathan families are found here and there.

It will be well here to dispose of the other Mahommedan settlers, that is, Mahommedans who do not own or cannot be traced to a Hindu origin. With the exception of the Pathans, their origin is, in fact, generally obscure and doubtless very mixed.

The name of Mogul is assumed by but few, and whatever the word may originally have been, it must be understood that it does not now in India in any degree mean 'Mongol.' There is no ethnological trace of Mongol immigration into India. Even the leaders who inherited Mongol claims had, in fact, changed their blood in passing through Persian and Affghan peoples. And on the Frontier, the term Mogul is now applied to Persian-speakers, as distinguished from Pushtoo-speaking Pathans. Most people will there tell you that 'Mogul' means a Persian, but it is really a somewhat wider designation. In Cabul, the Mahommedan population is simply divided into Pathans and Moguls (or non-Pathans), the latter being chiefly composed of Persian Kazzilbashes and the like. So then in the armies and followings of the Emperors of Dehli, Foreigners were divided into Pathans and Moguls; but while the Pathan settlers are many, the Moguls are, as I have said, very few.

In small Mahommedan countries there are numerous people claiming to be descendants of the prophet after the easy Mahommedan form of descent. Indian Syuds are generally mere loose waifs of low degree among the Urban population; but here and there we have considerable settlements of Syuds holding villages or jagheers, and where these occur, they generally claim and maintain a good deal of dignity and propriety, and are a superior and well educated, if sometimes somewhat bigoted, class.

It is generally said that a 'Sheik' means only a Mahommedan who is neither Pathan, Mogul, nor Syud. There are, however, a good many respectable landholders, and some village communities who bear the name of Sheiks; for instance, the old proprietors of Lucknow, when it was but a village, were Sheiks. It is impossible to trace the origin of these people, much less that of the loose Urban Mahommedan population. But I think it may be said that, generally speaking, the Mahommedans retain among them considerable traces of north-western origin. Dress and manners may have something to do with it, and there are of course many exceptions, but on an average they are fairer and show fewer marks of aboriginal intermixture than the Hindus. High-Arian features are not unfrequently to be seen among them. Even among those who do not directly claim to belong to Pathan and other tribes of the North-West, one often sees handsome faces, features, and beards, such as would make good 'wise men of the east,' or the very best of our oriental imaginings. It is impossible to attribute to these features, in Northern, Central and Eastern India, a Semitic origin (on the South Western borders it is another matter), and I attribute them to the hilly countries of the North-Western Arians.

Of the races which I call in some respect pastoral, I will take first

THE GOOJARS.

They have been long known to us as cultivators of predatory proclivities in the country about Dehli, and after 50 years of enforced peace and quietness, they distinguished themselves by breaking out into wholesale plunder all over that district within a few hours of the out-break of the mutiny, just as if the present generation had been accustomed to it all their lives. However, we must take a wider survey, for the Goojars are a far extending people, numerous in the Punjab and on the Northern Frontier. In fact, they now extend farther to the North-West than any other Indian people. I understand that they are still numerous in Swat and the adjacent hills, and they are said to have been the original inhabitants and owners of part of the Hazareh District, on this side the Indus, before they were in great degree dispossessed by the Swattees, themselves pushed forward by the Affghans. In the hills about Kashmere the Goojars are very numerous; and there more than anywhere else they have an actual pastoral character, being apparently somewhat vagrant in their habits, and at one season receiving the cattle of the Kashmeerees to graze, while at another they bring their own down for sale. Perhaps these are the Goojars who were dispossessed of their homes in Hazareh. It is supposed that in the event of any disturbance in Kashmere, they might visit the valley for other than pastoral purposes.

Descending into the plains of the Punjab, we find the Goojars about Goojerat and the country thereabouts in very much better repute than elsewhere, in fact they are there said to be among the best cultivators. They are very numerous, settled in prosperous communities, and give, it appears, their name to the town and thence to the district of Goojerat. There might be some question whether the word is not the Persian one, '*Goozerat*,' *i. e.* 'Fords' or 'Ferries,' in allusion to the ferries over several rivers thereabouts, but I understand that it is really Goojerat from Goojar. And there are frequent names in the Punjab derived from the same source. In fact, Goojars are very much mixed with Jats in all the northern, if not in all the Jat country, and form a considerable proportion of the population. About Dehli they are, as I have said, very numerous, and they are so in the Meerut and Seharanpore Districts of the Doab. They are numerous in all Northern Rajpootana, and extend into Malwa and the adjoining parts of Central India.* They there extend as far east as Bundlecund, where one of the chiefs is a Goojar. But in the other direction they do not approach Goozerat, and, so far as I can learn have never been known there. I believe that the Bombay 'Goozerat' is a name derived from some other source. Its proper form is said to be *Gurjarat*, derived from '*Gurjar*' Princes. I do not know the derivation of this last term, but there are *Gurjat* Chiefs in the Cuttack and Southern Nagpore territories, where there are no Goojars. I fancy, however, that I have heard it said (though I cannot now trace the source), that a similarity of names can be traced between places in Goozerat and in the Punjab Goojerat. If that be really so, it would open up an interesting inquiry. To prevent mistake, I should here notice that in the Bombay Presidency the word 'Goozar' is used, not to signify a Goojar in the northern sense, but merely an inhabitant of Goozerat, as thus 'Goozar Bramins,' 'Goozar Banians.'

The Goojars are generally a fair good looking people, especially towards the frontier, and have no aboriginal traces about them. Those located to the east trace their origin from the west. All, I think, to the north of Dehli are now Mahommedans; but those to the east and south of that place are sometimes half-Mahommedans, sometimes a sort of Hindus, though of so lax a character that I believe they are hardly admitted within the pale, and are considered to be in some degree a sect apart. They are sometimes said by the natives to have a language of their own; at least so I was told in the Punjab. It may not improbably be that this is only the patois of one province carried by them into another, but it would be interesting to inquire whether they may possibly have among themselves some sort of Gypsy tongue. Their most proper calling seems to be the keeping of cattle and buffaloes, not sheep; but they do not generally exercise this as a mere caste profession among the general population. They

* The last Nagpore Prince is stated to have been a *Goojar* adopted into the family, the son of 'Nane Goojar,' but I apprehend that there must be some mistake, as the Nagpore family were, I believe, Maratta Koonbees, of the same race as the Sattara family. Either 'Goojar' must be here a mere name or title of the individual, or the allusion must be to some supposed indiscretion of a lady of the family.

are usually settled in separate villages of their own, and in the absence of pastoral and predatory opportunities are cultivators, like other tribes, though in most places indifferent ones.

I shall here just mention 'Mewattees,' not because I am prepared to class them as 'Pastorals,' but because they are very frequently classed with Goojars, as "Goojars and Mewattees," with reference to their plundering propensities. In fact, although I have always been familiar with Mewattees as a very thieving tribe of cultivators found here and there along the south-western borders of the North West Provinces, I have not been able to make out what they really are. They seem to come from the Central country, from somewhere in Rajpootana or Central India, and their name might seem to indicate a connection with Mewar. I have seen mention of 'Mewassees,' hill chiefs, in those parts, but don't know if they are connected with the Mewattees. In fact, the Alwar country near Dehli seems to have been of late called 'Mewat.' Mewattees are mentioned as common in Malwa in the characters of irregular soldiers and depredators. They extend farther east than the Goojars. I think the villages razed to the ground in the station of Allahabad, for their predatory activity in the mutiny, were those of Mewattees. My impression is that they are mostly Mahommedans and not bad looking, but in truth I know and can find very little about them.

The Goojars are succeeded as cattle-keepers to the east and south by the 'Aheers,' who seem to be the pastoral element of the Rajpoot and Bramin countries, as the Goojars are of the Jat countries. Aheers and Goojars are sometimes spoken of as if connected, but that I believe is an error arising from mere coincidence of profession. Meeting as they do in the country east and south of Dehli, they keep entirely apart (in a social point of view), and are universally recognised as entirely separate and distinct castes, with no connection whatever. The Aheers are not a very strict sect of Hindus in the modern sense, and their widows re-marry, but still they are decided Hindus of the respectable position which their charge of the sacred animal demands. In the strictest days of caste there were a good many Aheers in the Sepoy army. They are good and upper-class-looking Hindustanees. Like the Goojars, they are not a mere cow-keeping caste, but have many independent villages, and in some parts of the country are in considerable tracts almost the principal landholding class. Under these circumstances they are very fair agriculturalists, only a little given to cattle-lifting, when opportunity offers. Besides the Aheer villages, families of the caste are much spread about the country as cultivators and herdsmen. 'Ghosees' also, common as buffaloe-keepers, are said to be related to the Aheers; they are, I think, Aheers converted to Mahommedansm. Except in the country occupied by Jats and Goojars, Aheers are found all over Hindustan, but do not generally extend east into Bengal. There are many of them just between the proper Jat and the Rajpoot country about the Ganges, to the east of Meerut and Allyghur, and on the other side in part of Rohilcund, and they seem to extend into the south-east of Rajpootana and of the Dehli territory, and are found about the Jumna near Muttra, and in many places farther east. In the Benares and Behar Divisions there are also many of them.

Thence through Central India I am not prepared to say what proportion of the population are Aheers, but they were certainly very famous in old time on the Southern frontiers of Hindustan, in Guzerat, and in the Maratta country. The famous Fort of Asseerghur derives its name from *Asa Aheer*, a noted leader of this tribe, and Aheers are still, I believe, found in those parts. They are said to have been once powerful in Goozerat and to be still numerous in Kattywar. That western country is stated in fact to have been formerly called 'Abhira' or the country of the Aheers. And thence southwards, it seems probable that Aheers were one of the principal Hindu races who along with the Bramins conquered and colonised Southern India. Bramins and Herdsmen are said to have been the first conquerors, and the Aheers may probably be the progenitors of the cowherd castes who are still numerous in the Southern Districts. One can only suppose Goozerat to have been a Goojar country, by assuming Goojars and Aheers to have been originally identical, which at any rate would require that we should go back a very long way. The subject is, however, worthy of inquiry.

Besides the Aheers known in the Maratta Districts, there seems to be in the south of that country and also in the Canarese country a quiet respectable class of cultivators called 'Dhangurs.' The word is translated 'Shepherds,' but I have also seen it stated that the

Dhangurs and Aheers are nearly the same. It would be well to know more on the point.

In Hindustan sheep and goat herds, 'Gaderias,' form a separate and very inferior caste and profession. They have no villages of their own, but tend sheep in the villages in which they reside.

In Bengal Proper and Orissa, the Aheers are succeeded by the Gwallas, whom I have already incidentally noticed as very different in their style, manners and occupations. 'Gwalla' is not a tribal name, but merely means a cowkeeper (from the old Sanscritic word, *go*, a cow), so that the name does not necessarily imply any tribal connection with the Gwallas of the south and elsewhere. The Gwallas (as I have before noticed) are, with their congeners the 'Satgopes,' by far the most numerous Hindu caste in Bengal; and as Bengal is not much of a grazing country, they constitute a large proportion of the cultivators, besides carrying palanquins, acting as domestic servants, and following some other avocations. In the jail returns they are about 13 per cent. of the non-Mahommedans, that is, of Hindus and Aborigines of all sorts taken together; and as Aheers prevail in Behar, it is probable that in Bengal and Orissa the Gwallas amount to fully 20 per cent.

There are no democratic villages in Bengal; indeed village communities in the proper sense, with anything like a municipal constitution of any kind, can hardly be said to exist; the Province is in that respect peculiar. Consequently it is unnecessary to add that the Gwallas are not in regular communities. They are scattered about the country. I believe that they have frequently acquired rights in the land and attained to respectable positions. They seem to be a quiet, decent set of people.

I am not well versed in the manners and customs of the Bengallees, and there seems to be a great want of information on the subject, which I trust may be supplied.

I have before hazarded a conjecture whether the Bengallee Gwallas may not have been formed on the basis of the Aboriginal Bhooyas.

Of the fine cultivators or gardeners, the most important are—

THE MALLIES,

to whom I have alluded as apparently allied to the Koormees, and who are not only the humble gardeners to whom Europeans ordinarily apply the name (as to a profession), but a considerable and far extended people. On the Frontier, above the Salt Range and extending up into Peshawar, there is a considerable class of 'Mulleals' who are I believe Mallies (though like most of the people of those parts now Mahommedans), and who are very industrious cultivators and gardeners.

Throughout the plains of the Punjab, there is again a very important and numerous class who seem to be allied to the above, called Raees or Raeens. These people have generally villages of their own, or hold divisions of villages on equal terms with Jats and others, and under a similar constitution. They chiefly affect the best lands and finer cultivation, where they pay a high revenue and are much appreciated by native governments; for they are probably, on the whole, the best cultivators in the Province. They are not martial, but are generally (like almost all Punjabee Mahommedans) fair and good-looking men. They are all, so far as I know, Mahommedans, which may account for their bearing a different name from their Hindu congeners, if congeners they be. So far as I am aware, they are not known by this name beyond the Punjab.

A little farther east, long before we come to the Koormees, we meet with Hindu Mallies. I know that between Umballa and Dehli, in the Khytul country (one by nature very little suited for gardening operations), there are a good many Mallie villages. In the North West Provinces I do not think that they are much known as independent landholders, but as gardeners they are scattered about. I find mention made of them as common about Ajmere and on the Southern frontier of Hindustan. Beyond Jubbulpore they are common, mixed with the Koormees. Thence going onwards to the Maratta country, in Nagpore also they share the country with the Koonbees, and are the class next in importance to these latter. In fact, in all this part of Central India, (the southern limits of Hindustan and the Maratta country), Koormees and Mallies seemed to be classed together. The Patels, I learned, were either Koonbees or Mallies, and they often divided the same villages. The two classes (I was told by the Patels of the Nagpore country) will eat together, but do not intermarry. In this latitude both Mallees and Koormees extend far to the east. I find mention of the former in Orissa, and of the latter in Maunbhoom and other districts of Chota-Nagpore.

The Lodhas I have already mentioned as connected with and of the same character as the Koonbees, though they are strictly speaking distinct from them.

The remaining classes of Northern India, whose proper profession is cultivation or gardening, have not generally, to my knowledge, villages of their own. There are, however, scattered through most villages in Hindustan many industrious Kachees and Koerees and Morows (tobacco cultivators) and Kumbohs, and some (though not many) who have no other caste name than that of 'Kisan' or cultivator. The farther we go down in the scale, the greater seems to be the infusion of aboriginal blood, the shorter is the stature, the darker the skin, and the more low-Arian the features; but in none of these decent castes of Hindustan do the features or the complexion and hair assume at all an aboriginal type.

In Bengal the names of castes are different, and *there* very many of the cultivators, the majority I believe in all Eastern Bengal, are Mahommedans, whose original caste and ethnological history I am at present unable to discover. Among Hindus, the most numerous castes after Gwallas, Bramins, and Kaists, are Bagdees (who are I am told of an inferior and aboriginal type), and a decent class of cultivators called Kyburtos. I am as yet altogether puzzled about the ethnology of the mass of Bengal ryots. Most of them, though dark, look Arian, but some are *very* dark, and have a decided tendency to a thickness of lip, and to some features either Aboriginal or Indo-Chinese. I am half inclined to think that there are two types among them. Some of them seem to have a great tendency to curly hair, and to a cast of features which I should be disposed to attribute to the influence of the black woolly-headed Aborigines, who may have stretched across from the Rajmahal to the Garrow hills. Others, especially the Ooryahs, with the Bhooyas of those parts and some of the Bengalees, seem rather to have straight hair with high cheek bones and complexions not very dark, which might suggest an Indo-Chinese element stretching from Burmah across the Soonderbuns. But I have acknowledged that I do not understand Bengal, and I hope that others will throw more light on it.

The inferior Helot classes, who generally, all over Northern India, cultivate to a considerable extent, either on their own account, or as the servants of others, I leave for another division of my subject.

It must, however, be understood that a good deal of cultivation, in most parts of the country, is carried on by miscellaneous cultivators of a great variety of classes, who by caste properly belong to other professions. Cultivation is the one profession which is open to all alike, and is occasionally followed by almost all. In a great part of Hindustan in particular, wherever Rajpoots and Bramins are comparatively few, and Koerees and Kachees are not numerous, there is in the present state of cultivation a large space not occupied by the classes which I have enumerated, and lists of tenant cultivators of these tracts present a very great variety. It is the same in Bengal. The caste of '*Telees*' are supposed to be properly oil-manufacturers, but whether (seeing the large growth of oilseeds) they were also in their origin oil-growers, or whether their multiplication is accidental, they certainly in many parts of the country form an important and respectable section of the agricultural community. Many of them are found both in Hindustan and in the Bombay Presidency, and in Bengal and Orissa they are particularly numerous and well-to-do. In Bengal the Tantees or weavers are also a prosperous class, and own a good deal of land.

The Chumars or leather workers form a large proportion of the population of Hindustan, and are both labourers and cultivators, but they may perhaps better be put among the inferior labouring classes.

For the rest the list of cultivating artisans and others would be endless. They must be classed under their own professions.

The Mercantille Classes.

First under this head, I will put—

The Khatrees.

Trade is their main occupation, but in fact they have broader and more distinguished functions. Besides monopolising the trade of the Punjab and the greater part of Affghanistan, and doing a good deal beyond those limits, they are in the Punjab the chief civil administrators, and have almost all literate work in their hands. So far as the Sikhs have a priesthood, they are moreover the priests or gooroos of the Sikhs; both Nanuk and Govind were, and the Sodees and Bedees of the present day are, Khatrees. Thus then they are in fact in the Punjab, so far as a more energetic race will permit them, all that the Maratta Bramins are in the Maratta country, besides engrossing the trade which the Maratta Bramins have not. They are not usually military in their character, but are quite capable of using the sword when necessary. Dewan Sawan Mull, Governor of Mooltan (and his notorious successor Moolraj), and very many of Runjeet Sing's chief functionaries were Khatrees. Even under Mahommedan rulers in the west, they have risen to high administrative posts; there is record of a Khatree Dewan of Badakshan or Koondooz, and I believe of a Khatree Governor of Peshawar under the Affghans. The Emperor Akbar's famous minister, Todar Mull, was a Khatree; and (though I was not before aware of it) a relative of that man of undoubted energy, the great Commissariat Contractor of Agra, Jotee Pershad, lately informed me that he also is a Khatree. Altogether there can be no doubt that these Khatrees are one of the most acute, energetic, and remarkable races in India, though in fact (except locally in the Punjab) they are not much known to Europeans. They are, either on account of their name confounded with Rajpoots (by those who only see the name), or more frequently, on account of their mercantile profession, are confounded with the Bunneahs or Banians, with whom socially (as matter of tribe and caste) they have no connection whatever. The Khatrees are staunch Hindus, and it is somewhat singular that, while giving a religion and priests to the Sikhs, they themselves are comparatively seldom Sikhs. And though, judged by a modern Hindu standard, they can hardly penetrate as they do into Central Asia with much regard for caste, they show their staunchness by never succumbing to the Mahommedan faith, where all the Indians around them have done so. I scarcely think that there are such people as Mahommedan Khatrees in latitudes where Jats, Rajpoots, and others are all Mahommedan; and even in Affghanistan they seem to maintain their faith intact. The Khatrees are a very fine, fair, handsome race. And as may be gathered from what I have already said, they are very generally educated. There is a large subordinate class of Khatrees, somewhat lower, but of equal mercantile energy, called Rors or Roras. The proper Khatrees of higher grade will often deny all connection with them, or at least only admit that they have some sort of bastard kindred with Khatrees, but I think there can be no doubt that they are ethnologically the same, and they are certainly mixed up with Khatrees in their avocations. I shall treat the whole kindred as generically Khatrees. Though the Rors have not usually risen to such high posts, at least one of Runjeet Sing's ministers was of this class.

Speaking of the Khatrees then thus broadly, they have, as I have said, the whole trade of the Punjab and of most of Affghanistan. No village can get on without the Khatree who keeps the accounts, does the banking business, and buys and sells the grain. They seem too to get on with the people better than most traders and usurers of this kind. Of course, like all people so situated, they are often a good deal abused, but in a Punjabee village I think that the Khatree is generally rather a popular character and on friendly terms with his clients; at any rate they appreciate the necessity for him, and are by no means anxious to get rid of him. In Affghanistan, among a rough and alien people, notwithstanding occasional exceptions, the Khatrees are as a rule confined to the position of humble dealers, shop-keepers and money-lenders; but in that capacity the Pathans seem to look on them as a kind of valuable animal, and a Pathan will steal another man's Khatree, not only for the sake of ransom (as is frequently done on the Peshawar and Hazarah frontier), but also as he might steal a milch-cow, or as Jews might, I dare say, be carried off in the middle ages, with a view to render them profitable.

I do not know the exact limits of Khatree occupation to the west, but certainly in all eastern Affghanistan they seem to be just as much a part of the established community as they are in the Punjab. They find their way far into Central Asia, but the farther they get, the more depressed and humiliating is their position. In Turkistan, Vambery speaks of them with great contempt as yellow-faced Hindus of a cowardly and sneaking character. Under Turcoman rule, they could hardly be otherwise. They have even found their way to St. Petersburgh and made money there. They are in fact the only Hindus known in Central Asia.

In the Punjab they are so numerous that they cannot all be rich and mercantile, and many of them hold land, cultivate, take service, and follow various avocations. But I do not think that there is in the plains such a thing as a Khatree village or Khatree community, such as I have described to be the social form of other castes. They are always mixed among other classes.

It is somewhat singular that the Khatrees, so important in Affghanistan, and who also push so far into Central Asia, are altogether excluded from Bramin Kashmere; they are not found there at all. In point of acuteness, I fancy it is an instance of 'two of a trade.' In the hills, however, the 'Kukkas' on the east bank of the Jhelum are said to have been originally Khatrees, (they are a curiously handsome race); and in the interior of the Kangra hills there is an interesting race of fine patriarchal-looking shepherds called 'Gaddees,' most of whom are Khatrees. There are some Bramins among them, and some of low caste, but the great majority are Khatrees, and their story is that they are the remnant of the former rulers of the plains of the Punjab, driven to the hills by conquering invaders. They are a very pleasant, frank, simple people, quite apart from their present neighbours, and a great puzzle. Khatree traders are numerous in Dehli, are found in Agra, Lucknow and Patna, and are well known in the Burra Bazar of Calcutta (though there they are principally connected with Punjab firms). But as soon as they pass east from the limits of the Punjab, they get into the mercantile field of the Bunneeahs, who are quite their equals in mere mercantile ability where little physical courage is required, and in the Bunneeah country the Khatree merchants are mere exceptions in large towns.

In Behar there seems to be a considerable agricultural class called Kshatrees, Chatrees, or Khatrees, who are distinct from and considered to be somewhat lower in rank than Rajpoots. They seem somewhat to affect a Military character, sometimes serve, I believe, as soldiers, and are well known as '*Darwans*' and the like in Calcutta. Buchanan seems to have been inclined to suppose that they are really Khatrees from the west, but I have not yet been able to ascertain whether they are in truth of the same caste as the mercantile Khatrees.

I do not know the exact limits of the Khatrees to the south. I have not visited Mooltan which is a great mercantile centre of the race, and cannot accurately distinguish between Khatree and Bunneeah sects called by their sub-tribal names. The term 'Mooltanees' seems to be applied to several trading sects in different parts of Central India, &c., some apparently wandering Pathan traders, and some,

I suspect, of some Khatree sect. The Khatrees do not seem as a rule to reach the western Coast; the Guzerat and Cutch traders appear to be Bunneeahs (or Banians) not Khatrees, and in the Bombay market I cannot find that they have any considerable place. In Scinde, however, I find (in Captain Burton's book) an account of a race of "pretended Khsatryas who are really Banians of the Nanuk-Shahi (Sikh) faith," and who trade and have a large share of public offices. These are evidently Khatrees. I had supposed the Lohanee merchants to be Pathans coming under much the same category as the "Povindeahs," but again Captain Burton makes mention of the "Lohanos, a Mooltanee caste of Banians," a robust and good-looking race who trade with Central Asia, and also with the Arabian Coast, who form a very large proportion of the Government servants in Scinde, and who also do some agriculture and labour. I cannot at this moment ascertain whether these Lohanos are really Banians or Khatrees, probably I think the latter. Palgrave again mentions among the Indian traders of the Arabian Coast, as distinguished from Banians, people whom he calls 'Loothians' or Loodianah men. I take it that these must be Khatrees, unless indeed they may possibly be Kashmeree shawl merchants. Loodianah is a large and thriving town of mercantile Khatrees, with a numerous colony of Kashmeree shawl-weavers.

The Khatrees claim to be the descendants of the old Kshatryas, and I am inclined to think that they really have the best claim to that honour. With all their enterprise, it is difficult to imagine them so completely domiciled in Affghanistan, among so alien a people, if they are entirely foreigners in that country. It is well known that the Pathans themselves have advanced into the North Eastern portion of the country which we call Affghanistan, within comparatively recent and historical times; and although the upper valleys of the Indian Caucasus have probably all along been held by pre-Hindu tribes, there seems to be little doubt that the lower valleys of the Cabul country were once Hindu. To this day the peaks of the 'Sufed Koh' between Jalalabad and Cabul bear the palpably Hindu names of "Seeta Ram" and such like.

The old Sanscrit books make the Bramins and Khsatryas to have remotely sprung from a common origin. May it not be that in early

Aryan days the Bramins of Kashmere may first have become literary and civilised, and ruled on the Saraswatee by peaceful arts, after the fashion of the earliest Egyptians before the art of war was invented, (See M. Renan's abstract of recent Egyptian inquiries); and that later a cognate tribe of Khatrees of the Cabul country, rougher and more warlike, may have come down upon them like the Shepherd Kings, and assumed the rule of the Military caste of early Hindu history? That warlike conquerors of one age should become astute money-dealers of another, is but the ordinary course of history—Jews, Greeks, Lombards and others are instances in point, and perhaps when the New Zealanders rule in England, the English may be known as the Khatrees of those parts.

The Bunneahs, Banians, Banees, or Wanees.

No race is more important in India than the Banees. What I have described the Khatrees to be in a mercantile point of view in the Punjab, that the Banees are in the whole of Hindustan and Western India. No village can get on without them. Unlike the Khatrees, they are for the most part confined to their proper mercantile business. A few of them are found in Government offices and such service, more properly the domain of the Kaists, but these are only rare exceptions. They have also under our system acquired by purchase large rights in the land, and take farms of more, but this is in fact with them a mere mercantile operation; they do not cultivate the land, but make the most of the rents payable by the ryots, and the ejected proprietors reproachfully term the British Government "Bunneah ka Raj" or the shopkeepers' rule. Bunneahs may cultivate a few fields, like any one else, or even reduced individuals may earn their livelihood as ryots or labourers, but so far as I know, a proper Bunneah village is nowhere to be found.

There is no doubt that in their own way the Banees are a people of wonderful energy and enterprise, and it is their energy that gives tone and sinew in a commercial, and to a great degree an industrial sense, to the greater part of India. Without the Banee to supply the sinews of war, little would be done. Their function permeates every operation of every village. In all the great cities of Hindustan, they are found in a position commanding much respect as Bankers and

Merchants, and they are also most daring speculators, as is well known in the markets of Bombay and Calcutta. Indeed they often carry the rage for speculation to the point of gambling. In respect of physical courage, however, the case is quite different. Both their habits and their religious ideas make the use of a sword a thing unknown to them, and they have no affectation of personal manliness.

If the Banees are not generally very tall or strong, they are not much the contrary, and they are generally very fair. For this latter feature their indoor avocations may in part account, but that alone is not, I think, sufficient. When one gets peeps of the faces of their women on the occasion of great religious gatherings and the like, they seem to be fair beyond almost any other Hindustanee caste. The men, though flabby and un-muscular looking, are, I think, to an unprejudiced eye often by no means bad looking. They have, however, none of the high-Arian sharpness of feature, but rather a sleek comely pudding-faced kind of countenance, something like those old Egyptian faces which are said to come nearest to the Hindu type. They are, I think, generally reputed more grasping than I have described the Khatrees to be; are more often accused of being hard on those in their power, and exercising a severe tyranny of the purse. But even in their case I believe that this is a good deal exaggerated, and that many of those who abuse them most, can least get on without them. Possessed as they are of so much capital and energy, there can be no doubt that, from an industrial point of view, the acquisition by them, from indolent and unprovident proprietors, of a good deal of the land is beneficial, when it becomes their absolute property. They, almost alone among superior landholders, perform something of the industrial functions of landlords, and they know too well the value of ryots, altogether to expend and sell up those in whom they have a permanent interest. There is to be set, on the other side, the political weakness resulting from the existence of large numbers of strong-armed pre-owners still, as they think, natural proprietors, side by side with new owners who in a difficulty will not fight. Still, if the Bunneahs will not fight, they may perhaps pay others to fight for them. It is only when they are set to 'exploiter' the ryots in a speculative way, as mere temporary lessees and middlemen under the great superior Zemindars, that they are often a great curse.

The great seat of the Bunneahs seems to be in the west, and most of them point to a western origin, or rather, speaking from a Hindustanee point of view, I should say south-western, not to the Punjab, but to Rajpootana and the Bombay country. There are a great many subdivisions among them, and my impression is that the different divisions do not intermarry as do those of Jats and Rajpoots. There may therefore be ethnological distinctions among them, but I do not know that it is so. The most famous of them are the Marwarees; and that is the name of the country, and not of the sect, intimating their habitat in Rajpootana. The red-turbaned gentlemen so conspicuous in the Calcutta Opium marts and Bombay share-markets are generally Marwarees. In Hindustan the highest class of Bunneahs are called 'Aggerwals,' and there are several other sects. The Bunneahs professing the Jain religion are called Srawaks, and under that name they seem to have been famous in very old times, even in parts of Central India which are now comparatively barbarous. In Hindustan, Hindu Boras are a sect of money-lenders and traders and, I imagine, Bunneahs. I believe the name is the same as that of the Mahommedan 'Borahs' of the Bombay side; but the latter, with some peculiar Mahommedan tenets, have probably got some traces of transmarine blood, and I shall reserve them for the category of 'Borderers.' Towards the south of Hindustan I have heard of a sect of inferior Bunneahs called 'Jashwals' who, unlike the race generally, are lax Hindus and even permit their widows to remarry.

So far as I can make out, the proper Banees are not thoroughly and completely domiciled in Bengal proper, and to the want of that element (or of anything equal to it) I attribute the absence of enterprise and practical achievement, which seems to be remarkable among the Bengallee, notwithstanding the great value acquired by the land under the permanent settlement, and the accumulation of wealth during a hundred years of peace. In Calcutta most of the considerable trade and banking business and all the Hindu speculation is done by up-country Marwarees and other Bunneahs, not by Bengallees. In the Bengal districts, though a good many Banee colonists are settled in towns and considerable places, the money-lending and shopkeeping business seems to be in great part in the hands of a variety of other classes. Bramins do, I believe, a good deal of money-lending, and the goldsmith class are also Bankers in Bengal. Then there is a class of *Sahoos*, whose proper profession is spirit-distilling and vending, but who have a large share of the general trading business. The common 'Modees' or grain-sellers, instead of being almost universally Banees as in Hindustan; are, I understand, of various castes, and there are separate spice-sellers, oil-sellers, &c. If there are not so many enterprising Banees to make the most of the land, there is at any rate this advantage that, I believe, the ryots are now not nearly so much rack-rented in Bengal as they are in Behar and other parts of Hindustan, where the lands of great landholders are almost invariably farmed to speculators.

In Goozerat, Forbes describes the Wanees as very universal and very grasping. But at any rate the traders of the Coast of Goozerat and Cutch are very enterprising. The Banian of those parts is an important institution all over the coasts of Arabia and Africa on the opposite side of the Ocean. And in Bombay, Premchand and other Banees have made their names famous. In the Maratta country, the higher trade and banking seems to be done by Marwarees, the village business by local Wanees. Farther south, in the Canarese country, the classes of trading proclivities called, 'Banijagas' seem to be very numerous, but as the name is derived from the Sanscrit 'Banij' a trader, I cannot be quite sure that the northern and southern traders are related by blood. Inquiry is necessary on this point.

Almost all the Banees are strict Hindus, that is, strict in their own form of the faith; for in some sense Jains and such like may be said not to be proper Hindus. In Hindustan, though there are a good many Jains, the great majority are proper Hindus. They may be considered to be in religion very high Hindus, and carry to a great extreme respect for animal life. This tenet, I think, connects them with the western Jains and others, the foundation of whose faith is really the doctrine of metempsychosis and the transmission of souls from one creature to another. The Banees are, I think, really the most sincerely religious among the Hindus, and much attached to their tenets. Among many other Hindu classes, religion is little better than form. In the west country, Jain tenets very much prevail at the present day among all the Banee classes, and seem to have had a very ancient hold upon them. In the south, the Banijagas are, it appears, now chiefly Lingamites and, as such, scarcely Braminical Hindus. But at one time the Jain form quite prevailed among them. In fact, in all the west and southwest the Jain religion appears to have been at one time predominant. The Jains seem to assert that the Rajpoots were once of their faith. The Pali language and character would seem especially to belong them.

What then is the origin of the Banees? That is a very puzzling question. I cannot account for them in any historical way, but the speculation which has occurred to my mind is, whether they may not originally have been immigrants by sea from the west who brought with them the Phallus or Lingam, and those ideas of a continually self-reproducing procreative power which took shape in the worship of Siva, and eventually gave birth to Buddhism and to Jainism, and which finally, meeting and amalgamating with the Braminical faith, produced modern Hinduism. If this be so, we might suppose that the Banees had done much to civilise the Central and South of India, before the Bramins got so far. But, as I have said, this is mere speculation; much farther inquiry is necessary.

Among the mercantile classes of the north (as well as of the south) should be classed the well-known Banjaras or wandering grain merchants, men of great energy and usefulness in their day. Though they carry on their trade all over the country, they have in some places fixed homes. On the borders of Rohilcund, towards the Terai, they have in fact considerable settlements, are considerable landed proprietors and altogether important people.

I now come to the Writer classes:—

The Kaits or Kayasts.

Important as this caste now is, I am totally at a loss to imagine how or why it came into existence. In old Hindu times, with a great Bramin class occupying something the position which Bramins now hold among the Marattas (by no means confined to sacerdotal duties, but performing all literate functions), one can see no room for a separate Writer class. If the Rajpoots, coming in as conquerors, wished to put aside the Bramins, they would probably have found Khatrees and Banees ready to assist them. The Mahommedans, we know, had always among them a large educated class of their own, so much so that in the early days of our rule in Upper India most of our public servants were Mahommedans. Yet somehow there has sprung up this special Writer class, which among Hindus has not only rivalled the Bramins, but in Hindustan may be said to have almost wholly ousted them from secular literate work, and under our Government is rapidly ousting the Mahommedans also.

Very sharp and clever these Kaits certainly are. They are looked on by Hindus as rather a low caste, and their appearance is not aristocratic. Most of them are decidedly dark, generally spare thin men, and, I should say, on the average short, with often sharp weasel-like features, small and quite low-Arian. They are somewhat lax in their ways, given to drink, and on their great annual festival, when they worship the pen, it is rather the correct thing than otherwise to have a good debauch.

They have generally the office of Patwaree, or village accountant; and of high office, having always had a good share, they are getting more and more a monopoly. They are, in fact, first-rate men of business, and without pride ready to adapt themselves to our ways, they have become almost indispensable to us. They have acquired much landed property, some by honest means, some by dishonest means, when very loose practices prevailed in our courts. And of course, with dignity and wealth the respect with which they are regarded from day to day increases. What I have said of loose ways, is only applicable to the lower and more common members of the sect. It is only fair to acknowledge that there are now many high officers and worthy proprietors of this class, whose respectability is great and conduct unimpeachable. I never remember to have heard a conjecture as to the origin of the Kaits. They are never found in separate villages, but are scattered about rather as a separate profession than a separate race. There are a good many illiterate men among them who earn their bread as they best can; but most of them are educated. I should not say that they anywhere in Hindustan form a very large population. One may suppose that when the Bramins got indolent, this class grew up as a sort of low-caste clerks to the Bramins, who ruled by supplanting their masters. But whence did they get their talent? Some of the Aboriginal races seem to have activity and bodily energy, but none of them mental talent.

In Bengal the Kaits occupy a higher relative position and are very numerous. It is related as a historical fact that they accompanied the Bramins into Bengal from the North-West, and indeed it would seem as if the Hindustanee colonists in Bengal had been almost exclusively Bramins and Kaits; there are scarcely any other castes of well authenticated Arian descent, while a large proportion of the inhabitants show some aboriginal traces. In Bengal then the Kaits seem to rank next or nearly next to the Bramins, and form an aristocratic class. According to the Jail Returns, they are 7 per cent. of the Hindus incarcerated in Bengal, Behar and Orissa, and in the general population they are probably in still larger proportion. They have extensive proprietary rights in the land, and also, I believe, cultivate a good deal. Of the ministerial places in the public offices they have the larger share. In the educational institutions and higher professions of Calcutta, they are, I believe, quite equal to the Bramins, all qualities taken together, though some detailed information of the capacities of different classes, as shewn by the educational tests, would be very interesting. Among the native pleaders of the High Court, most of the ablest men are either Bramins or Kaits; perhaps the ablest of all, at this moment, is a Kait.

Not knowing where else to put them, I shall here mention a caste who are, so far as I know, peculiar to Bengal, the Boidyas or physicians. They are not very numerous, are, I believe, often learned and respectable men, and rank high among Hindus, but in truth I do not know very much about them. It would be interesting to know more.

The Kaits extend west all through Hindustan, are numerous in Malwa and are found in Goozerat. But in this latter Province we come upon either another caste of the same kind, or a branch of the same bearing a different name, and called—

Purbhoos or Purvoes

who are very conspicuous in that part of India and in the town of Bombay, where they do most of the work of clerks. I cannot make out whether Kaits and Purbhoos are in the main the same or different. Of two well informed native gentleman whose opinions have been sent me, one seems to think that they are mere sub-divisions of an original writer class, another, that they are different. Those whom I saw in Bombay seemed to me different in appearance as well as very different in dress from the Hindustanee Kaits; they are, I should say, generally fairer and better looking. I should much like to know more about them.

The Artisans.

For ethnological purposes it would be useless to go through the long lists of professional castes, as they cannot, so far I know, be distinguished as representing races, but are merely the modern Hindu social division into professions. It will nearly suffice to say that in Northern India almost every possible profession has its separate caste, and that there is no grouping of them together, either into right hand and left hand, or into such groups as the Punchalas of the south. Nothing of the kind is known; Carpenters, Blacksmiths, Goldsmiths, Bricklayers, Potters, Barbers, Confectioners, Washermen, Spirit-sellers, and very many others, have all their own separate castes, and they eat and marry within those castes. Some are more and some less strict Hindus. All are of a low-Arian type, and I am not prepared to suggest any ethnological differences, except that they are better looking in the Punjab, and less so to the east and south. I doubt, whether substantial differences can be found till we get lower, to tribes exhibiting more decided aboriginal traces. Most professions bear different names in Bengal from those in Hindustan. I do not know much of these classes in Goozerat and the Maratta country.

The Hindustanee Kahars or Palkee-bearers are a considerable class, and are strong hard-working men, rather good looking than otherwise. They stand well among Hindus, whose water-carriers they are, and who will therefore generally drink from their hands. They are also fishermen and cultivate a good deal. They have by caste nothing whatever to do with cow-keeping, though they may own cows, like other people. I believe that they are quite distinct both from Bengal Gwallas and from south country Buis or Booes. They are found in parts of the Punjab as well as in all Hindustan, but not in the west of the Punjab.

The Inferior and Helot Classes.

Finally I come to the inferior labouring classes, the Helots and out-castes, among whom, if anywhere, the aboriginal blood should show itself in a marked way.

Castes originating in a difference of races, it may be pretty safely assumed that Helot races represent conquered peoples; but it sometimes happens that the form remains when all substantial difference has disappeared, just as in fossils we have the form although in fact the substance is stone like that which surrounds it. In the hills of the extreme north, where we have the high-Arian race in its purest and most unalloyed state, even the form of a Helot caste is wanting; which is just what we might expect in a country where the Arians themselves are the aborigines. There are no out-caste Pariahs. In Kashmere a tribe called Wattals are said to be low, but they appear to be rather immoral than ethnologically low, a gypsy kind of tribe which supplies dancing girls and prostitutes. The women are notoriously among the handsomest in the valley, so they are not at all Helots such as I mean. In all these hills, the "Chooras" of the plains are altogether wanting.

In the plains of the Punjab there is a thorough Helot tribe. The arrangement of castes is there generally more simple than elsewhere, and a single low caste tribe are both the ordinary labourers who do all the inferior Coolee work, and at the same time the out-caste scavengers of the community. They are in fact all considered to be of the lowest sweeper caste, and are called 'Chooras.' As in most democratic communities there has generally been under the freemen a Helot class (the Helots of Greece, the Slaves of Rome, the Negroes of South and the Irish of North America), so also every Jat village has its Helot quarter, where the low caste people, fewer, but still considerable in number, reside. They sometimes cultivate on their own account, but more generally act as labourers, and do all that is done by the Chamars in Hindustan. When a traveller of rank arrives at a village in Hindustan, the Chamars are called out to carry his baggage; the Chooras in the Punjab.

These Punjabee Helots are in fact fine powerful men and tolerably good looking. They were well-known under native governments as good soldiers, fit to be expended on desperate enterprises. The early Sikh reformers, preaching their doctrines of equality, tried to bring these men within the pale, but with very partial success, though a few were admitted to a respectable position as Sikhs. They were only occasionally used as soldiers by chiefs who were hard-pressed.

It has been reserved for us to enlist them in regular regiments, and to try to raise them to a good position. Like most low-placed men, they look low, when in low case performing low offices; but that they are well grown and powerful, is always clear. I had recently an opportunity of looking at them carefully, in a body drawn up on Regimental Parade, and looked especially with the view of seeing whether I could detect any ethnological peculiarity. I was quite satisfied that nothing of the sort is to be found. There may not be so large a proportion of good looking men as among the higher castes, but as a body they are fine Arians, not very materially inferior to the other people of the country. The only physical peculiarity that I have noticed among people of this class in the Punjab is, that a large proportion of them have only one eye. I apprehend, however, that this is not an ethnological peculiarity, but the result of inferior labour in a dry and dusty country, as may be seen in Egypt.

In Scinde also the low caste people are mentioned as large men of Punjabee origin and speaking the Jatee language. They are there called 'Bale Shahe' or Royal, a term also I believe applied to the sweepers in some other parts of India, and which may seem ironical, but may possibly be founded on some traditions of their former rule.

In the Punjab, in addition to the functions which I have mentioned, the Chooras are generally the village watchmen; and it may be observed that this office is all over India very generally held by the representatives of the oldest races, especially when they possess any fighting capacities. It may be supposed that when conquerors came in, they would find the headmen of the conquered races best acquainted with the localities, and most capable of dealing with those of their brethren who had taken to the jungles. I should always be inclined to look to the watchmen for ancient ethnological traces. The same races who do the watching also often do the thieving, and the Punjab Chooras have done a good deal of theft and robbery and some thuggee. What may be the origin of these Punjabee Helots, I must leave to conjecture. Either they may represent an old aboriginal tribe, whose features have been wholly absorbed by infiltration and intermixture, and who have left no ethnological traces but a dark tinge in the colour of the Punjabees and Affghans of the lower hills, or they may be early Arian inhabitants, conquered and enslaved by subsequent tribes of Bramins, Khatrees, Rajpoots, and Jats.

At any rate it may generally be said, that the whole population of the Punjab, both high and low, is above the average Arian type.

I have before mentioned that the lower class of cultivators and labourers in the Simla hills are called "Kolees." I have not noticed among them any marked aboriginal features.

I have alluded to the Chamars as the labourers of Hindustan, but *there* the functions of the Punjabee Helots are divided; the Chamars are the labourers (besides their own proper profession of curing skins), and the out-caste sweepers are an entirely separate and lower class. I have never quite made out whether the Chamars are considered to be properly Hindus. They are not considered absolutely offensive to the touch like the unclean out-castes, but their name is commonly used to signify a low man, and the greatest insult commonly proposed is to beat a man by the hands of Chamars.

They used to be sworn in a court by a peculiar Gooroo of their own, not by the ordinary name of God; and the sweepers again had a different Gooroo. They really are the modern Sudras of Hindu society, and no Hindustanee village could get on without them. Like others, they do not appear to advantage when engaged in menial offices, but to judge them fairly we should take them clean and decently fed and dressed. Most of our Hindustanee Syces are of this caste, and any one in Northern India may among them satisfy himself of their general style. It seems to me that they are a good specimen of the lower grade of the low-Arian type. An ancient proverb, quoted by Sir H. Elliott, speaks of a black Bramin and a fair Chamar as perversities to be avoided. In these days I think many Bramins may be found darker than many Chamars; but as a rule and on an average the Chamars are very decidedly dark, also rather small, though active and well knit. In features they are as it were quite the opposite of the high-Arian; there is a want of prominence, a simplicity as it were of feature; but still they do not I think show anything whatever that can really be called aboriginal. Judged by a European standard, and colour and size apart, I think that their features are quite as good as the average of Europeans of inferior degree.

The Chamars have never been soldiers, though I believe that we have enlisted some of them since the mutiny; nor have they generally held the office of watchman; that is more frequently held by the unclean out-castes. In their own trade as leatherworkers and shoemakers, they are clever intelligent men, and they are the same as Syces and sometimes Coachmen, and as Coolees and hired labourers. In some parts of the country, a good deal of the cultivation is in their hands; but I have not heard of their acquiring considerable landed rights or rising high in the world, except in Chateesgurh in the Central Provinces, where I understand that a colony of Chamars of a reformed faith have come to occupy quite an aristocratic position.

The Chamars generally are apt to be somewhat foul feeders; the lower people of the race habitually eat the dead cattle which they skin. They are also a good deal given to drink, when they can afford it.

The unclean outcastes are generally by no means numerous in Hindustan, and are for the most part confined to their own proper functions. There are various sub-divisions of them, and they are somewhat indiscriminately known by various names, Bhangees, Mehters, &c. General Briggs, in an ingenious paper, tracing the names of provinces to aboriginal tribes, makes the Bhangees the Aborigines of Bengal, but the term is a Hindustanee one, not Bengalee. The term 'Dome' is somewhat generally applied to these people, or if specially, I should say that their particular function is more particularly connected with dead dogs. It would appear, however, that in the north of Hindustan under the Himalayas, the Domes were once a considerable tribe, and in the Kumaon hills, they are still a numerous Helot section of the population, being in fact the only inferior class, and assuming the functions of artizans as well as those of ordinary labourers.

They are there described as very black, with curly hair, and altogether very aboriginal in appearance. I had not myself noticed this, but when I knew Kumaon I had not much taken up ethnology. In the plains where races have been longer and more mixed, and where, as I have said, the lowest caste are few in numbers, they do not, I think, exhibit aboriginal features. The fact is that so small a class has been recruited by people turned out of other classes, to a degree which has quite obliterated their original type. There are now many decidedly good-looking people among them, and their women often take up with men of other caste. On the average, I should say, that they are now decidedly better looking than the quiet decent Chamars.

The result is that, in my view, in Hindustan, after 3,000 or longer years of juxta-position, the Arian element has quite prevailed in feature over the aboriginal type, and the population, take them all in all, are in this particular about as Arian as Europeans, but dark in skin and usually smaller.

It is on the authority of one of the most learned native members of the society that I have alluded to the *Bagdees*, one of the most numerous non-Mussulman castes of Bengal, as aboriginal, but I have no particular description of them; and though I have observed the much greater frequency of aboriginal feature in Bengal, I am not sufficiently acquainted with the people to distinguish the special personal characteristics of the different inferior classes. The Bagdees seem to be cultivators, fishermen, watchmen, and dacoits. On the borders of Bengal and Behar, the work of labourers is done by Rajwars, Bhooyas and other aboriginal tribes whom I have noticed. The unclean tribes seems to be very various, and to have among them a system of castes more particular than that of many Bramins. I was lately obliged to dismiss the lowest servant in my establishment, an excellent man, because he respectfully but firmly declined to wash the cat, as impossible under the rules of his caste.

In the Prison Returns there is a large entry under the head of 'Chandals,' the orthodox low caste name, and others appear under the titles of 'Dosads,' 'Harees,' 'Bhoomallees,' &c. Altogether they must be numerous in Bengal. There is in the list a considerable caste of 'Mooshers,' but I cannot find what they are.

I consider that in Bengal there is still a very great field for ethnological exploration.

In the plains of Goozerat, the Kolees seem to fill the place of the inferior grade in the social scale, as labourers and lower cultivators, being there rather members of the ordinary community that a separate aboriginal tribe. The unclean outcastes are there called Dhers and Olganas.

In the Maratta country, the 'Mhars' seem to perform the functions of 'Begars' (forced bearers of burdens), watchmen, and Helots generally, much as the Punjab Helots do among the Jats. There is also a low caste of Mhangs. The lowest unclean caste are called 'Dhers' there too, but I have also seen it asserted that the 'Mhars' are really the same as the "Dhers." There is a low caste called "Parwarees" in the country below the Ghats. They are found in the Bombay army. They, also, seem to be much the same as Mhars. Everything seems to point to the reasonable expectation, that if we could but trace the matter back far enough, the Goozerattee language would be found to be the tongue of the Rajpoots and Koormees with an infusion derived from the Koolees, and the Maratta that of the Koormees and Mallies with a considerable infusion derived from the aboriginal Mhars. I have not any good description of the personal appearance of the modern Mhars. The Ramooses of the south of the Bombay country, seem to have been a bold robber caste, now settled down to cultivation. They came apparently from the Telagoo country and are not aboriginal to the Maratta districts.

Besides the settled lower classes, there are also in the north some tribes of a character which is apparently more common in the south; people who are a kind of half-tamed huntsmen, watchmen, and thieves, doing little regular labour. In all Oude and in some of the neighbouring districts to the east, there prevails a very peculiar tribe called "Pasees" who almost monopolise the office of village watchmen and who are in their way extremely good active men. They are also huntsmen and thieve extensively, also to some degree cultivate and labour. On the whole they are superior to most of these tribes.

Then there are several wandering tribes of Bhoureahs, Sansees, Harnees, Koonjars, Dhanuks, and others who go about on pretext of trapping vermin and the like, and are great robbers. There are also everywhere the gypsy 'Nuts' or 'Sirkie-bashes' (dwellers under reed-mats), but Gypsies are too well-known all over the world to need farther specification here.

The Tribes of the South.

I have already avowed my ignorance of the Telinga country, and without a good knowledge of the races there existing, it would be impossible to trace the Aryan tribes in their progress from North to South—for I find that a very large proportion of the tribes farther South refer to Andria, the Telinga country, as a former stage in their southward progress. That country seems in fact to have been a great nursery of the southern tribes. Whether "Andria" is another form of

"Ariana" I am unable to say. The change, on the southern frontier of the Maratta country, to a Canarese population seems to be abrupt, and there are few traces of progress of the tribes southwards at that point. I am inclined to think that the aborigines held out in the hilly country about Sattara and Poonah till a more recent date, and that the Arian immigration into the south principally occurred by a route farther to the east through the Telinga country, which may possibly have been then more extensive than it now is. In this I put aside the question of maritime immigration from the west.

The Telinga country seems, from some source, to have been civilised at a very early date, and there appears to be reason to believe that a good deal of the country about Warangal and thence eastwards towards the sea, was in a better state than that into which it has since fallen. Much of the ancient Telinga country is said to have been taken from the Koles who (in the sense in which I have used the word) are not now adjacent—the Gonds intervening—and the country was it seems anciently called "Kalinga" which may be another form of Coolie-land. The old Telingas seem to have been a maritime people, and it was probably they who carried Hindu ideas and perhaps some Hindu blood into the Eastern Isles. To this day the Hindus of the Eastern Coast are called "Klings" on the opposite side of the Bay and in the Islands, a name evidently derived from Kalinga or Kalinga. It is then much to be hoped that we may obtain some better knowledge of the Telinga country.

The Bainjagas, who are very important in the Canarese country, are stated to be comparatively humble in the Telinga country and reduced to the condition of cultivators and labourers, while the mercantile business is in the hands of Comtees or Comatiyas, claiming to be a race of pure Arian Vaisyas. The dominant classes are others of Arian character, whom I shall presently mention so far as I know them. All this would seem to indicate that if the Banees, being according to my speculation western immigrants, ever reached the Telinga country as Srawaks or Lingamites, or with some earliest forms of that type of faith, they have since been reduced and humbled by Northern Arians.

The principal people of whom I find mention in the Telinga country are Aylmas or Velmas, said to be "the Rajpoots of the

South," and apparently somewhat like them in character, a dominant agricultural tribe of military proclivities. But of the nature of their settlements I have no information. Another similar tribe are mentioned as " Ratsawars."

Another fine tribe called Reddies and found in the Northern Canarese country, are also stated to be a Telinga tribe, but of their location in the latter country I have no particulars.

The original Telinga " Andras" seem to have come from the North West by the valleys of the Godavery and Wyngunga. The better classes of them would seem to be taller, fairer, and better looking than most of the southerners. The " common Telinga peasantry" are described as people of spare form and dark complexion, with little spirit or enterprise, but it is added that they do well in the Madras Army. I cannot make out what are the common castes of these people.

'Naik,' a word known in the native army and elsewhere, is in some sense a Telinga, but more properly I believe an aboriginal word. There are I think some people called Naiks towards the Eastern Ghats, but in most places 'Naik' is the title of a headman. The Telinga villages, I find it stated, are not compact and fort-looking like those of Northern India and the Maratta country, but loose and detached, which would seem to be rather an approach to the very loose Bengal form. There are a good many Gonds in the North East, but the common low tribes are 'Dhers' and 'Beders' who have their Helots' quarter in each village.

The Telinga palanquin-bearers are widely spread over the south and are, I imagine, the Buis of whom I have before made mention. The bearers who ply at Madras itself and on the East Coast seem to come from Ganjam and the Northern Circars, which also furnish many of the so-called " Coolee" emigrants to the Mauritius.

The Canarese country is a remarkable instance of the way in which names are transposed in India. The Canarese name is given to everything that is not Canarese, and to nothing that is. What is called in Bombay the " Southern Maratta country," because the Marattas conquered it (the districts of Dharwar and Belgaum and the country about Beejapore) is for the most part ethnologically Canarese, while the Canara districts on the West Coast (though there is some Canarese intermixture and they were once ruled by a Canarese dynasty) are principally inhabited by races alien to the Canarese, more akin to the Marattas in the extreme north, and akin to the Malayala people in the south. About and under the Ghats, the Marattas and Northern Bramins run farther south than they do on the plains of the Deccan.

On the other side of the Peninsula, the Carnatic, wholly Non-Canarese, will always be called the Carnatic, because a dynasty seated in the Canarese country once had authority there.

The real Canarese country is, the southern part of the Bombay Presidency, part of the adjoining Nizam's territory, part of Bellary, and nearly the whole of Mysore. The Canarese can scarcely be said to be Hindus, the Lingamite sect so much prevails, and those Lingamites so entirely ignore Bramins, and so completely make their Lingam worship a separate faith. Most of the people are called 'Lingamites' or 'Sibahtagars,' a name which conceals various castes and races; for it is only a religious designation, and Lingamites are of many castes. So far as I can gather, the chief people of the Canarese country are the Banijagas who both trade and hold land, and are very numerous.

In the north of this country the Reddies, whom I have already mentioned, are described as a fine handsome powerful race, capital cultivators, living together in large villages, and raising much cotton, which with other produce they often export as well as grow. They pay their revenue well, but are jealous of interference in their village concerns, and somewhat litigious. This is an old account, and it seems very like what might be said of Jats. I do not know what is the present condition of these communities. The widows of the Reddies remarry. They are much superior to their southern Maratta neighbours in an industrial and personal point of view.

Farther south the chief castes of Hindu cultivators are 'Wokuls' or 'Ooculagas,' said to be called by the Mahommedans 'Koonbees,' and whom the Abbe Dubois considers to be in essentials the same as or similar to the Tamul Vellallers, though they will not eat or marry together. Whatever they may originally have been, they are evidently now a different caste from both Koonbees and Vellallers. I have few particulars regarding their character, but they seem to be on the whole good cultivators. The headmen of Canarese villages are called

'Gaudas,' and under native governments not unfrequently farmed the rents. There also seems to have been the village communal system in some degree, but in most places not democratic. The Wokuls are indifferent soldiers, but serve as Militia. They eat flesh freely and are not a strict class. There are, it seems, a number of sub-divisions among them. One of the chief are called Gungacara, but whether that indicates a northern origin, I can't say. In truth Wokul seems to be a very wide word. A considerable proportion of the cultivators, in several parts of this country, seem to be settled and reclaimed aborigines, sturdy "Beders" and "Malawa" or "hillmen," and there are a class allied to the Billiaru and Teermen of the Western Coast.

The low Helot outcastes are numerous and called "*Hollayers.*" Some of this caste seem to be still aboriginal in the Western Ghats, they are mentioned as coming down to the Coast nearly or quite naked; but most of them are agricultural labourers and serfs. They are said to correspond to the "Dhers" to the north and to the Palli or Pallers to the south. "Halaya" means ancient, and the word Hollayer perhaps only means "the ancient race." The Gollars, Golavadu or Gwallas seem to be few, but the "Dhangars," mentioned as connected with Aheers, extend a good way south, and there is a large class of the aboriginal shepherds the "Carambers." There are Banjaras called also "Lambadi," and I believe also "Warali" or "Katode Warali," but I am not sure whether these last are not a kind of Gpysies found also in the Bombay country.

The Buis and Bustars are palanquin-bearers, fishermen, ferrymen and distillers.

The old Canarese dynasties and most of the people were at one time Jain, but those of that faith are now few, they have returned to the worship of Siva and the Lingam, which seems to be their ancient faith. This former Jain profession seems to be, however, a link of connection with the Banees farther North.

My impression, in passing through the country, has been that the Canarese as a body are fairer and better looking than most of their southern neighbours; and as the tribes of a northern character seem to prevail among them less than in the Tamil and Telagoo country, it may be a question whether their features are influenced by an infusion from the west. It seems that the ancient name of the Canarese people and language is "Arabee," but I have been unable to trace the origin or derivation of that name. There are some vague traditions of former Arab conquest in those parts, but I have not been able to connect them with the Canarese name. The language is certainly, like the other languages of the South of India, Dravidian with Sanscrit super-imposed, but it is an undoubted fact (as we shall see when we come to the Western Coast) that a succession of immigrations has occurred there, and one of them seems to a considerable extent to have flowed over into the Canarese country. Perhaps still more ancient immigrations may have flowed farther, and it might be well worth while minutely to inquire whether any Himyaritic or Egyptian importations can be traced in the Canarese tongue.

In the Tamul country there is little suspicion of Western blood. The dominant tribe is of a very decided Northern character, while the mass of the lower classes is probably more aboriginal than in any other part of India. Consequently most of the Tamul people are small and black, and there seem to be among them frequent traces of aboriginal features.

The superior agricultural class, owning and cultivating most of the land and in possession of many chiefships, &c. are the "Vellallers," a people of whom their own traditions of immigration from the North, coupled with their laws and institutions, leave in my mind no doubt that they belong to the class of later democratic tribes. Much has been done to dissolve the old communal system, but the early descriptions of Vellaller villages, their apportionment of the lands and mode of self-government are exactly such as would describe a Jat village of the present day.

The term Vellaller, like the Canarese Wokul, seems to be used to express a cultivator of the soil, in fact may be translated zemindar or cultivator, just as "Jat" is synonymous with zemindar in the Punjab. Whether the Vellallers are directly connected with the Velmas of the Telagoo country or with the Bellalla Rajas (who, ruling in the Canarese country, carried their arms into the south), I am unable to say. They appear to burn their dead, but are Hindus of the looser sort in their religious observances, and in their rules respecting marriage, &c. Like most of these tribes, they do not ordinarily marry more than one wife, unless the first fails to bring children. They have apparently some Poojarees of their own caste, but also to some degree accept Bramins as priests. Some of them are educated, or at least some sections of them are quite literate.

Of this sort I have mentioned the Modelliars, who are distinctly stated to be a branch of them, but I am not quite sure whether it actually is so as regards the Pillays. The Vellallers are the principal tribe among the Tamul population in the north of Ceylon. The whole race seems to be an industrious good people.

The cowherds in the Tamul country are it appears called "Idayan," and I have alluded to the learned branch of the cowherd race called Yadavas. I have not been able to ascertain who are the merchant class among the Tamul people, whether Modelliars, Pillays, &c. or whether there are any Banijagas.

The artisans in the south generally seem to be classed in groups, one caste comprising several different handicrafts, the principal of which is that of the Panchalas or Pancham-Bandams, comprising carpenters, blacksmiths, coppersmiths, masons and another which has escaped me.

The principal low caste tribes are the Palli or Pallers, and the Pariahs, who, though somewhat similar in name, are quite distinct and in fact seem to be a good deal opposed to one another one (the Pallers ;) forming the lowest grade of what are called the right hand castes, the other (the Pariahs) holding the same place among the left hand castes. Then there are the robber castes, Kallars and Marawars. I have been unable to make out accurately whether these are the same or different, whether Marawar is the name of the tribe and Kallar only means robber, or whether there are two tribes. However predatory their disposition, they are not all now robbers, but seem to form a considerable portion of the settled inhabitants of the extreme south of the Peninsula. In one place I find the Marawars described as very aboriginal in feature, and in that respect giving much ground for the belief that they are descended from the monkeys who assisted in the conquest of Ceylon, while in another place they are said to be well made and featured and of a martial disposition. Probably they vary very much, accordingly as they are more or less crossed with Arians. The Tondimans people are, it appears, mostly Kallars. There seems to be a great resemblance between the position of the

Ramooses of the southern parts of the Bombay territory, the better Beders of the centre of the Peninsula, and the Kallars and Marawars of the south. All are of a sturdy, semi-military, predatory character. They have generally, in times of trouble, acquired considerable position, and their chiefs have risen to be Polygars. Evidently they are superior to the simpler aborigines. The Ramooses are described as ill-favoured, but not altogether different in appearance from the ordinary population. They have many customs which seem to indicate some connection with the northern democratic tribes (see full particulars in the Madras Literary Journal), and have the Rajpoot-like traditions of the Sacred Horse, &c. It is in such tribes that I think an infusion of Yavana blood may well be suspected.

The Pallers are probably related to the Puliars of the Pulney hills, but as settled inhabitants they seem to be decent cultivators of low degree. They are very numerous, and seem chiefly to cultivate kitchen gardens and small farms. They bury their dead, and have Poojarees of their own caste, eat animal food when they can get it, and drink freely. Like most non-Arian tribes, they appear to practice polygamy when they can afford it.

The Pariahs are well known, their name having become proverbial. *They* also seem to be numerous, and somewhat lower in degree than the Pallers, being under native rule a sort of serfs, and living in serf quarters attached to the Vellaller villages. I think that traces of the thick lip and something of the prognathous jaws of their ancestors may sometimes be traced in those whom we see in service. Yet they are certainly very intelligent good servants. It appears that they are sometimes educated, and that there have even been Pariah authors. Perhaps their masters sometimes found them intelligent, and had them educated.

A strong mark that even yet Hindu ideas and manners have not fully taken hold of the extreme south, is this that *there*, as it appears, even some pretty decent and respectable castes bury, instead of burning their dead.

The division into right hand and left hand castes, which prevails all over Southern India is very extraordinary and unexplained. They are sometimes violent factions, and yet, for anything that we are told, there is as little occasion for the feeling as for the feud between the three-year-olds and four-year-olds in Ireland. The Canarese Banijagas seem to be the chief of the right hand castes, with the lower cultivating classes of Hollayers and Kallars under them—while the better classes connected with the land appear to be the left hand, with the Pariah serfs under them. The Abbé Dubois seems rather to reverse this arrangement as respects right and left, but the more recent statements are probably the better. The artisans seem to be divided. I think that the subject deserves farther inquiry. Possibly these factions may represent two different streams of civilisation and domination meeting in the south.

The old dominant tribe of the South Western Coast are the Nairs, who seem long to have dominated that country from the Western Ghats. These Nairs are the chief people of Malabar and Travancore, and the Bunts, who occupy a similar position in Canara, are cognate to them, as are the Coorgs above them. They are chiefly notorious for the singular custom of polyandry, and the consequent order of succession through females. Polyandry is not now universally practised (though not uncommon), but the rule of succession through females is at this day the actual unvarying law of this people. They are a good-sized well-featured race, but rather dark, especially compared to the other inhabitants of this Coast. They are not only soldiers and landholders, but are also often educated, and are then considered to be remarkably good accountants. I have mentioned the prevalence of Bramins in this part of India. They seem to get on very well with the Nairs, and share the land with them. Indeed, it is said, that the Nair women are not always satisfied with their own polyandrical arrangements, and that a good deal of Bramin blood has been infused into the Nair aristocracy by the channel of female descent.

There seem to be a considerable number of the Agrestic slaves of Malabar, the black aboriginal Chermars, to whom, as well as to the Nagadies (if possible still lower), I have already alluded. The remaining important sections of the population of this part of India I shall soon come to, but with regard to the effect of immigration upon them, I shall class them under the head of Borderers.

The system of village communities does not prevail on this Western Coast. The land is there considered to be the private property, in full right, of private landholders who hold separately, more after a modern

European fashion. It is also a general observation that in all hilly and broken countries (such as are the Western Ghats and their spurs on either side) village communities are neither required, nor can be easily formed. In the midst of great plain countries, the cultivation of a community is concentrated within fixed and not distant limits, and concentration of habitation is required for defence. In hilly countries, the occasional spaces fit for cultivation are occupied by petty scattered hamlets and individual habitations.

I have never heard any attempt to account for the singular polyandry of the Nairs. My impression, however, is that polyandry is only a step in advance of the custom which is well-known as existing both among the old Jews and among almost all those modern Hindu tribes which permit remarriage, as well as among some other races, viz., that the wife of one brother passes on his decease to the next brother. Among the Jats, the men strenuously assert this right, and the women generally as strenuously deny it; but as we do not enforce it, it has never been decided which is in the right. At any rate it is always asserted. Now when the woman is recognised to be family property, and when moreover the Hindu and older than Hindu doctrine of joint family property is brought to bear on the matter, it seems to require but a little pressure and a little philosophy to convert a successive holding into a joint contemporaneous holding; especially when childless elder brothers are getting old, and younger brothers are rising up who may supply the want. In an early state of society, we know that in war the women are always carried off as the prize of the victors; consequently, as the fortune of war varies, tribes must often be left with a deficiency of women to an inconvenient degree, which the polyandrical arrangement among brothers (already possessed of contingent remainders in the same woman) obviates. This result seems to have followed among some of the Scythian tribes, and there is a tendency to the same thing among some of the Arian tribes of the Himalayas. In this last case, the cause assigned often is, that the women being good-looking and much prized in the plains, fathers have great temptations to make advantageous matches for their daughters (to sell them, rude people say), and women become scarce in the hills.

We may suppose that the Nairs were perhaps a tribe who had

pushed far ahead of their base of operations, possibly their baggage and most of their women had been cut off, and being left with a scant supply of wives in their new settlements, they may have adopted the present arrangement. Yet it seems one which has little to recommend it to permanence. The extraordinary thing then is, that it appears that in some parts of the Malabar Coast, parts of other tribes have actually to some degree borrowed the practice from the Nairs. There can be nothing about the country unfavourable to the propagation of women. Any cause tending to female infanticide would also tend to polyandry, but this has not been assigned as the reason in Malabar.

In the Canara districts, the Jains are still numerous, many of the Bants, &c. being of this sect, and it appears that this country (known also as the Tulu or Tulava country) was formerly a great stronghold of the Jains and ruled by Jain Rajas.

THE BORDERERS.

The Teermen or Islanders of the South West Coast.

On the Malabar Coast there is a numerous class called Teers or Teermen. They are generally a fair good-looking race, but considered to be of very low caste. Caste ideas are there carried to an extreme unknown in Hindustan, where, with the exception of the unclean scavenger caste, mere contiguity and general intercourse is not supposed to affect caste, and all classes mix freely together. In Malabar and Travancore, the Nairs do not pretend to be more than Soodras, but they make out the Teers and Shanars (who are much the same) to be so infinitely below them, that they must get out of the way when a Nair calls out to announce his approach in the public road. And yet the Teers are by no means a low and degraded caste; on the contrary they are, as I said, a good-looking, and they are also a thriving prosperous people, who are largely educated in the Government schools, obtain much public and private service, are acquiring land, and are in every way well-to-do.

They have (it seemed to me in Malabar) not the least aboriginal trace, but are fairer and in appearance more refined looking than the Nairs. The Shanar women of this class are those about whose liberty to cover themselves a disturbance was made in the Travancore country by the classes who considered them too low for this decent practice. All the Teer and Shanar people are said to be by caste or profession palm-growers or toddy-drawers, in allusion to the principal product of their native regions. 'Teer' it seems means 'Island' and the Teermen are generally understood to be Islanders or immigrants by sea. Their relationship to the Maldivians is spoken of, but that is a petty group, and the only people to whom it is clear that they are related are the Singhalese. I am not acquainted with Singhalese ethnology, but the Singhalese whom I have seen seemed, I think, to be a fine-featured straight-haired people with no dash of the Indian Aborigines and like the Teers, only somewhat darker and somewhat different in dress, &c. Caldwell speaks of the Teers as being a reflex of the previous Hindoo emigration to Ceylon. Yet if all the accounts be correct, it is difficult to suppose all the congeners of the Teers to have come from Ceylon. Not only are the Teers very numerous in Malabar, where they form a great proportion of the population, but all the Shanars farther south are stated to be of the same race, as are the Billiaru (said to mean 'Bow men'), the lower race in Canara, and a considerable number of people related to the latter who are found in Mysore, and there called Halaya Paika or old Paiks. Some of these people are, however, I believe much darker and less good looking than the proper Teers. The latter are also said to have contributed to form the Moplahs. If so large a population has immigrated, it must have been a long time ago. I said I think that there can be little doubt of their relationship to the Singhalese. It would seem from the published accounts, that the Singhalese are not Dravidian in language and manners, but derive the main portions of their language and religion, and perhaps of their civilisation, from Bengal and Magadha. That they received their present Buddhism from Magadha, and much of their language from a Sanscritic source, there can, I believe, be no doubt. But here also Western elements may be mixed with the other, and very careful inquiry is necessary.

It would be curious if it proved that, as it were in the three extremities of India, in Cashmere in the north protected by mountains, Bengal in the east protected by the marshes of the Ganges and Berhampootra, and parts of Ceylon and Malabar on the south protected by distance and water, there remain three remnants of the older and softer Indian civilisation, not swept over by the democratic tribes of the north-west, and still retaining considerable points of resemblance among themselves.

The Southern Christians.

I have not been able to find any precise ethnological description of the Christians of the Southern Coast, but so far as I can learn, they are principally Shanars.

The Moplahs.

I believe that the notoriety of certain events has led most people at a distance to suppose the Moplahs to be a small sect of religious fanatics on the West Coast. Nothing can be a greater mistake. They are a large, most energetic, and most prosperous people; in some industrial respects perhaps the best population to be found anywhere in India. In point of numbers alone they are very considerable. In a large portion of the Malabar country, they form full half the population, and in the Malabar district their total number by census is not far short of half a million. They are also numerous in Canara and very numerous in Travancore. The Lubbays of the Tinnevelly Coasts seem to be as nearly as possible the same race. It is evident then that they are numerous enough to form a small kingdom, and in point of wealth and individual comfort and prosperity they certainly exceed any similar number of any other race in India. I confidently assert that no one can see the comfortable, neat, superior two-storied houses and homesteads of the Moplahs of the West Coast, without feeling that he has come upon a people non-Indian in their vigour, progressiveness, and whole style. One hardly feels oneself in India. There is no doubt that the Moplahs have a very large share of Arab blood. I have not been able to ascertain particulars of the date of their immigration, nor of the parts of Arabia from which, and the tribes from among whom they come, which latter points would be important now that Mr. Palgrave has led us to distinguish among Arab and quasi-Arabs; but the general native belief, which is probably correct, is that the Moplahs are a cross between Arabs and Teermen. The result is a fine, stout, manly, good-looking race. Their religion and much of their energy and manners are Arab, but at all events they are Arabs of an industrious money-getting stamp. They have most of the trade of the Coast in their hands, and they are rapidly acquiring a larger and larger share in the land, not only inferior rights by settlement and lease, but also superior rights by purchase and mortgage. As respects their religious fanaticism, I believe it will generally be found that fanaticism is most frequently used as an instrument of political warfare, and that in the most sincere it is but a symptom of political discontent. In spite of Mr. Palgrave, I think that when Arabs beyond their own country are Mahommedans, they are pretty zealous, especially when they find themselves confronted with unbelievers. Probably the Moplahs are as good Mahommedans as are usually found, and in time of political discontent there is no lack of religious leaders from Arabia; but in fact I understand that it is perfectly clear to those acquainted with the matter that the Moplah outrages of which we have heard so much, are really political, or perhaps I should rather say social, outbursts of a few individuals among an energetic people, directed not against the British Government or Christian rule, but against Hindu landlords. The land question is at the bottom of it all. It is the old story of an inferior race with the law in their favour, and a more energetic race who wish to progress somewhat more rapidly than a conservative law allows. The more serious attacks on European officers have been made on them, not because they are Christians, but because they have not taken a view sufficiently favourable to the Moplahs in questions between them and the Hindu landlords.

They are a sturdy and independent as well as an intelligent and educated race, and though they make, I believe, capital public servants when they enter our service, they do not much seek it, and circumstances seem to have rendered them somewhat apart and over-independent. There is perhaps less intercourse and friendly feeling than is desirable between the governors and the governed. Still the Moplahs are an ethnological fact, and a strong and rapidly progressing fact; we can't get rid of them, and we must try to guide their energy in the right direction. After all, their outbreaks have been those of a very few individuals, and have only been serious on account of their extreme pluck and energy, with which only European soldiers can cope.

Mixed and immigrant races on the Bombay Coast.

The Mahommedan Borahs, with equal mercantile energy, are a pleasant contrast to the Moplahs in their quiet demeanour and ready acceptance of British rule. They seem to be of the sect of Ismaleahs or Assassins, who are supposed to hold murder among their tenets; but the Borahs are very mild, peaceable, shop-keeping assassins indeed. I believe that the name is that of the Hindu mercantile Borahs, but there is an evident infusion of immigrant blood, which probably came in together with their religion. It is probable that they are a cross between immigrants from the Persian Gulf and Hindu Borahs. Whether called Gulf-Arabs or Persians, the population of the countries at the Northern end of the Gulf is evidently more Persian than Arab, and *there* also seems to be a chief seat of the Ismaleah sect. The Borahs seem to some extent to cultivate and hold land, but their proper avocation is trade; and a most useful and prosperous race they are. They are very numerous in Bombay, and thence west and north-west; they have a large proportion of the trade of Western India, and form an important class in all the large towns up to about the centre of India. Boorhanpore is, I believe, the "city of the Borahs" to which they attach peculiar importance, and where they desire to lay their bones; and they are found in Ellichpore, Nagpore, Indore, Nusseerabad, and many other places in those directions. They are generally a fair good looking people, and deal largely in all sorts of Europe and foreign goods.

The Parsees are so well-known that I need say little of them. They must form altogether a considerable population in the west of India, comprising many humble members in service, &c. as well as merchants. They are, I think, in feature, in the main, of a high-Arian type, somewhat intermixed perhaps after a very long residence in India, and somewhat blunted and thickened as compared to the sharper and more chiselled northern faces; but still there is generally the prominence of feature which we might expect from an extraction originally Persian.

I believe that there are some black Jews on the Western Coast, but the comparatively recent Jew settlers somewhat numerous about Bombay, and who form a considerable community in Calcutta, are one of the most striking and, I think I may say, handsome of all races. A remarkably showy oriental dress, setting off a complexion almost European, no doubt goes for something ; but still the people themselves are very remarkable. Far from the dingy old-clo' looking complexion which we are apt to associate with European Jews, their complexion is the most bright and transparent looking to be seen anywhere, and the blood seems quite to over-master the faint tinge of olive in their skins. The features are large and prominent, almost to excess, and their forms tall and goodly. I believe that these people are all connected with the Persian Gulf, and that they derive their blood from thence. After Mr. Palgrave's description of the true Arab physique, one may well believe that their traits are really rather Persian than Semitic.

The Scindees.

I have already noticed the people of Upper Scinde. The people and language properly called 'Scindee' are almost confined to the lower part of the Province, and I have reserved them to be classed among the Borderers, because they are not altogether an extension of any of the Indian Arians of whom I have treated, but a composite race largely influenced by other elements. The Arabs seem to have conquered Scinde some centuries before India at large was overrun by Mahomedans of other races; and at this day there is both much Arabic in the Scindee language, and probably a good deal of Arab blood in the Scindee people. There is also probably some Persian, some Hindu, and perhaps some aboriginal Koolee blood. In short both the people and the language are altogether composite. The amalgamation does not seem to have had the good industrial result shown in the Moplahs and Borahs. The Scindees are described as well grown and rolust, but dark in skin, debased in morals, and idle. The Delta and the country of the Lower Indus seem to be very ill and insufficiently cultivated ; and the people are given to hunting, fishing, and pastoral pursuits quite as much as to cultivation.

The Belochees.

I have not alluded to the Belochees as an element in making up the Scindees, because it would seem as if the Belochees themselves were a composite people, made up of the blood of Persians and Arabs, and I don't know what besides. However, if that is so, it is not now a mere mixture, but a chemical union of the elements thrown together, and the Belochees, if their language is composite, are still now a people of distinct traits and nationality. They acquired, as is well-known, at a comparatively recent time the dominion of Scinde, and they are pretty well-known as settlers in the North-West of India, say to about as far as Dehli; but they have there none of the dignity and station of the Pathan settlers. I dare say there are decent cultivators among them; but they are more often camel-drivers and such like, and they have not a good name, being generally supposed to have considerable robber and cut-throat proclivities. I don't think they have any villages of their own; they are generally only scattered about in the capacities which I have mentioned. They are fine powerful men, but rather dark. Those whom I have seen of the families of the Ameers of Scinde are fair and good looking, but even in Belochistan I believe it may be said of the Belochees generally, that they are a good deal darker than the Pathans. They are similarly arranged in tribes, and are similarly predatory upon the border; but I understand that they are a good deal less democratic in their constitution, and more amenable to the authority of their chiefs than the Pathans. This too may make them preferable as mercenary soldiers. It is somewhat curious that, while in the west of India Arabs are entertained in that capacity, on the Coasts of Arabia itself and of Africa, Belochees are the people so employed by the chiefs. They are in fact the Swiss of those parts.

I have alluded before to the Brahooes, and as I believe that they are not known as residents within Indian limits, I need not recur to them.

The Afghans or Pathans.

I have included the Indian Pathans among modern Indian tribes, and have sometimes called the Pathans proper "Afghans," to distinguish them, and in deference to English habit. But among the people themselves, the name Afghan is hardly known.

Physically these people are among the very finest on the earth. And they have a pleasant, frank, simple, unaffected way, that makes a man at once feel, when he gets among them, that he is out of India. A European will really more amalgamate with a Pathan in a week than with a thorough Indian in seven years.

The Pathans are decidedly high-Arian in feature; and if their features are less universally very high and chiselled than those seen in the northern hills, they have on the other hand more of a broad, robust, ruddly, manly look, and the people are in fact a hardier and bolder people. About Cabul they are fair, but some of the tribes in the lower and hotter hills and valleys adjoining India have somewhat dark skins. Rough, simple, and frank as these people generally look, they are in fact by no means simple. I believe that some of the more isolated tribes, Wazeerees, &c., have more simple virtue, but the great majority of the Afghans, partly probably by nature and more in consequence of long dealing with many nations (holding as they do the portals of India), have the reputation of being a very astute, intrigruing, ambitious, avaricious, and crafty people. Great allowance must, however, he made for their situation and temptations. One cannot but feel that so energetic and fine a race, living in a country so poor, but the highway of so many nations, must of necessity learn to live a good deal on their neighbours. I am told by officers on the frontier, that in point of bold unblushing lying, a Hindu is a mere child to a Pathan. I suppose this habit comes from long living by their wits. The character of faithfulness, however, is in the main injurious to the Pathans. They are distrusted as mercenaries. It is felt that if they are always ready to do any work when it is made worth their while, they are also people of a calculating disposition, who are very likely to turn, when the advantages preponderate in favour of another policy; as the Persians found to their cost in the last century, when they too much availed themselves of the services of the Afghans. At present they are very popular in our native army, and certainly make capital soldiers. But they are fickle and uncertain, and seldom serve long without a break. A man gets a message to say that it is absolutely necessary that he should come home and murder his uncle, and off he goes with or without leave. They come back, however. It is a thing to be understood that the Ameer of Cabul pretends to no authority whatever over the Eastern Afghan tribes. They are avowedly politically quite independent, while in one sense, without our attempting to interfere in their internal affairs (that they will not permit for an instant), they are becoming more and more our military retainers. A very large number of them pass though our service, and a steady income is derived from it.

The Pathans south and south-west of Peshawar are pure and rough, but the Eusofzies and tribes to the north seem to differ considerably in character. In fact, as I have before mentioned, the Pathans are comparatively recent conquerors and colonists of the northern hills and valleys. They have there mixed much with people of an Indian type, pre-Hindu it may be, but probably the ancestors of Hindus. These people have not the Hindu caste which, for the most part, prevents amalgamation on the part of the Khatrees, and I think there can be little doubt that their blood has much influenced the character of the Eusofzye clans. The purer Afghans are extremely illiterate, and the very opposite of bigots in matters of religion. The Eusofzies are perhaps all the fairer and handsomer for the intermixture of blood; they are also more civilised in their manners and much more literary. And they have imbibed very much of that veneration, that religious capacity, which distinguishes the oldest Indian branch of Arians. Mahomedans as they are, they really seem to have some religious zeal, and they are very much priest-ridden. In fact the Akhoond of Swat and other priests have, to some extent, induced the tribes to submit to a certain and partial religious government, if it can be called by that name. The priests seem to have considerable grants of land, and at any rate succeed in levying a regular tithe from the landholders and cultivators, whose differences they settle as far as they can. It is among these people that discontented Mahomedan immigrants from Hindustan have found some sort of shelter. It should be understood that intermixture has not destroyed the military qualities of the Eusofzies themselves. With an inferior population at home to cultivate their fields, they are amongst the most notable Pathan soldiers who have pushed their fortunes in India.

The proper Afghan constitution is democratic in the extreme, so much so that any sort of government on a large scale is almost impossible, and the Ameer's authority is confined to a few open valleys (for the most part cultivated by inferior races) and to a very uncertain feudal chiefship over the western clans. They have their regular system of democratic representation and self-government by the assemblies of Jeergahs and Oolooses; but like most rude people so situated, no man's nationality goes beyond his own clan (just as in civilised Greece, it did not go beyond his own city), and within the clan order is very insufficiently maintained. Afghan individuality in very irrepressible.

A considerable population of proper Pathans are now our subjects in the districts of Peshawar and Kohat, and it would be very interesting to examine critically, how far their constitution is really different from that of the Jats and other democratic Indian tribes. It is generally said that as a people they are very different, and non-Indians must be very different from Indians. The language too shows that, Arian though they be, the Pathans are a branch separated by a wide interval. But still I have not been able to discover by cursory inquiry that their constitution is other than that of the more democratic Indo-Germans. I rather incline to think that they are probably of the same stock as the Jats and other tribes, but of a common ancestry, long anterior to the entrance of the latter into India. It may be that while some tribes poured into India, others have been gradually working their way though the hills, dispossessing the Khatrees and Khasas and more aboriginal Caucasians who held what is now modern Afghanistan.

The Aboriginal Arians of the Indian Caucasus.

I have lately called attention to our ignorance of these most interesting people, probably the remains of the pre-Hindu ancestors of the earliest Hindus. Of the Kaffirs of the most inaccessible portions of the range, between the Kashgar river and Bameean, we have heard a great deal, but learned almost nothing. They are thought to be related to Europeans, because they sit on chairs and drink wine copiously. They must be a sturdy race, to have maintained their independence so long. All the other tribes seem to be more or less Mahomedans. There are the "Neemchahs" or half breeds on the southern slope of the Caucasus, between the Afghans and the higher peaks, speaking a language with a strong affinity to the Indian tongues, and which also seems to present some curious affinities to the Latin. In the lower country near the debouchure of the Kashgar river, the people speak a mixed language called "Laghmanee." In the upper valley of that river, the name Kashgar seems to mark the trace of early Khasas.

The ancient language of Swat seems to have disappeared, and the country is now Pathan, with a subject race of aboriginal blood, that is pure Arian aborigines. But farther north, in the valleys of the Ghilghit river, running into the Indus from the West, we have an Arian people speaking a language of their own, which is cognate to the tongue of the tribes east of the Indus in and about the country called "Chilas." Some of these latter are independent and scarcely known, but most of this country, and also Ghilgit, is now subject to the Maharajah of Cashmere. The "Dards" seem to be among these tribes.

It may be asserted of all these Caucasian tribes (excepting the Kaffirs of whom we know so little) that, while they are physically as handsome and fine as possible, they are not so democratic and sturdy in independence as the Afghans. We know very well what an undertaking it is to subdue, still more to rule, an Afghan tribe in their own country. But the Afghans have certainly subdued many of these Caucasians. The Maharajah of Cashmere has conquered and governs many more. Those in contact with our own frontier are quiet and not troublesome. And in Kashgar it is understood that the people submit to their rulers, in a way which Afghans will never suffer. Altogether it may be assumed that this race is less independent (though it may be more intellectual) than the democratic races; more amenable to Rajas and Priests, and altogether just such a people as we might expect to give birth to Khasas and early Braminical Hindus. Living in countries most favourable to the Vine they seem to be generally given to the use of wine. Whether the use of chairs extends beyond Kaffiristan I cannot say. We have in fact everything to learn about these people and their languages.

The Northern Borderers of mixed Tartar or Thibetan blood.

The Mongolians and Arians seem to cross well. Most of the tribes falling under this heading are physically vigorous and industriously energetic.

I have before alluded to the Hazarahs beyond Cabul and Ghuznee, who come down to Peshawar and the Punjab for labour. This name "Hazarah" has no connection with that of the Cis-Indus district so called from a town of that name. These Hazarahs are Persian in speech, Sheeah in religion, and decidedly Mongol in feature, characteristics, which would seem to tally with the story of their having been a body of slaves in the train of some Mahomedan conqueror; but whether this is really historical, I cannot say. They are very independent and industrious, decidedly a good race.

The people of Ghilgit are the farthest Arians of the country whence the Indus flows. To the north the people are of Turkish race, and in the valley of the Indus above the junction with the Ghilgit river are the Bultees of Iskardo, &c. The language of the Bultees is decidedly Thibetan, and their features show a large proportion of the blood of that race. Some of it may be, as they say, that of Alexander, for anything I know to the contrary; but we should hardly have heard of it, if they had not been Mahomedans. They are Sheeahs, as are several tribes in those higher countries, a circumstance which has not been explained. They seem to be a good, stout, quiet race. The Maharajah of Cashmere (who rules the country) has enlisted many of them into his service, apparently with advantage.

In the upper valleys of the Sutlej, in Spiti, Kanawer, &c. there are mixed races exhibiting much Thibetan blood, and apparently more Buddhist than Hindu in religion. A very Thibetan-looking colony used to be settled at Mahasoo just beyond Simla, and people of that race did much of the heavier work, carrying wood on their backs. They are powerful, ruddy-looking people, and as entirely unlike Indians as anything one can imagine. The women especially are remarkably fine females in an industrial sense; but in other respects, whatever they may be from a Turanian point of view, they are not likely to be dangerous to the Arian visitors to the sanatarium.

From this point for many hundred miles to the east, all the passes, the very crests and centres of the passes through the snowy range, are occupied by a peculiar tribe who almost monopolise the trade across, principally carried on upon the backs of sheep. They also cultivate some land. They are known as the "Bhooteas," but that is so wide a word (in fact identical with Thibetan) that it is little guide to us.

I believe that there are some very curious tribes in valleys near and immediately beyond the snows, but I have not the means of specifying them.

As respects the Himalayas generally, the following may, I think, be said. From Cashmere eastwards, all the easily accessible portions of the Himalayas are occupied by perfectly Arian Hindus, as far as the eastern border of Kumaon and the Kalee river, separating that Province from the Nepal dominions; the Thibetans being here confined to the valleys about and beyond the snow. Throughout the whole length of Nepal again people of Thibetan blood have partially flooded over into the Nepal country, have there met and intermixed with other races, and have formed mixed tribes who appear to be generally (the proper Goorkhas perhaps excepted) more Thibetan than Indian in physiognomy and speech, but are or affect to be more Indian than Thibetan in religion and manners, doubtless under the influence of the dominant "Khas." East of Nepal, in Sikkim and Bhootan, Thibetans are altogether dominant, and the Hindu element almost disappears. The soldiers whom we erroneously call 'real Goorkhas' are mostly of the Gurang and Magar tribes of western Nepal. Their features are ultra-Mongolian, but they are small, whereas the Thibetans are generally large. Of their pluck and energy there can be no doubt. At the Simla Government School, the children from a Goorkha Regiment were found at least to equal, in fact rather to beat the Hindus. They themselves affect to be Hindus, and stoutly deny being Buddhists, though they are free from most disagreeable Hindu prejudices. The Newars, the cultivating peasantry of the valley of Nepal, are stated to have Thibetan looking features, with a fair and ruddly complexion. Both their language and that of the Gurangs and Magars seem to be in the main Thibetan, at least in the fundamental numerals, pronouns, &c. Still more is it so as regards the languages of the tribes farther east, Kerantis, Murmis, and others, of whom I know little.

The Lepchas of Sikkim and Lopas of Bhootan are unmitigated Buddhist Thibetans. There seem to be several tribes of "Rong," "Khampas" or Kambas, and Limboos, who come from different parts of Thibet, and there are some differences of language. The Lepcha tribes are described as a dirty, good-natured people, in character said to be something like the Mongols from beyond the Chinese wall, as described in recent accounts. The Lopas, &c. of Bhootan seem to be more difficult to deal with. Farther east are, I believe, still wilder Thibetan tribes. All these people are idle, but very powerful; and when they do work, they carry enormous loads, both men and women. They are said to carry up to Darjeeling as much as 250 lbs. in a single load. And at some of the Hill Stations on the Eastern Frontiers of Bengal, I understand it is the fashion that a European visitor is carried up the hill in a basket on the back of an old woman.

The people of the Eastern Frontier.

The people of the very lowest hills of Bhootan and of all the low country at their foot are of another race, the Meches or Mechis (before alluded to in marking the boundaries of the Indian Aborigines), who are apparently the same as Hodgson's "Bodo." They are, it appears, now quite ascertained by their language to be Indo-Chinese of the Lohitic or Burmese branch of the Turanian family, a connexion which their physiognomy confirms. They seem to be a good-sized, fair, but rather yellow-looking people. They are described as rude in their agriculture (using the hoe, not the plough), and erratic in their habits, but good-natured and tolerably industrious. They profess a kind of debased Hinduism, but are very omnivorous in their habits. The Dimals are a smaller but somewhat similar tribe, speaking a language which in some degree differs.

Passing over the Garrow and Cossya Hills to Cachar, the Cachar people again are of the same race as the Mechis. So, it would appear (so far as I can gather), are the Nagas, Abors, and some other tribes in the hills bordering on Assam. There are aboriginal tribes of Tipperah and Munneepore, but of their ethnology I am not informed. In the Cossya hills are an isolated body of people of the Taic or Siamese race. Of this race were the Ahoms who once ruled Assam, as are, it appears, the Khamtis and some other tribes of the more distant hills of that Province; also the Shan tribes of the Burmese interior. The Karens are, I rather think, Lohitic. It is evident, however, that on this Eastern Frontier I have got into a vast ethnological region, with which I have no personal acquaintance, and with which I cannot deal farther than to point out the vast field for inquiry, and to suggest how great a service any one would render, who would briefly classify and describe these tribes. There are endless distinct tribes, even the names of which I do not attempt to give.

POSTSCRIPT.

When this paper had nearly passed through the Press, Colonel Dalton's paper on the Kols (to the want of which I have alluded) was received in the office of the Society, and it will be printed along with this. I have only had an opportunity of hastily glancing at it, but have seen enough to be sure that it will admirably fill up just what was wanting in regard to our knowledge of the aboriginal tribes, and will be read with extreme interest. The two papers, thus published together, having been written without concert, may be found to express or assume different opinions on some points; but I hope that the general result of Colonel Dalton's paper will tend rather to confirm than to contradict most of that which I have written. In regard to the general Negrito character of the Dravidian tribes he fully bears me out. At the same time he seems to point to a considerable difference in the type of the Moondahs, Hos, Sontals, and others speaking the language which I have called Kolarian. He seems in some degree to support Major Tickell's account of the superior physical qualities of the Hos, but he also tells us that other tribes of this race are much more degraded and less good looking. In fact, the principal tribes of the race, the Moondahs and Sontals, are now extremely well known, and it is patent to all that they are among the ugliest of mankind. The Sontals are a proverb for a combination of simple good nature and ugliness. Still, I quite admit that most of these people are less black and Negrito-looking than the Savage Dravidian tribes. I think I have already suggested, and I am inclined to repeat, that they look in some respects more like Hottentots than Negroes. It is very much to be desired that a more complete study of their language should in some degree break through the complete isolation which has been hitherto attributed to it. It seems to have no affinity to the more Eastern tongues so far as has yet been discovered.

I have been struck by those parts of Colonel Dalton's description, which would seem to show, among the more civilised of these tribes, some institutions akin to those of the modern Hindoos. Not only does it appear that the Kolarian tribes burn their dead, but also I notice that the systematic division of their tribes is very similar to that which I have described among the Hindoos, and especially that they have the peculiar rule which forbids intermarriage among people of the same tribe, and imposes on every man the necessity of taking his wife from another tribe. The question will be, whether the practices common to Kolarians and Hindoos are borrowed by Kolarians from Hindoos, or by Hindoos from Kolarians. Many interesting subjects of inquiry may be opened out.

Colonel Dalton's account of the tenacity with which some of the tribes cling to their ancient rights in the soil, seems somewhat at variance with the information which I had noted respecting their ready emigration. That many of them do emigrate, is certain; but perhaps my information has reference to the Dravidians and less settled tribes,

Colonel Dalton in one place speaks of the Kolarian Hos as more dignified and more like North American Indians, and the Dravidian Oraons as more like light-hearted Negroes; but in other places he seems rather to confirm my suggestion that the Kolarian Sontals and Moondahs are an especially light-hearted race, and the Dravidians less so; the Dravidian Oraons having, he says, learned their songs and dances from the Moondahs and other Kolarians among whom they have settled. Certainly the flat and broad-faced Sontals and Moondahs seem to bear no resemblance to the North American style of feature.

Colonel Dalton more than confirms what I have said in regard to the increase of numbers of the Kolarian tribes of the Chota-Nagpore division. He tells us that, notwithstanding their tendency to drink, they increase rapidly. He evidently takes a most favourable view of them, and I think it impossible to doubt that we have in these tribes, in a healthy and accessible country in the immediate vicinity of the Capital of India, a people whom it behoves us to cherish and utilise—a people comparatively free from the peculiar vices of the modern Indians, simple, truthful and ready to receive our religion and the impress of our manners—possessed moreover of much industrial energy, laboriousness, and ductibility. To make such a people thoroughly our own—to render the central and healthy plateau occupied by them a completely Christian and Anglicised country, would be (higher considerations apart) a very great source of strength and comfort to the English in India. I think that every effort should be made in this direction.

Colonel Dalton has sent with his paper a grammar of the Oraon language by the Rev. Mr. Batsch. This is a Dravidian tongue. The Rev. Mr. Phillips has published a grammar and introduction to the Sontal language, but he has put it in the Bengallee character, somewhat unfortunately, as I think—for although I have not advocated the Romanising of the written vernacular languages, I should prefer to give to the Kolarian tribes, hitherto entirely without a written character, our own Roman letters, rather than those of the foreign and hated Bengallee. Since then Mr. Phillips's work is not available for my present purpose, I propose to re-publish, for comparison with Mr. Batsch's Oraon grammar, the brief grammar of the Kolarian "Ho" language, published by Major. Tickell in an old number of the Society's Journal. I hope then, by placing, as appendices to the present publication, vocabularies of test words both Arian and Aboriginal (including in the latter both Dravidian, Kolarian and Indo-Chinese dialects), and the sketches of Dravidian and Kolarian grammar, to supply the rough elements for a comparison of all the dialects of India. And I trust that if a beginning is thus made, we may hereafter obtain much information, more full, ample, and complete.

The "Kols" of Chota-Nagpore.—By Lt.-Col. E. T. Dalton, *Commissioner of Chota-Nagpore.*

[Received 27th July, 1866.]

The country called Chota (or properly Chuttia) Nagpore is the eastern portion of the extensive plateau of Central India on which are the sources of the Koel, the Soobunreka, the Damoodah and other less known Indian rivers. It extends into Sirgoojah and forms what is called the Oopur Ghat or highland of Juspore, and it is connected by a continuous chain of hills with the Vindhyan and Kymore ranges, from which flow affluents of the Ganges, and with the highlands of Omerkuntuck on which are the sources of the Nurbudda. That the population of this watershed is found to be, for the most part, a heterogeneous collection of non-Arian tribes, is in itself a fair proof that these tribes were at one time the inhabitants of the plains who, driven from their original sites at different periods by Braminical invaders, gradually fell back, following converging lines of rivers in their retreat, till from different directions, nations, some bearing marks of common origin though separated for ages, others bearing no trace of such affinity, met at the sources of the streams, and formed new nationalities in the secure asylum they found there.

The plateau averages more than 2,000 feet above the sea level; it is on all sides somewhat difficult of access, and it is owing to the security thus given, that the primitive tribes, still found on it, retained for ages so much of their independence and idiosyncracy. After overcoming the difficulties of the approach, these first settlers must have rejoiced at finding they had not merely reached the summit of a range of hills, but had ascended to a new country, well suited to their wants and out of reach of their enemies; and here they made their final stand.

They found a genial climate at this elevation and a well-wooded undulating country, divided and diversified by interior ranges of hills uplifting the fertilizing streams, or breaking out in rocky excrescences, sometimes in vast semi-globular masses of granite, like sunken domes of gigantic temples, sometimes in huge fragments piled in most fantastic forms, viewed with awe by the new settlers as the dwelling places of the local gods.

The total area of the plateau thus occupied is about 7,000 square miles, and the present population may be estimated at a million; more than half of whom are of the race best known to us by the name of "Kol."

This word is one of the epithets of abuse applied by the Braminical races to the aborigines of the country who opposed their early settlement, and it has adhered to the primitive inhabitants of Chota Nagpore for ages. It includes many tribes; the people of this province to whom it is generally applied, are either Moondah or Oraon; and though these races are now found in many parts of the country occupying the same villages, cultivating the same fields, celebrating together the same festivals, and enjoying the same amusements, they are of totally distinct origin and cannot intermarry without loss of caste.

The received tradition is, that the Moondahs first occupied the country, and had been long settled there, when the Oraons made their appearance. The Moondahs believe themselves to be autochthonous, or at all events declare that they are all descended from one man and woman, who were produced or established themselves, at a place called Satyomba, which is revered by the whole tribe as the cradle of the race.

Satyomba is the name of a pergunnah on the edge of the plateau overlooking the valley of the Damoodah. It is not improbable that the Moondah race had previously occupied a position on that river, and that, in departing from it, the division took place which separated them from their brethren the Sonthals. The Sonthals, unquestionably a branch of the same people, have to this day a veneration for the Damoodah, and call it their *sea;* and the ashes of their dead are always preserved till they have the opportunity of disposing of them by throwing them into that stream or burying them near its banks. The Sonthals, remaining in the plains, had easy access to the river and retained their veneration for it. The Moondahs, settling on the highlands, were less faithful to it, but from its name they might claim it as their own; for, though Damoodur has been adopted as one of the sacred names of "Krishno," does not Dah-Moondah in their own language mean "the water of the Moondah?"

We find the Moondah settlements chiefly in the eastern and southern parts of Chota-Nagpore, the Oraons predominating in the western; and this strengthens the hypothesis that the Moondahs ascended from the eastern side of the plateau.

The intimate connection between the Sonthals, the Bhoomij and the Chota-Nagpore Moondah tribes has long been known. I have pointed out their affinity with the Korewahs of Sirgoojah and Juspoor, and have given some account of that wild clan.* I have now to add to the list the "*Kheriahs,*" another aboriginal tribe settled on the plateau of Chota-Nagpore, and the "*Juangas*" of the Cuttack tributary mehals, whose women are so conservative in their notions, that they still adhere to the fashion in dress first introduced by mother Eve and wear nothing but leaves. I had often met with individuals and families of the Kheriah tribe, living in mixed communities, but from contact with other races they had lost much of their individuality, and I found it difficult to place them.

This year, I happened to come upon some of their principal settlements in pergunnah Bussiah, on the southern borders of the portion of the plateau occupied by the Moondahs, and collected round me the elders of the tribe. These settlements all lie near the Koel, one of the streams from the watershed of Chota-Nagpore, which, after its union with the Sunkh in Gangpore, becomes the Bramni and terminates its career at Point Palmyras.

The Kheriahs venerate the Koel as the Sonthals the Damoodah. They were in all probability once settled on its banks in the low-lands, and clinging to it in their retreat and adopting the place of refuge that it led to, regard it still as communicating with their fatherland, and with this idea the urns containing the ashes of their dead are dashed into a rock-broken rapid of the river, so that their contents may be rapidly borne away by the current to mingle with the ashes of their forefathers.

They say their first settlement was Pora, a village on the Koel, and that there were no Moondahs in the country, at least in that part of it, when their ancestors first came there. There is sufficient resemblance between the Kheriahs and Moondahs in language and customs

* As. Soc. Journal, Vol. XXXIV. p. 1.

and appearance, to make us certain of their consanguinity, and at the same time sufficient divergence to lead to the inference that the relationship is a remote one, and that the two branches of the family had been long separated when they met again on the banks of the Koel. These points of resemblance and divergence I will describe, when treating of the manners and customs of the race generally.

The Juangas or Puttoons (leaf-clad) are noticed in a paper by Mr. E. A. Samuells.* They are found in the Cuttack tributary mehals of Keonjur, Pal Lehra, Dhekenal and Hindole. They are thus isolated from all other branches of the Moondah family, and have not themselves the least notion of their connection with them; but their language, a specimen of which is given in the table appended, shews they are of the same race, and that their nearest kinsmen are the Kheriahs, a fragment of the tribe left behind when the remainder ascended the valley of the Koel. The Hos of Singbhoom have a tradition that they once wore leaves only, and not long ago threatened to revert to them, unless cloth-sellers lowered their prices!

The Bhoomij form the majority of the population in all the estates of the Manbhoom district to the south of the Kassae river. As they approach the confines of Chota-Nagpore, they appear to be called indiscriminately Moondahs or Bhoomij, and they intermarry. More to the east the Bhoomij have become Hindooized, or rather Bengaleeized, to a great extent, and many of them have acquired considerable estates, like the Mankees of Chota-Nagpore, and positions of influence as "Sirdar Ghatwalls," the hereditary custodians of the passes.

The characteristics of the tribe that they most tenaciously cling to, are the national dances and songs. The Bhoomij appear to have been the first to colonise the large pergunnah called Dhulbhoom or Ghatsillah, attached to the Singbhoom district. The Rajah or Zemindar is, in all probability, himself a Bhoomij by race, though (without thereby improving his pedigree, so far as I can see) he endeavours to conceal his extraction under one of those hazy traditions that Bramins always have ready for families in want of them. His ancestor, according to their version, was a washerman, a Dhoby who

* As. Soc. Journal, Vol. XXV. p. 295, 1856.

saved the goddess Kali when, as Runkini, she ran away from Pochete. Discredit has attached to the Bhoomij and Sonthal in consequence of the human sacrifices offered at this shrine of Runkini, but the whole establishment and ritual are essentially Braminical. The Bhoomij and Sonthal races personally do not much care for the blood-thirsty goddess. The Bhoomij is the branch of the Moondah race that has spread farthest in an eastern direction. Bhoomij are to be found in Mohurbhunj and Keonjur, though perhaps not so much at home there as in Dhulbhoom.

The Sonthals are now chiefly massed in the Sonthal Pergunnahs, but they muster strong in Mohurbhunj, and there are several colonies of them in the Singbhoom district. They are an erratic race, and their ancient traditions are lost in the history of their modern migrations; but my idea is that their chief settlements in Bengal were once on the Damoodah river, and that they gave way to the Koormees, an industrious Hindoo race, who now form the bulk of the population in that part of Manbhoom.

In a southerly direction the next tribe of "Dasyus" that we come across are the Khunds, but I am unable to trace any point of resemblance between them and the Moondah, either in their religion with its morbid superstitions and horrible human sacrifices, or in their language.

To trace the further ramifications of the Moondahs we must proceed west, not south, and take up the link in the hills and highest tablelands of Sirgoojah and Juspore, where we find the wildest of the race in the Korewahs. I have given a brief note on them in the paper above quoted, and have only to add that the Korewahs are quite unaware of the connectionship between themselves and the Kols. They do not acknowledge, and do not see, that the languages are almost identical. This would not, I conceive, have been the case if the Korewahs had broken off from their Satyomba kinsfolk.

The Korewahs are another branch of the family, and the history of their migrations is no doubt an independent one. It is probable that they were forced back into the hills they now occupy by the Gooands, as a Hindooized clan of that people became the dominant race in the plains of Sirgoojah. Moreover, as pointed out by Mr. G. Campbell, at a late meeting of the Society, we have in this Journal* a brief notice of a tribe called "Coour Gooand," and a vocabulary which proves them to be not Gooand at all, but another branch of the great family we are describing, occupying the Gavilghur range of hills near Ellichpore. Dr. Latham mentions in connection with them another tribe which he calls Chunah, but I have no further information about them. If the investigation is carried out, we shall, no doubt, find connecting links in the intervening ranges of hills.

Thus we have in the Coours of Ellichpoor, the Korewahs of Sirgoojah and Juspore, the Moondahs and the Kheriahs of Chota-Nagpore, the Hos of Singbhoom, the Bhoomij of Manbhoom and Dhulbhoom, and the Sonthals of Manbhoom, Singbhoom, Cuttack, tributary mehals, Hazareebagh and the Sonthal Pergunnahs (the author of the introduction to the Sonthal language, the Rev. J. Phillips, adds "Nâkâles and Kodas," I do not know where they are to be found,) a kindred people sufficiently numerous, if united, to form a nation of several millions of souls. They were, in all probability, one of the tribes that were most persistent in their hostility to the Arian invaders, and thus earned for themselves the epithets of "worshippers of *mad* gods," "haters of Bramins," "ferocious lookers," "inhuman," "flesh-eaters," "devourers of life," "possessed of magical powers," "changing their shape at will."† To this day, the Arians settled in Chota-Nagpore and Singbhoom firmly believe that the Moondahs have powers as wizards and witches, and can transform themselves into tigers and other beasts of prey, with the view of devouring their enemies, and that they can witch away the lives of man and beast. It is to the wildest and most savage of the tribe that such powers are generally ascribed; and amongst the Kols themselves the belief in the magic powers of their brethren is so strong, that I have heard converts to Christianity assert they were first induced to turn to our religion, because sorcery had apparently no power over those who were baptized! The upper classes of the Moondahs, those who aspire to be Zemindars, have assumed the "*poita*" and taken to Bramins and Kali, but the mass of the people adore their "mad gods" still, after their own primitive fashion. The great propitiatory sacrifices to the local deities or devils are carousals

* As. Soc. Journal, Vol. XIII. p. 19.

† See Muir's Sanscrit texts.

at which they eat, drink, sing, dance and make love, but though the austere "munis" of old must have stood aghast at such wild ebullitions of devotion, it is a fact that whilst the mass of the Kols have not taken to the worship of any Hindoo idols, the Hindoos settled in the province think it expedient to propitiate the gods of the Kols. It is gratifying that the darkness in which this primitive and interesting people have so long dwelt, is now being dispelled by a brighter light: that their paganism is at length yielding to the gentle influence of Christian teaching; that there is abroad amongst them a widespread feeling that a change is necessary, a change more perfect than can be typified by the adoption of a "*poita.*"

As the Moondahs first settled at Satyomba spread over the country, they formed themselves into communities called Purhas, or the country was divided into Purhas, each consisting of twelve or more villages under a chief. They do not appear in their earlier days to have acknowledged any chief, superior to the head of the Purha; the ordinary business of the community was conducted by him, and on extraordinary occasions, the Purha chiefs met and took counsel together.

Vestiges of this ancient system are still met with in many parts of the country. Though ignored as geographical or fiscal or territorial divisions, the Purhas still exist in the eyes of the people, and they still have chiefs whom they call Rajahs, men of influence and weight, who preside when a meeting is called to adjudicate regarding breaches of social observances, and who take the lead on the great hunting expeditions and national festivals.

It is said that the Moondahs were in a very wild state, occupying but a small portion of the plateau, when the Oraons, driven from the Rhotas hills, swarmed into the country, and sought and obtained permission to occupy it jointly with the Moondahs. Both Moondahs and Oraons declare there was on this occasion no fighting. The former were glad to obtain assistance in reclaiming the country they had adopted, and the Oraons are said to have come with large herds of cattle and implements of husbandry previously unknown to the Moondahs.

It is probable that the Moondahs of those days were not more advanced than are to this day their brethren, the hill Korewahs of Sirgoojah, a tribe that know not the use of the plough: but they were great hunters, and could sing and dance and make merry. The Oraon youth and maidens speedily acquired the songs and the steps, and this I doubt not aided greatly the harmonious blending of the two peoples.

There are no ancient temples or other antiquities on the plateau of Chota-Nagpore to indicate that the early Braminical races or Buddhists ever obtained a footing there; there is no tradition even of the "Munis" having sought retreats amongst its rocks or by its waterfalls for their devotional exercises. We find such monuments in Sirgoojah to the very foot of the western face of the plateau; and, as I have recently described in a paper dovoted to the antiquities of Manbhoom, we find numerous remains of Arian colonization close to its southern and eastern approaches, but none on the platean itself. Left to themselves, the Kols increased and multiplied, and lived a happy arcadian sort of life under their republican form of government for many centuries; but it is said that a wily Bramin at last obtained a footing amongst them, and an important change in the form of government was the result.

The Rajah of the Purha of which Satyomba was the head quarters, was a Moondah named Madura. His occupation of the supposed cradle of the race gave him precedence in the confederate councils; and a child of his house, reared in it if not born there, was, through his influence and by the advice of a Bramin he had taken into his service, elected supreme chief over the whole confederacy; but as it would not suit the noble family, his descendants, to have it supposed that their ancestor was one of the despised race called Kol, they have adopted the following legend as their origin:—

"When Jonmajoya, Rajah of Hustinapoor, attempted the destruction of the Nags or Serpent race, one of them, Poondorik, assumed the form of a Brahmin and went to the house of a Bramin at Benares to study the 'shasters.' The Benares Bramin, pleased with the intelligence and grace of his pupil, gave him his only daughter 'Parbutee' to be his wife. Poondorik and his wife, Parbutee, together visited Juggernath, and on their return, passing through this country, then called 'Jharkhund,' the forest land, she was seized with the pains of labour near Satyomba, and gave birth to a child and died.

"Madura's Bramin happening to pass, bearing an image of the sun worshipped by the Moondahs, saw the child sleeping and protected by a snake with expanded hood. This snake was Poondorik, relapsed into his original form. He addressed the Bramin, told his own story and the story of the child's birth, declared that the babe was destined to be a great Rajah, and that his name was to be Funimatuk Roy, 'the snake hood crowned,' a worshipper of the sun, whose image the Bramin bore, and the Bramin was to be the family priest. The snake then vanished. The child was taken to Madura's house and adopted and brought up with his own son, a boy of much the same age. When Funimatuk Roy was twelve years of age, Madura convened the Purha chiefs, and it is said the neighbouring Rajahs, including the Rajah of Sirgoojah and the Dytya Rajah, and suggested that one of the two lads should be selected as the Rajah of Nagpore. The lads were subjected to an examination, when it was found that the snake boy had already acquired all the accomplishments necessary for his destined position, whilst the other was a mere rustic. It was then (according to the annals of the Nagbunsee family) ruled, that Funimatuk Roy and his heirs for ever should be the Rajahs, and that the Moondah's child and his descendants should bear burdens, and thus all who claim to hold lands as descendants of the Moondahs and Oroans that first cleared them, are bound, when called on, to bear the burdens imposed on them by the Rajah and his assigns!"

It is frankly admitted in the annals I quote from, that a difficulty arose regarding Funimatuk's birth, when he sought in marriage the daughter of the Sikurbhoom (or Pochete) Rajah. The Sikurbhoom family priest was sent to examine the certificates of birth and found none: but Rajah Matuck Roy prayed for the intercession of his *ophidian* parent; he had calmly contemplated his position and put it to his father, that if the Sikurbhoom priest was not satisfied, a Moondah or an Oroan girl should become Queen of Nagpore. This was not to be thought of. So the Nag once more entered an appearance, satisfied the Bramin by a relation of wonders, and since then the Nagbunsis have always intermarried with the best Rajpoot families. It is particularly noted that at Funimatuk Roy's wedding-feast the Oroans and Moondahs all got drunk and began to fight, and the Rajah of Nagpore and Madura had to obtain the assistance of his guests, the

Rajah of Sirgoojah and the Dytya Rajah, to separate them. The Dytya Rajah was, I presume, the Rajah of Patkoom, as that family bear the surname of Adytya to this day.

The marriage was celebrated at Satyomba, and there the first Rajah resided in a mud fort. The fourth in descent from Funimatuk moved his court to Chuttia, where we have the remains of a fort with masonry walls and some stone temples ascribed to him. Subsequently Doisa was chosen as the seat of Government, and here are some fine buildings, shewing that the family were improving in art and in civilization, when they moved there. This site also has been abandoned, and the present Rajah lives in a very mean house at Palkote.

The sway of the Rajah of Chota-Nagpore does not, in early times, appear to have extended beyond the plateau or fringe of hills which divide it from the plains, but the Moondahs overran those limits and formed colonies in what are now called the five pergunnahs—Silli, Tamar, Barundah, Rabey and Boondoo—which did not acknowledge the Rajah-elect of Satyomba. In time, each of these pergunnahs elected a Rajah of its own, who (their descendants declare) were each of a divine or miraculous birth, like Funimatuk Roy; and on the strength of it they all call themselves Chuttrees and wear the cord. They intermarry amongst themselves or with the petty Rajahs of Manbhoom who are of similar origin; so their claim to be Chuttrees, or at all events Hindoos of respectable caste, is not disputed. According to their own tradition, the Rajahs of the five pergunnahs first forfeited their independence by submitting to pay tribute to the Rajah of Cuttack. Eventually, however, they were subjugated by the Maharajah of Chota-Nagpore, and submitted to pay tribute to and accept the "Tilluck" or symbol of investiture from him. The Moondahs comprise about two-thirds of the population of the five pergunnahs, and all who are not Moondahs are settlers of no very ancient date.

In the northern and western parts of Chota-Nagpore, the authority of the old Moondah or Oraon chiefs has been almost effaced by the middlemen who have been introduced by the Zemindars as more profitable farmers, or by the Bramins, Rajpoots and others to whom, for religious or secular services, grants have been made by the Maharajah and members of his family holding under him. In many instances, the Kols have been entirely dispossessed of the lands their ancestors brought under cultivation, and ryots from other parts of India, more subservient to the wishes of the farmers, have been introduced. In some villages the peasant proprietory right of the aborigines has been entirely extinguished, and the few of that class that remain are found in the position of farm labourers.

In the southern parts of Chota-Nagpore the Moondah chiefs, there as in Singbhoom called Mankees, have managed to retain their position, first, by resisting in open arms all attempts to encroach upon it, and lastly, by a settlement suggested and brought about by the officers of the British Government and concluded with the Maharajah shortly after the Kol disturbances in A. D. 1833.

These Mankees have each under them about as many villages as formerly were included in a "Purha," and they pay a quit rent to the Maharajah as a commutation of the service and tribute in kind formerly paid to him as Lord Paramount, and they collect this and a little more as the contribution for their own support from the heads of villages, who again collect according to ancient custom at fixed rates from the villagers. There is fixity of tenure throughout, from the Maharajah to the cultivator, notwithstanding the intervention of the Mankee, the village Moondah, or Mohto. This is no doubt a living exemplification of the relation that, in older times, subsisted between the cultivator of the soil and his chief in most parts of India.

In the Hoor Lurka Kols of Singbhoom we have a people who, till recently, had no notion of what it was to pay rent to any one, or even to give pecuniary support to their chiefs. They had their Mankees and Moondahs, but no one exercised any right arising from a title in the land except the cultivators. We have a very interesting description of the Hos, their country and their languages, by Colonel Tickell,* and to this, before proceeding further with my memoir, I will add a brief sketch of their history.

The Singbhoom district is of a singular interest to the ethnologist. That portion of it called the Colehan, the Ho-desum or country proper of the Hos, is a series of fair and fertile plains, broken, divided and surrounded by hills; about 60 miles in length from north to south, and from 35 to 60 in breadth from east to west. It has to the south and south east the tributary estates, Mohurbhun. Keonjur, Bonai

* As. Soc. Journal, Vol. IX. pp. 783, 997, 1063.

and Gangpore, inhabited by Ooriah-speaking Hindoos, to the east and north the Bengalee pergunnah of Dhulbhoom and district of Manbhoom, and north and north-east the Hindee district of Lohardaggah, and it is occupied by a race totally distinct by descent, custom, religion and language from any of the three. A people on whose smiling country covetous eyes have often been directed, but into which no one ever attempted with impunity to intrude.

It is impossible to say when the Hos first entered Singbhoom; but as we find that the Chota-Nagpore Moondahs more and more assimilate to the Hos, as we approach Singbhoom from Chota-Nagpore, we may safely infer that the Hos came originally from that country; and this is their own tradition. They appear to have brought with them and retained their system of confederate government by Purhas, but in Singbhoom the word now used to express it, is Pirhi or Peer. Thus the Colehan is divided into Pirhis, each under a Mankee as chief of the Pirhi, and each village having its Moondah as headman.

According to their own tradition, the Hos displaced a nation of Jains settled in the eastern parts of Singbhoom, some remains of whom are still extant, and a nation of Bhuyahs from the western and southern parts, driving them out of, and appropriating to their own exclusive use, the richest part of the country. From these early times, probably more than 2,000 years ago, they have proudly held the country they acquired; and, in my humble opinion, they have the right to say they never submitted to rulers of an alien race, till they were forced to do so by the power of the British Empire.

At the commencement of the present century, Singbhoom was only known to the British Government as a country under the rule of certain Rajpoot chiefs, all of one family, whose independence, when we first occupied the Orissa Provinces, Lord Wellesley promised to respect. After the final cession of all the surrounding districts in 1819 these chiefs, occupying a territory that embraces the Colehan, voluntarily submitted to the British Government, and immediately sought the assistance of that Government in reducing the "Hos" to submission, asserting that the Hos were their subjects then in rebellion; but they admitted that for fifty years they had exercised no authority over them, and I find no proof that the Hos had at any former period ever submitted to them. It is not pretended that they were conquered, but supremacy was claimed by the Rajpoot Rajahs over the Ho tribes next to them, thus dividing the country and the people amongst four Rajpoot chiefs, the Rajahs of Mohurbhunj and Porahat, Koer of Seraikilla, and Thakoor of Khursowan.

It is true that the chiefs of Singbhoom, ancestors of the Rajahs of Porahat, Seraikilla and Thakoor of Khursowan, obtained great influence over their wild neighbours. They were gradually induced to believe tales which gave to the founder of this family a miraculous birth in their country, and they accorded to him divine honors, whilst they repudiated the idea of his being their temporal chief. The oldest surviving member of the Porahat family tells me that no regular tribute was ever received from the Colehan, but they were treated and employed rather as friendly allies than as subjects, and at certain seasons presents of trifling value were received from them and presents given in return.

When a division of the estate of the Singhoom chief occurred, the brothers each took, with the share assigned to him, a share in the goodwill of the Hos. Thus the Seraikilla and Khursowan families claimed the allegiance of the tribes nearest to them. The claim of the Mohurbhunj Rajah sprang up as the Kols extended their cultivation, till it touched or ran over his boundary. But it is admitted that all recorded attempts of the Rajpoot chiefs to subdue them had been signally defeated.

On the last occasion, the great grandfather of the present Maharajah of Chota-Nagpore, at the head of 20,000 of his own men co-operating with the forces of the Singbhoom Rajpoot chiefs, entered the Colehan. The Hos allowed him to do this; they then fell on his army in masses, and, routing it with immense slaughter, ignominiously expelled him, pursuing him into his own territory, and severely retaliating on the border villages of the Maharajah and his allies.

It was no doubt in retaliation for these attacks on their independence that the Hos now became, as they were found to be when first brought to our notice (in 1819-20), the scourge of the inhabitants of the more civilized parts of Singbhoom and of all the surrounding districts. They shewed no mercy to the Braminical inhabitants of the villages they attacked and pillaged. A long line of Bramin villages on the Bramin river in Gangpoor was laid waste by them and has remained depopulated ever since. No traveller ever ventured to pass through their country. No Bramin, Rajpoot or other Hindoo caste, or Mussalman was suffered to reside in it.

In 1820, the Agent Governor-General, Major Roughsedge, entered the Colehan at the head of a force consisting of a battalion of infantry, with cavalry and artillery. He was surprised to find the wild race, of whom he had heard such disparaging accounts, in possession of an open undulating and richly cultivated country, studded with villages in groves of magnificent tamarind and mango trees, abounding in unusual indications of rural wealth. He was allowed to enter on this scene unmolested, but the slaughter of some of his camp-followers, who had incautiously strayed into one of the villages, demonstrated the hostility of the people, and an attempt to capture the murderers brought about the first collision between the Hos and our troops. A party of cavalry, sent to the offending village, was met in the open field by 300 warriors, who undauntedly advanced to meet the charge, rushed between the ranks of the horsemen, hacking especially at the horses with their formidable battle-axes, and shewing no disposition to yield or to turn, till half their number had been sabred or shot. In the village where the murder was committed, was found a reserve of 60 men who fought desperately and were all killed! The same evening another body of Lurkahs* attacked the rear of the column and cut off a convoy of supplies. It became necessary to act with vigour, and the old Hos of the present day describe the retaliation that now fell upon them as dreadfully severe. Eventually some intercepted mails were restored uninjured, as a token of submission, and the Lurka chiefs in the vicinity entered into engagements to acknowledge and pay tribute to the Rajah of Singbhoom.†

Major Roughsedge met with further opposition in his progress towards Sumbulpoor through the Southern Peers: he had in fact to fight his way out of the country; and on his leaving it a war broke out between the Kols who had submitted, and those who had not. One hundred Hindustanee burkundazes under a Soobadar were sent by the Agent to the support of the Rajah and his Lurka allies, and this for a time gave them the advantage; but the Soobadar having

* "Laraka," the fighters, a common name for the Hos.

† Major Roughsedge's dispatches.

been induced to enter the Colehan to assist in levying a contribution, was attacked, and he and the *whole of the party cut up !*

In 1821 a large force was employed to reduce the Lurkas to submission, and after a month's hostilities, the leaders, encouraged by a proclamation surrendered and entered into engagement, binding themselves to subjection to the British Government, and agreeing to pay to the chiefs at the rate of 8 annas for each plough. It was now noticed that the Lurkas evinced a perfect willingness to be guided and ruled by British officers, and the utmost repugnance to the authority arrogated over them by the Singbhoom chiefs ; and it would have saved much blood, expense and trouble, if this feeling had at the time been taken advantage of. Made over to the chiefs, they soon again became restive and reverted to their old practices of resistance and pillage. The circle of depredations gradually increased, till it had included Dhulbhoom, devastated Bamunghatee, and extended to some parts of Chota-Nagpore. The chiefs under whom the Lurkas had been placed could not control them, and for some five years, from 1830 to 1836 the Hos, maintained this hostile attitude.

In consequence of this unsatisfactory state of affairs, a proposal made by Captain Wilkinson in August 1836, to employ a force and thoroughly subdue the Lurkas, and then to take the whole tribe under the direct management of British officers, was favourably received by Government and promptly acted on. Two Regiments of Infantry and two Brigades of guns entered Singbhoom in November 1836, and operations were immediately commenced against the refractory Peers ; and by February following all the Mankees and Moondahs had submitted and bound themselves by fresh engagements to obey and pay revenue to the British Government, and no longer to follow the orders of the chiefs to whom they had previously been required to submit. Six hundred and twenty-two villages, with a population estimated at 90,000 souls, of whom more than three-fourths are Hos, were thus brought and have since remained under the immediate control of the British Government. Since then, the population and spread of cultivation have immensely increased, and the people are now peaceful, prosperous and happy. From the region round about the station, Chybassah, 170 miles due west from Calcutta, the waste lands have entirely disappeared. Colonies of Hindus may now be found settled in the heart of the Colehan, occupying villages apart from the Hos, but without demur placing themselves under the Ho Mankees of Peers. For their own system of government is, as far as possible, preserved, and the Mankees are officers of police as well as the tuhsildars or rent-collectors of their circles. One great change is now being peaceably introduced, the old system of assessment on ploughs is under process of commutation to a light assessment on the land.

This is undoubtedly the nucleus of the Moondah nation, the most compact, the purest, most powerful and most interesting division of the whole race, and in appearance decidedly the best looking. In their erect carriage and fine manly bearing, the Hos look like a people that have maintained and are proud of their independence. Many have features of sufficiently good cast to entitle them to rank as Arians; high noses, large but well formed mouths, beautiful teeth, and the facial angle as good as in the Hindu races. The figures both of male and female freely displayed by the extreme scantiness of the national costume are often models of beauty; but this description applies only to the people of the highly cultivated part of the country who have seldom been subjected to severe privation and who generally fare right well. The inhabitants of the imperfectly reclaimed hill forests are more savage-looking, but they seldom deteriorate to the almost simian physiognomy that the Oraons are found with under similar circumstances. When the face of the Moondah varies from the Arian or Caucasian type, it appears to me rather to merge into the Mongolian than the Negro. High cheek bones, small openings for the eyes, having in some rare instances a tendency to the peculiar oblique set of the Mongolian, and flattish faces without much beard or whisker. They are of average stature, and in colour vary from brown to tawny yellow.

II.—The Oraons.

The Oraons have a tradition that they were once settled in Guzerat. They were expelled from that part of India, and, retreating east, made a stand at fort Kalinjur where they fought the "Loorik Sowrik" of "Palipipri," were defeated, and, retreating still east, settled on the Rhotas hills. Here they say, they remained unmolested till attacked and driven from the hills by the Mahomedans in the reign of the emperor Akbar, but as they aver this occurred fifty-two generations ago, there is an anachronism somewhere. I think they were settled in Chota Nagpore centuries before the days of Akbar, but it is probable that some of the clan remained in the Rhotas hills until the Mahomedans constructed their fortress there.

The accounts of ancient Guzerat faintly confirm the Oraon tradition. I find from Thornton's Gazetteer that there is a race settled there from remote antiquity who are called Coolies; but there is nothing in the name, which, as I observed before, appears to have been applied very generally to the aborigines by the Arians, and the account given of the Coolies does not lead me to suppose they are of the Oraon family. There is, however, a short description of what appears to be a remnant of a tribe, which would answer perfectly for the Oraons,—"A small, active, well built race, engaged to some extent in cultivation, but by choice deriving their subsistence, as far as possible, from the chase, fishing, or the collecting of wild fruits and the marketable produce of the jungles for sale. Their peculiar pursuits, little relished or shared in by the rest of the community, caused them to be viewed with dislike and dread, and the reputation of possessing great powers in sorcery subjects them to much cruel treatment."

Every word of the above description applies to the Oraon tribe, and the name given to this remnant of a people viz. "Dunjas," is an Oraon word not unlike the term Dhangurh, so commonly applied to the Oraons in the countries to which they emigrate for work.

The names traditionally handed down amongst the Oraons, as Loorik Sowrik, allude probably to some tribe of Sravacks or Sowoks or Jains, and the Palipipri might refer to the Palithana mountains, the Jain temples on which are amongst the most interesting architectural works in India. The etymology of the word Oraon, I have not been able to trace satisfactorily, but it may have been applied to the tribe in consequence of their migratory habits. They call themselves "Khoonkir."

Between the language of the Oraons and the language of the Moondahs and their cognates, I can trace no similarity either in pronunciation, formation, construction or general character. With pretty copious vocabularies before me, I can find no analogues, and whilst the language of the Moondahs is soft and sonorous, that of the Oraons is guttural and harsh. Doctor Latham, in his descriptive ethnology, has noticed the near connection of the Oraon, Rájmahal hill and Tamul languages, and especially observes on the similarity of the personal pronouns.

English.	*Rajmahal.*	*Oraon.*	*Tamul, &c*
I	En	En	nam, En.
Thou	Nin	Nin	Nin
He, she, it	Ath	As	Ata
We	Nim	Em	Nam
Ye	Nina	Nim	Nim
They	Awar	Ar	Awar

Out of a vocabulary of about 24 Oraon and Tamul words, I find the following analogues.

English.	*Tamul.*	*Tuda.*	*Oraon.*
Man	Al	Al	Al
Eye	Kam	Kan	Khan
Tooth	Pal	Paroh	Pulla

But I find in the language now spoken by the Oraons, words of Sanscrit origin not in common use, as "*puph,*" flower, "*amb,*" water, "*kesh,*" hair, indicative of their having occupied some country in common with people speaking a Sanscrit or Prakrit dialect.

The annexed notes on the language with which I have been favoured by the Rev. Frederic Batsch, senior Missionary at Ranchee, will, I hope, throw some light on the subject. The resemblance between the Oraon and Tamul language does not invalidate their own migratory traditions, for it is not more marked than the relation between the Tamul and the language of the Gonds and others.

Their physical peculiarities are as different from those of the Moondah as are their linguistic characteristics. The Oroans must be regarded as a very small race, not short and squat like some of the Indo-Chinese stock, but a well proportioned small race. The young men and women have light graceful figures and are as active as monkies. Their complexions are, as a rule, of the darkest; but if we take as our type those who dwell in mixed communities, we find great variety in feature and colour. If we take those who, living in isolated positions, may be supposed to offer us the purest blood, we find them generally dark and ill-favoured. They have wide mouths, thick lips and projecting maxillary processes, nostrils wide apart, and no elevation of nose to speak of, and low though not in general very receding foreheads. I have seen amongst them heads that in the woolly crispness of the hair completed the similitude of the Oraons to the Negro. It may be said that the class I am describing have degenerated in feature from living a wilder and more savage life than others of their clan; but I do not find this degeneracy of feature amongst the Jushpore Korewahs, who are to the Moondahs of Chota-Nagpore what the Jushpore Oraons are to the Oraons of the same district.* I found the Korewahs mostly short of stature, but with well knit muscular frames, complexion brown not black, sharp bright deep set eyes, noses not deficient in prominency, somewhat high cheek bones, but without notable maxillary protuberances. In the more civilized parts of the province, both Oraons and Moondahs improve in appearance. The former indeed still retain their somewhat diminutive appearance, but in complexion they are fairer, in features softer, some even good looking, and the youthful amongst them all pleasing from their usual happy contented expression and imperturbable good humour.

Driven from the Rhotas hills, the Oraons, according to their own tradition, separated into two great divisions. One of these, moving east, found a final resting-place in the Rájmahal hills; the other, going south, sought refuge in the Palamow hills, and wandered from valley to valley in those ranges, till they found themselves in Burway, a hill-locked estate in Chota-Nagpore proper. From thence they occupied the highlands of Jushpore and formed the settlements in the vicinity of Lohardugga, on the Chota-Nagpore plateau, where they still constitute the bulk of the population. The Satyomba Moondahs had not effected settlements so far to the west.

The identity of the language spoken by the Rájmahal hill people (not the Sonthals) and that of the Oraons is full and sufficient confirmation of the tradition of their common origin, and of the division of the tribe spoken of above; but a comparison of the customs of the Rájmahal hill people, who being isolated must have retained those they brought with them to the hills, with the customs of the Oraons, demonstrates that the latter are derived from the Moondahs.

* Asiatic Society's Journal, Vol. XXXIV. p. 15.

Referring to Col. Walter Sherwill's account of the Rájmahal hill people,* I find, in regard to marriage, that it is customary for the young couple to sleep together on the same bed before marriage. The Oraons would consider this a very indecorous proceeding, though a public recognition that the young couple have slept together after the marriage is with the Oraons an important sequel to the ceremony. In the Rájmahal hills, says Col. Sherwill, the dead are buried. The Rig Veda and Ramayun tell us that this was the custom of the Dusyas, but the Moondahs and their cognates all burn their dead, and the Oraons follow their example.

The Rájmahal hill men swear on salt, the Oraons have a veneration for salt, but swear on *dub* grass,† *huldee* and rice.

The Oraons know nothing of Bedo Gosain, the invisible spirit adored by the Rájmahalies. Their supreme deity is the sun under the title of Dhurmo, but as that and the Rájmahalee term are both of Sanscrit origin, it evinces that neither race have in their own language any word for the Deity.

Lastly, the hill man is described as less cheerful than the Sonthal, less industrious, and as not joining in the dances that the people of the Moondah stock are so devoted to. In Chota-Nagpore the Oraons are more lively than the Moondahs, quite as industrious, and the most enthusiastic and nimble-footed of the dancers.

The two races, Moondah and Oraon, must have been for ages the only colonists of the plateau; it is singular that they have no tradition of any disqute having arisen between them. Affecting jealously to guard against admixture of the races by sexual intercourse, they in other respects lived as one people, the Oraon conforming more to the customs of the Moondah than the Moondahs to the Oraon, and in many instances adopting the Moondah language and losing their own.

In villages east of Ranchee, though inhabited wholly by Oraons, the Moondah, not Oraon, is the language spoken; but the Moondah language is not much known in the vicinity of Lohardaggah or in Jushpore.

The village systems of the two people became almost identical in form. The village priest, called the Pahan, is probably an Oraon institution, as, I think, amongst the Moondahs the principle is that the head of the family is priest; but the Moondahs of Chota-Nagpore

* Asiatic Society's Journal, Vol. XX. p. 544. † Agrostis linearis.

adopted it, and in their villages, as well as in those of the Oraons, there is always a Pahan. The village system now existing is such as it became after many encroachments by the Rajah and the middlemen introduced by him. Still as bearing the impress of a very primitive form of government, it is worth describing, and in doing so, I will make use of a very elaborate report on the subject written by Doctor Davidson in 1839.

The actual descendants of the men who formed the villages are called Bhuinhurs. They are a privileged class, who hold their lands at low fixed rates or rent-free, but they are bound to do service to the chief or his representative. The head of the Bhuinhurs is called the Moondah, and is generally the representative of the old Moondah chief of the village. He presides when meetings are held to settle disputes about social customs; and all demands for service on the Bhuinhurs by the proprietor or farmer are made through him. He holds his lands as Bhuinhurree, and has no other emolument.

The Mahto, though second in point of rank, is the most important functionary in the village. He has the assessment and settlement of all lands not held by the hereditary cultivators; collects all dues and rents, and is responsible for them to the farmer or proprietor. He holds for his services one *powa* of land rent-free, and in some villages gets a fee of one or two pice annually from each ryot. The office is not hereditary.

The Pahan is the village priest. He is a Moondah or Oraon by caste, but all observances for propitiating the village gods or devils are performed by him. No Bramins are permitted to interfere. The office of Pahan is generally hereditary, but is not necessarily so. He has under his charge the land called "Dalikhatari," and from the proceeds of this land, he has to support himself and to provide the rice and rice-beer required for the great festivals.

The Bhandari assists in the collection of rents, summoning ryots who have to do work or whose attendance is required by the Zemindar or farmer, and in looking after the collections made in kind. He has an allowance of one *powa* of land, and gets from each ryot one *kerai* or bundle of each crop as it is cut.

There is a Gorait for each village, and a Kotewar for one or more villages. The former is the messenger of the Zemindar or his representative, the latter is the Police officer.

The villagers maintain a blacksmith and a Gowala or herd; the latter takes care of all the village cattle, and is supposed to be responsible if any are stolen. They each get a maund of dhan for every plough and three *kerais*, bundles, of other crops.

According to the tradition of the Kols, the Rajah is entitled to the rent of only half of the land in each village. The remainder is Bhuinhurree, or rent-free under some other denomination, but in most villages rent is now taken on from two-thirds to three-fourths of the land. The land is thus divided:—

I. Rughus—the land that pays rent to the owner or his representative.

II. Bhetketta, a certain portion of the Rughus which each ryot, not a Bhuinhur, is allowed to cultivate free of rent, but for which he has to perform various services to the landlord or farmer.

III. The land allotted to the Mahto, the Pahan and the Bhundari.

IV. Munghus—the land at the disposal of the landlord or his agent or the farmer of the village. For the cultivation of this land, the holder of the village can make any arrangement that he pleases.

V. Bhuinhurree is the land held rent free by the descendants of the founder of the village, who are, however, bound to render certain services to the Rajah or his representative.

VI. Bhootketta—the land, the produce of which is appropriated to the expense of the great village poojas and festivals; a portion of this called "Dalikhatari" is assigned to the Pahan for the ordinary annual poojas, and the proceeds of the remainder are reserved for the triennial sacrifices and extraordinary occasions.

The rent is assessed on the wet land only. The cultivator is entitled to upland in proportion to the wet land for which he pays. If he cultivates more, the custom is for a payment in kind called Muswur, to be made when the crop is harvested.

The Bhuinhurs cling most tenaciously to their Bhuinhurree lands. Insurrections have followed attempts to disturb these tenures, and even now such attempts are sure to lead to serious affrays. The Kol insurrection of 1833 was, without doubt, mainly caused by the encroachments of alien farmers and sub-proprietors on the rights of the descendants of the old settlers. The first burst of the outbreak was a pretty broad hint, a general conflagration of the houses of alien farmers and sub-proprietors, and the massacre of all that the incensed Kols could find.

The Kols of Chota-Nagpore, generally a good-tempered, mild, inoffensive race, become wild with excitement on this question, and nothing can reconcile them to a decree or order which in any way infringes on what they consider their proprietary right. According to their theory, dispossession for generations can no more annul their right in the land than it can extinguish the ties of blood. The courts will not always accept this doctrine, and the Kols cannot regard as equitable any decision that excludes it.

An Oraon family lives very promiscuously in a small, indifferently constructed and untidy looking hut, and their village often consists of a street or court of such huts. In all that relates to their inner domestic life, they are less susceptible of improvement than the other tribes. They have no gardens or orchards attached to individual houses, but the groves of fruit-trees that they plant outside the village form a beautiful feature in the scenery of Chota-Nagpore, and they have generally, in and about the village, some fine trees which are common property. In every Oraon village of old standing there is a house called the "Doomcooreea" (Bachelor's Hall), in which all unmarried men and boys of the tribe are obliged to sleep. Any one absenting himself and spending the night elsewhere in the village is fined. In this building the flags, musical instruments, yaks' tails, dancing equipments and other property used at the festivals are kept. They have a regular system of fagging in the Doomcooreea. The small boys have to shampoo the limbs of their luxurious masters, and obey all orders of the elders, who also systematically bully them to make them, it is alleged, hardy. In some villages the unmarried girls have a house to themselves, an old woman being appointed as Duenna to look after them. She is always armed with a stick to keep the boys off. A circular space, in front of the Doomcoorea, is kept clear as the village dancing ground. It is generally sheltered by fine old trees, and seats are placed all round for spectators or tired dancers.

The Doomcooreea is never used by boys of the Moondah tribe. It is an institution quite unknown to the Hos, but the Moondahs and Hos build themselves houses in which all the family can be decently accommodated. Their houses are more isolated, occupy much more space and are in appearance much more civilized than those of the Oraons, with verandahs, well raised plinths and separate apartments for the married and single members of the family. Every Moondah village has its dancing place, though it has no Doomcooreea. The best Korewah villages consist of about forty houses built round a large square, in the centre of which is the dancing arena; but as the Korewahs are nomads, changing their abodes every second or third year, their villages may be regarded as mere standing camps. The Kheriahs build substantial comfortable houses like the Hos. It is curious they have the same word "O" for a house and the sky. The Moondah word "Ora" is, like the Turkoman "Ova," a house or tent. The flags kept in the Oraon Doomcooreea appear to be an Oraon institution. Every village or group of villages, probably the head quarters of each "Parha," has its peculiar flag, and we have actually had cases in courts praying for injunction against villages charged with having assumed flags that did not belong to them!

I will now proceed to review the customs of the Moondahs and Oraons together, taking care to note all points of divergence that are known to me.

After the birth of a child, the mother has to undergo purification, and on the same day that this ceremony takes place, which is simply a process of ablution, the child is named. Elderly females or matrons, friends and relations assemble for this purpose, and a vessel containing water is placed in the midst, and as the name first selected is pronounced, one of the women drops a grain of rice into the water. If the grain of rice sinks, that name is discarded, and the experiment is repeated with the second name on the list, and so on till, as the name is pronounced, the grain floats. (Tho Garrows of the eastern frontier have a similar method for divining the name of the spirit they ought to invoke on particular occasions.) If the name of some friend is chosen, it is considered as establishing a tie between the child and his namesake, resembling that which subsists between a Christian child and his godfather. The person whose name is selected is always called Saki or Sakhi, a word of Sanscrit origin meaning friend, so that in "nam Saki" we have in meaning and sound our word namesake. The following are some names of girls, Jambi, Jima, Jingi, Turki,

Sulgi,* Pongla, Madhi, Makoo, Roomeea Saggi, Dinli, Natri, Akli, Bangi, Julli, and the Hindoo names of the days of the week are very commonly given. The following are the names of boys—Rumsi, Birsa, Somra, Daharoo, Singra, Satri, Dubroo, Doolkoo, Didoo, Runka, Biggoo. But they have adopted many foreign names, and the names of British officers they have known and esteemed, are thus preserved amongst the Hos of Singbhoom, and may be handed down from generation to generation. Thus "Major" and "Captain" have become common names in the Colehan, originally taken from Major Roughsedge, the first British officer they ever saw, and Captain Wilkinson (now Col. Wilkinson) whom they regard as their greatest benefactor. Doctor, Tickell, &c. are also common. Girls, when three or four years of age, receive their mark of caste. Three lines tattooed on the forehead and two on each temple, four dots on the chin and one on the nose. It does not appear to be connected with any religious custom, nor is it applied with any ceremony, and as neither the Moondahs nor the Oraons have any particular term for it in their own language, it is probable that they adopted it from the Sudhs or Hindoos. Some Moondah girls of Chota-Nagpore have different marks. Those of Singbhoom have adopted the arrow, appropriately enough, as the national weapon of their lords and masters.

The Kheriahs and Juangas, though isolated from the Moondahs and Oraons, have the same triple and double marks on the forehead and temples. The Oraon boys are marked, when children, on the arms by rather a severe process of puncturation, which they consider it manly to endure. The only reason I have heard assigned for this custom is, that through it even the naked dead may have a distinguishing mark.

When a girl approaches maturity, it is incumbent on her to bind up her hair, and from that period of her life she is restricted to food prepared by her own people. As a child with her hair loose, she is permitted to partake of whatever is edible, no matter by whom prepared. Young men enjoy this liberty of appetite till they marry. They then, to use their own expression, put salt in their flesh, and must not partake of food prepared by aliens. The Oraons have a veneration for salt, and they are not absolutely prohibited from partaking of

* A common name and also the name of a goddess, and the name, I see, of one of the young ladies from the Andaman Islands.

plain rice cooked by others, provided they are left to salt it themselves. The salt, it would appear, thus applied, removes the "Taboo," and makes *fas* what is otherwise *nefas*.

As a rule, marriages are not contracted till both the bride and bridegroom are of mature age. It is sometimes left to the parents to select wives for their sons, but the young people have ample opportunities for studying each others characters, love-making and following the bent of their own inclinations; and it very often happens, that plans concocted by the parents are frustrated by the children.

In Chota-Nagpore, amongst the agricultural classes, and in Singbhoom amongst all classes of Kols, the girls have all a price fixed upon them, and this the lover or his friends must arrange to pay, before the parents of the bride will give their consent. In Singbhoom, the price is so high, especially for young ladies of good family, that marriage is frequently put off till late in life; and girls valued not so much for their charms and accomplishments as for their pedigree, often grow grey as maidens in the house of their fathers. Singbhoom is perhaps the only place in India in which old maids are found; they have plenty of them there. But though urged to change this practice by all who take an interest in them, the old Mankees of Singbhoom are inflexible, not only in demanding a high price for their girls, but in insisting that it shall be paid, according to ancient custom, chiefly in cattle. A Mankee of the old school will not take less than forty head of cattle for his daughter; but the eyes of the rising generation are opened to the absurdity of the practice, and some of us may live to see it changed.

In consequence of this custom, the grown up boys and girls are quite a separate institution in every Kol village; there is very little restraint on their intercourse, they form a very pleasant society of their own, from which the old people sensibly keep aloof. If a flirtation is known to have gone too far, the matter is generally settled by the young man being made to pay the price for the girl and marry her.

In Chota-Nagpore the daughter of a Mankee was, some years ago, valued at about 36 Rs, but they are gradually adopting the custom of the Hindoos in regard to their marriages, and giving up the objectionable practice of putting a price on them. The price paid by the common people ranges from 10 to 12 rupees. These disagreeable preliminaries having been arranged, the bridegroom and a large party of his friends of both sexes enter with much singing and dancing and sham fighting the village of the bride, where they meet the bride's party and are hospitably entertained.

The bride and bridegroom are now well anointed with turmeric, and bathed, and then taken and wedded, not to each other, but to two trees! The bride to a Mowa tree, the bridegroom to a Mango. They are made to touch the tree with "*seendoor*," (red lead), and then to clasp it in their arms. On returning, they are placed standing face to face, the girl on a curry stone over a ploughshare supported on sheaves of corn or grass. The bridegroom stands ungallantly treading on his bride's toes, and in this position touches her forehead with the red lead; she touches his forehead in the same manner. The bride's maids then, after some preliminary splashing and sprinkling, pour a jar of water over the head of each: this necessitates a change of raiment, and apparently concludes the ceremony, as the young couple going inside to change, do not appear again till the cock-crowing announces the dawn or its approach. At the first crow the bride's maids, who with the young men have been merrily keeping it up all night with the song and dance, burst into the nuptial chamber and bring forth the blushing bride and her bashful lord; and then they all go down to the river or to a tank to bathe, and parties of boys and girls form sides under the leadership of the bride and bridegroom, and pelt each other with clods of earth. The bridegroom next takes a water vessel and conceals it in the stream or water for the bride to find. She then conceals it from him, and when he has found it, she takes it up filled with water and places it on her head. She lifts her arm to support the pitcher, and the bridegroom, standing behind her with his bow strung, and the hand that grasps it lightly resting on her shoulder, discharges an arrow from the pretty loophole thus formed into the path before her. The girl walks on to where the arrow falls, and with head erect and still bearing the pitcher of water, she picks it up with her foot, takes it into her hand, and restores it to her husband with a graceful obeisance. She thus shews that she can adroitly perform her domestic duties and knows her duty to her lord and master, whilst he, on his part, in discharging an arrow to clear her path of an imaginary foe, indicates that he is prepared to perform his duty as her guide and protector through life.

In the Oraon marriages, many of these symbolical ceremonies are omitted, and the important one of exchanging the "*sindoor*" is differently performed. The bridegroom stands behind his bride with his toes on her heels, and stretches over her head to touch her forehead with the powder. She touches his forehead by reaching back over his shoulder. The cold bath completes the ceremony, they go to their own apartment to change their clothes, and do not emerge till morning.

The price paid for a girl in cows is called "*Sukmur*" by the Kheriah tribe. They have no word for marriage in their own language, and the only ceremony used appears to be little more than a sort of public recognition of the cohabitation. They have learned to call this "*biha*," but they admitted to me that this public recognition was often dispensed with.

It takes place in this wise. After the settlement of the usual preliminaries, the bride is brought to the village of her intended bridegroom by her own people and their friends, and they halt and bivouac in the village grove. The bridegroom and his friends join them in the grove where they all regale themselves and dance, and during these nuptial dances the bride and bridegroom are each borne on the hips of one of their dancing friends; they are not allowed to put their feet to the ground. Thus wildly dancing, they proceed into the village, and the bride and bridegroom are taken to the latter's house and anointed with oil; they are then brought outside, and the ceremony of touching each other's forehead with the "*sindoor*" is performed, followed by the splashing and sousing which becomes a general romp. Then the young couple are left to themselves till morning. The bride's maids arouse them as the cock crows, and after the public ablution of garments and their wearers the party breaks up.

The gestures of the dancers on these occasions, and the songs, all bear more directly than delicately on what is evidently considered as the main object of the festivities.

In Singbhoom, marriages, notwithstanding the lateness at which they take place are generally arranged by the parents, but their wishes are not unfrequently anticipated by love matches. In the various journeyings to and fro that are found necessary when a match is being arranged, omens are carefully observed, and the match is broken off, if they are unfavourable. At the actual marriage there is much feasting and dancing, but little ceremony. The turning point of the affair is, when the bride and bridegroom mix and drink off some of the beer they have each been helped to ; the boy pours some of the beer given to him into the girl's cup, she pours from her cup into the boy's cup, and they drink and thus become of the same "*keeli*" or clan, for the Hos, Moondahs and Oraons are all divided into families under this name, and may not take to wife a girl of their own *keeli*.

This division of the primitive races into something having a semblance to caste, will be found in the North Eastern Frontier as well as in this province. The Garrows, for instance, are divided into what are called "maharis," and a man may not marry a girl of his own mahari.

It is obvious that the custom does not spring from any such notion of caste as are found amongst the Hindoos, and that it is not one which these races have adopted from the Hindoos, because with a Hindoo, caste is destroyed by a marriage *out* of it. It is equally opposed to the custom of the Jews, whose daughters (at least if heiresses) were obliged to take husbands of their own tribe.*

In Singbhoom the bride and bridegroom do not touch each other with "*sindoor*", as is the custom in Chota-Nagpore. The Oraons and Moondahs may have adopted the custom from the Hindoos, and the primitive practice of the race is probably as it is found amongst the more isolated Hos.

A very singular scene may sometimes be noticed in the markets of Singbhoom. A young man suddenly makes a pounce on a girl and carries her off bodily, his friends covering the retreat (like a group from the picture of the rape of the Sabines). This is generally a summary method of surmounting the obstacles that cruel parents may have placed in the lovers' path ; but though it is sometimes done in anticipation of the favourable inclination of the girl herself, and in spite of her struggles and tears, no disinterested person interferes, and the girls, late companions of the abducted maiden, often applaud the exploit.

The Ho husband has to pay a high price for his wife, and it is

* Numbers xxxvi. 6.

certain that he highly appreciates her. Although he is not known to have for her any more endearing epithet than "my old woman," yet by no civilized race are wives treated with more consideration than by the untutored Ho. The whole of the domestic arrangements are under her exclusive management. She is consulted on all occasions, and I know one or two husbands whom I am almost inclined to regard as henpecked. The Kols seldom take a second wife during the lifetime of the first, but I know instances of their having done so. The wife always cooks for her husband, and when the dinner is ready, they sit down and eat it together like Christians; but the Oraons have followed the Hindoo custom of making the woman eat the leavings of her lord.

It is customary with all these tribes to pay particular attention to omens, when any of them set out to arrange the preliminaries of a marriage. The Hos who are more under the influence of this superstition than their cognates or than the Oraons, have a long list of deterrent signs, which have been described by Tickell in his paper above quoted. I subjoin the most noticeable of those that are observed by the Oraons.

1. On leaving the house "to win a bride", they look out for omens. If a cow calls and the calf responds, it is good. If there is no response, the wooing is postponed or abandoned.

2. If they find a dead mouse on the road, they must stop and make a diagnosis. If ants and flies have possessed themselves of the carcass, it is good, they go on. If the insects appear to have shunned it (which is not very likely to happen), they go back.

3. It is not good to meet oxen or buffaloes with their horns crossed, or to see a hawk strike a bird, or to come upon women washing clothes. It is good to see people burying a dead body, and to find on their road a cow giving milk to her calf.

4. If they see a man cutting a tree, and the tree falls before they can get past it, it is very bad. If they pass before it falls, it is all right. A certain bird heard on the left gives a note of joy; if heard on the right, he is a harbinger of woe.

5. If, on approaching the village of the girl, they come on women with water-pots full, it is a happy omen. If they meet a party with empty water-pots, it is a bad one.

The Nagpore Kols, whether of the Moondah or Oraon tribe, and all the cognates of the Moondahs that I know of, are passionately fond of dancing, and with them dancing is as much an accomplishment as it is with the civilized nations of Europe. They have a great variety of dances, and in each different steps and figures are used, of great intricacy, but they are performed with a neatness and precision that can only be acquired by great practice. Little children are hardly on their legs, before they begin to learn their dancing steps; and the result of this early training is that, however difficult the step, the limbs of the performers move as if they belonged to one body. They have musical voices and a great variety of simple melodies. It is a fact that, when we raised a corps of Kols, their early practice in keeping step and time greatly facilitated the operations of drill; and the Missionaries have availed themselves of the musical talents and taste of the Kol converts to produce congregational singing that would be a credit to an English country church.

The dances are seen to the greatest advantage at the great periodical festivals called "Jatras." They are at appointed places and seasons, and when the day comes, all take a holiday and proceed to the spot in their best array. The girls, on these occasions, put on their best dress, generally a white "*saree*" with a broad red border. They tastefully arrange flowers in their hair and plumes of the long breast feathers of the paddy-bird. The young men wear Turkey red turbans, and add a snow white cloth to their usually scanty garb, and also adorn themselves with flowers and peacock's feathers. As parties from the different villages come near the trysting place, they may be observed finishing their toilettes in the open fields; when all is ready, the groups form, and their approach from different sides, with their banners and yak's tails waving, horns and symbols sounding, marshalled into alternate ranks of lads and lasses all keeping perfect step and dress, with the gay head-dresses of the girls and the numerous brass ornaments of the boys glittering in the sun, forms a very lively and pleasing picture. They enter the grove where the meeting is held in jaunty dashing style, wheeling and countermarching and forming lines, circles and columns with grace and precision. The dance with these movements is called "khurriah," and they are held in all months of the year, a series of them following each other at short intervals at different places all over the country, and the attendance, at some that I have seen, could not be under 5,000 people, all enjoying themselves.

When they enter the grove, the different groups join and dance the khurriah together, forming one vast dancing procession. Then each takes its own place and plants its flag and dances round it till near sunset, when all go dancing home. This is followed by a carouse in the village, after which the dance is often continued at the "*akrah*" all night.

At each of these "Jattras," a kind of fair is held, and fairings and refreshments are to be had in abundance. The young men can treat their partners with sweetmeats and do so. As already observed, there is a place in every village called "*akrah*" set apart for dancing and ceremonies. This is a circular arena with a post in the centre, and around it are benches for the spectators or for the dancers when wearied, the whole being generally shaded by fine old tamarind, the most beautiful of village trees.

The season dances in the village open with the *kurrum* in July, at the commencement of the planting season. There is a movement in this dance called "*hojar*" when the girls suddenly kneel and pat the ground in time to the music, as if caressing and coaxing it to be productive. On the day appointed for the ceremony, the boys and girls go in procession to the *kurrum* tree, cut and bring back to the village some branches, which are planted in the *akrah*. An old man with a liberal allowance of beer is placed to watch these, whilst the young people refresh themselves. They all, old and young, then assemble in the *akrah*, and one of the elders harangues them, and after giving them much good advice, concludes by directing them to commence the dance. The songs sung on this occasion are in Hindee, and contain allusions to the flooded state of the rivers and fields. They also sing an ode to the Satyomba Rajah. The *kurrum* is kept by the Soodh or Hindoo population as well as by the Kols.

After harvest of the earlier crop of the planted rice, in November, the "*matha*" is danced by the boys and girls in the village. The girls, moving in a semicircle and clasping each others hands, dance with a very lively step and bowing motion of the body to the men who sing and play to them. The girls have another dance at this season called "*angua*," because it is danced in front of the house instead of the *akrah*; to this and to a feast held on the occasion the young men are not invited.

The "Jadoor" dances commence on the completion of the great harvest of the rice crop, and continue till the commencement of the hot season. This is one of the most characteristic dances, from the peculiar way in which the arms are interwoven and clasped behind the back of the performers.

Then comes the "Sarhool," at the close of the month of Phalgoon or early in March. The Sarhool is the flower of the Saul tree which now blossoms. The boys and girls make garlands of these flowers, weave them in their hair and decorate their houses with them. The dance on this occasion, called the "Baihini," is a very frisky one. The boys and girls dance to each other, clasping hands and pirouetting, so as to cause "*dos-à-dos*" concussions which appear to constitute the best part of the fun. Yet the subject of the song sung at the Sarhool feast is a sad one. A girl who had married out of the village is supposed to return to it in affliction, and to sit weeping at one side of the house, whilst her former associates are revelling at the other. The songs are in the Moondah language.

They have besides different dances for weddings, and a dance called "Jumhir" which is suited to any occasion. The dances above briefly noticed are all more or less connected with some religious ceremony, but this is left to the elders. The young people seem to me to take little interest in that part of the festival, which is, in proportion to the dancing, in importance like the bread to Falstaff's sack. They are always ready for a dance, and night after night in some villages the *akrah* drums collect the youths and maidens after the evening meal, and if you go quietly to the scene, as I have done, you may find that, whilst some are dancing, others are flirting in the most demonstrative manner, seated in detached couples on the benches or on the roots of the great trees, with arms round each others' waists, looking lovingly into each others' faces.

Next to dancing, that which most engrosses the mind of the Kol is the belief in and fear of witchcraft. All disease in men and in cattle is attributed to one of two causes, the wrath of some evil spirit who has to be appeased, or the spell of some witch or sorcerer who should be destroyed. The fear of punishment and, I may add for some of them, the respect they bear to the orders of their rulers, restrain their hands, and witch murders are now very rare, but a village is soon made too hot to hold one who is supposed to be a witch.

When a belief is entertained that sickness in a family, or mortality amongst cattle, or other misfortune has been brought about by sorcery, a Sokha or witch-finder is employed to find out who has cast the spell. By the Sokhas various methods of divination are employed. One of the most common is the test by the stone and "*poila.*" The latter is a large wooden cup shaped like a half cocoanut, used as a measure for grain. It is placed under a flat stone, and becomes a pivot for the stone to turn on. A boy is then placed in a sitting position on the stone, supporting himself by his hands, and the names of all the people in the neighbourhood are slowly pronounced, and as each name is uttered, a few grains of rice are thrown at the boy; when they come to the name of the witch or wizard, the stone turns and the boy rolls off!

There is no necessary collusion between the Sokha and the boy; the motion of the hand throwing the rice produces *coma*, and the Sokha is, I suppose, sufficiently a mesmerist to bring about the required result when he pleases.

The Singbhoom Kols or Hos, left to themselves, not only considered it necessary to put to death a witch thus denounced, but if she had children or other blood relations, they must all perish, as all of the same blood were supposed to be tainted.

In 1857, when, in consequence of the mutinies, Singbhoom was temporarily without officers, the Ho tribes of the southern parts of the district, always the most turbulent, released from a restraint they had never been very patient under, set to work to search out the witches and sorcerers who, it was supposed, from the long spell of protection they had enjoyed, had increased and multiplied to a dangerous extent. In a report on this subject from the district officer, in 1860, it is stated that "the destruction of human life that ensued is too terrible to contemplate; whole families were put an end to. In some instances the destroyers, issuing forth in the dusk and commencing with the denounced wizard and his household, went from house to house, until before the morning dawn they had succeeded in extinguishing, as they supposed, the whole race." On the suppression of the disturbances, the return of the refractory Hos to order was as sudden and decisive as had been their relapse into barbarism. The survivors of the families who had suffered at once emerged with confidence from their hiding-places, and of the cases of witchcraft-murder, thus or otherwise brought to notice, the perpetrators were in almost every instance prosecuted to conviction.

It was melancholy to have to condemn men who themselves artlessly detailed every incident of the crime with which they were charged. The work of retribution was a sad task, but it was rigorously carried out, and we have not since then had a siugle case of witchcraft murder in the Colehan. That the belief in the existence of witches and sorcerers is consequently extirpated, cannot be hoped. Nothing but their conversion from paganism could effect this. I am convinced that in most instances the prisoners, who in their examinations detailed the most marvellous effects of imputed sorcery, were sincere believers in all that they narrated.

One of them, named Mora, saw his wife killed by a tiger, which he followed till it led him to the house of a man named Poosa whom he knew. He told Poosa's relations what had occurred, declaring to them that Poosa had, in the form of a tiger, killed and eaten his wife. The relatives appealed to, did not for a moment discredit the charge. They said they were aware that Poosa did possess the imputed power of metamorphosis. They brought him out and, delivering him bound to his accuser, stood by whilst Mora deliberately put him to death.

In explanation of their having so acted, they deposed that Poosa had one night devoured an entire goat and roared like a tiger, whilst he was eating it; and on another occasion he informed his friends he had a longing to eat a particular bullock, and that very night that very bullock was killed and devoured by a tiger!

From their having lived so long together, it is not surprising that we should find the religious ceremonies of the Oraon and Moondah almost identical. The Oraons have adopted the religion of the Moondah, but they retain some features of their original faith which indicate that it was in many essential points different from that to which they have conformed.

I have already observed that the Pahan or village priest is in all probability an Oraon institution. The Rajmahali have a similar functionary called 'Demam,' who foretells events, offers sacrifices, regulates feasts and exorcises devils. In the Ho and Moondah villages, all priestly functions may be performed by the head of the family, or, if the occasion be one in which the village generally is concerned, by any elder of the requisite knowledge and experience. They worship the sun, "Singbonga," as the supreme being, the creator, the preserver; and a number of secondary gods, all invisible; material idol worship they have none. The paganism of the Ho and Moondah in all essential features is shamanistic.

The Oraons, in addition to the Pahan whose business it is to offer sacrifices for the benefit of the community, have recourse to a person called "Ojha" whom they consult regarding the proper spirit to be invoked and the nature of the sacrifice that is required of them, and whose functions appear to me to bear a strong resemblance to those of the medicine man of the African tribes. The Oraons have wooden images or stones to represent the village and domestic spirits that they worship. Thus a carved post in the centre of their dancing arena represents the tutelary deity of the village, "Daroo;" and they have objects of some kind to represent their domestic gods, *penates*.

They never build a house, or select a new site for a village or even a new threshing-floor, without consulting the ojha and omens. When a new house is ready for the reception of its owners, an ojha is called, and he takes earth from the hearth and charcoal, and mixing them together, marks on the floor a magic circle. In the centre of this he places an egg, and on the egg a split twig of the Bel tree. The egg is then roasted and eaten by the people who are to occupy the house. This is followed by a great feast and dancing—a regular house-warming—on the top of the house an image of a fish is hung to avert the evil eye. These peculiarities in the paganism of the Oraon, and only practised by Moondahs who live in the same village with them, appear to me to savour thoroughly of feticism: before affirming this positively, it would be advisable to examine more minutely the customs of the Rajmahal hill tribes; but the elephant gods, depicted by W. Sherwill as seen in their villages, are very fetish in appearance.*

* Vide Journal, Asiatic Society Bengal, No. VII. 1851, page 553.

The Moondahs, without applying to an ojha or medicine-man, consult auguries in choosing the site of a house, with prayer to Singbonga. A small quantity of rice is placed in holes made at the four corners of the selected site, where it is left all night; and if found undisturbed in the morning, the site is good. The same process is gone through in selecting a new site for a village. Prayer is offered to Singbonga twice, first, that the test applied may truly indicate if the site be good or bad; secondly, for a blessing on the chosen site.

It is the fashion to call the religion of the Kols 'devil worship,' but this is not strictly correct; for although the minor deities may be mostly of a malevolent nature and therefore devils who have to be propitiated, still Singbonga is worshipped as a beneficent god. This worship of the sun as the supreme deity is the foundation of the religion of the Oraons as well as the Moondahs. By the former he is invoked as Dhurmi, the holy one. He is the creator and the preserver, and with reference to his purity, white animals are offered to him by his votaries. He is not regarded as the author of sickness or calamity; but he may be appealed to to avert it, and this appeal is often made, when the sacrifices to the minor deities have been unproductive.

But besides these occasional sacrifices, all Moondahs who hold to the faith of their ancestors, are especially bound to make a certain number of offerings to Singbonga during their tenure of the position of head of the family. He may take his own time about them, but he will not be happy in his mind till he completes his complement and clears the account. I obtained this information from the Kheriahs, and on speaking about it to some ancient Pahans and Moondah elders, was told that it undoubtedly is the orthodox practice, but it has been neglected. The sacrifices are five in number: 1st, fowls; 2nd, a pig; 3rd, a white goat; 4th, a ram; 5th, a buffalo; and they must be offered in the open plain in front of an ant hill, or with an ant hill as an altar. Sacrifices to other gods are generally offered in the "Saerna,"* the sacred grove of Sal trees, the remnant of the primeval forest left for the spirits when the settlement was first made.

The names and attributes of the inferior deities are nearly the same amongst the Hos in Singbhoom, the Moondahs and Oraons in Chota-

* Or 'Saran,' 'Charan.'

Nagpore, and amongst the Sonthals 'passim.' Marang Booroo and Pongla his wife; Desaoolli, Jaer Boori, Eekin Bonga, Boora Bonga, Charee Desoolli and Dara are invoked in Chota-Nagpore.

The Sonthals have Marang Booroo, also Maniko his brother and Jaer his sister. Tickell's paper in Vol. IX, part 2nd of this Journal gives the Singbhoom gods and their attributes. They too have Marang Booroo and Pongala, Desaoolli and Jaer Boori or Jaer Era and others. In cases of sickness the Ho, after ascertaining by augury which of the gods should be propitiated, will go on offering sacrifices till the patient recovers or his live stock is entirely exhausted.

Next to Singbonga I am inclined to place the deity that is adored as "Marang Booroo." Booroo means mountain, but every mountain has its spirit, and the word is therefore used to mean god or spirit* also. Marang Booroo is the great spirit or great mountain. Not far from the village of Lodmah in Chota-Nagpore one of the most conspicuous hills on the plateau is called Marang Booroo, and here the great spirit is supposed to dwell. It is worshipped by the Sonthals, the Bhoomij, the Hos, the Moondahs and the Oraons. The two latter make pilgrimages to it. The Hos have some vague notion of its situation; the more distant members of the family canonize some hill more conveniently situated.

The Marang Booroo is especially venerated as the lord of rain. Before the rains the women go to the top of the hill, under the leadership of the wives of the Pahans, with drums, which are on this occasion only played on by young ladies, and with offerings of milk and leaves of the Bel tree. On the top of the hill there is a flat mass of rock on which they deposit their offerings.

The wives of the Pahans now kneel down, and with hair loosened invoke the deity, beseeching him to give their crops seasonable rain. They shake their heads violently as they reiterate this prayer, till they work themselves into a phrensy, and the movement becomes involuntary. They go on thus wildly gesticulating, till a "little cloud like a man's hand" is seen. Then they arise, take up the drums, and dance the Kurrun on the rock, till Marang Booroo's response to their prayer is heard in the distant rumbling of thunder, and they go home rejoicing.

* Thus they have for their altars groves and high places like the idolatrous Jews.

They must go "fasting to the mount," and stay there till "there is a sound of abundance of rain," when they get them down to eat and drink. My informant tells me it always comes before evening. We must conclude that the old women are wonderfully clever at taking a 'forecast,' and do not commence the fast till they sniff the rain.

All the villagers living in the vicinity of the hill make offerings of goats, whenever they think it desirable to propitiate this spirit; but he is not invoked in cases of sickness, unless the ojha declares it necessary. Sometimes bullocks are offered.

The next in importance in Chota-Nagpore appears to be the spirit Dara, whom the Oraons and Moondahs living with them adore in the form of a carved post stuck up where the great *jatras* are held, or in the village dancing place. Dara appears to be a god of rather bacchanalian characteristics, worshipped amidst much revelling and wassail. A sacrifice to him of fowls is followed by a feast in his honour, at which all the elders drink themselves into a state of sottish drunkenness, whilst the young people dance and make love; and next day comes the *jatra* which all the country attend.

The Penates are generally called the "old folks." They are in fact the *manes* of the votaries' ancestors; votive offerings are made to them when their descendants go on a journey, and they are generally the first that are propitiated when there is sickness in the family. By the Singbhoom Kols, the *manes* of the ancestors of the principal lady of the house are also honoured. The offerings to them are made on the path by which she was brought home as a bride. Desaoolli and Jaerоolli are propitiated for harvests and for cattle, Chandoo Seekur, the same probably as the Chanala of the Hos, for children.

The Pahan has to solemnize regularly the following festivals. The Hurihur, at the commencement of the planting season. Every one then plants a branch of the Belowa in his field and each contributes a fowl, a pitcher of beer and a handful of rice to the feast. The sacrifice is offered to Desaoolli, Jaer Boori and others, in the Saerna.

During the Sarhool—when the Sal tree blossoms—the sacrifice of a goat and fowls is offered in the Saerna by the Pahan to the *manes* of the founders of the village and to Dara. The introduction of the Sal blossom, in memory of the forest that was cleared when the village was formed, is very appropriate. At the khurria Poojah, when the rice is harvested, the sacrifice is offered and the feast takes place on the Pahan's threshing floor.

Dalikattari: every second year a fowl, every third year a ram, every fourth year a buffalo. To provide what is required for this feast, the Pahan holds the Dalikattaree land.

I have already alluded to the division of the Moondahs and their cognates into "Keelles" or clans. Many of the Oraon clans and some of the Moondah in Chota-Nagpore are called after animals, and they must not kill or eat what they are named after.

Thus the Moondah "Enidhi" and the Oraon "Minjrar" or Eel tribe will not kill or eat that fish. The Hawk, Crow, Heron tribes will not kill or eat those birds. Livingstone, quoted in Latham,* tells us that the sub-tribes of the Bitshaunas (or Bechuanas) are similarly named after certain animals, and a tribe never eats the animal from which it is named, using the term, "*ila*," hate or dread, in reference to killing it.

The above curious coincidence tempts me to give a few more details regarding the Oraon clans.

The "Tirki"—have an objection to animals whose eyes are not yet open, and their own offspring are never shewn till they are wide awake.

The "Ekkar"—will not touch the head of a tortoise.

The "Katchoor"—object to water in which an elephant has been bathed.

The "Amdiar"—will not eat the foam of the river.

The "Kujrar"—will not eat the oil of the Kujri tree, or sit in its shade.

The "Tiga"—will not eat the monkey.

The Ho chiefs could give me no signification for the names in which their families rejoice. The following are the most aristocratic, the Boorioolli, the Poorthi, Sincoi, Baipoi, Soondee, Bandri.

I do not know of any people who are more careful in regard to the disposal of their dead than are the tribes of whom I am treating, especially the Singbhoom Kols and best classes of the Moondahs.

On the death of a Ho or Moondah, a very substantial coffin is constructed and placed on faggots of firewood. The body, carefully

* Latham's Ethnology, Vol. II. p. 160.

washed and anointed with oil and turmeric, is reverently laid in the coffin, and all the clothes and ornaments used by the deceased are placed with it, and also any money that he had about him when he died. Then the lid of the coffin is put on and faggots piled above and around it, and the whole is burned. The cremation takes place in front of the deceased's house. Next morning water is thrown on the ashes and search made for the bones; all the larger fragments are carefully preserved, the remainder, with the ashes, are buried then and there. The selected bones are placed in a vessel and hung up in the house in a place where they may be continually viewed by the widow or mother. Thus they remain till the very extensive arrangements necessary for the final disposal are effected. A large monumental stone has to be selected, and it is sometimes so large that the men of several villages are employed to move it. It is brought to the family burial place, which with the Hos is close to their houses, and with the Oraons generally separated from the village by a stream. A deep round hole is dug beside the stone, and when all is ready, a procession is formed consisting of one old woman carrying the bones on a decorated bamboo tray, one or two men with deep sounding wooden drums, and half a dozen young girls, those in the front rank carrying empty and partly broken pitchers, and brass vessels. The procession moves with a solemn ghostly sliding step, in time to the deep sounding drum. The old woman carries the tray on her head, but at regular intervals she slowly lowers it, and as she does so, the girls gently lower and mournfully reverse the pitchers and brass vessels, to shew that they are empty.

In this manner the remains are taken to the house of every friend and relative of the deceased, within a circle of a few miles, and to every house in the village, and as it approaches, the inmates come out and mourn, as they call to mind all the good qualities of the deceased. The bones are thus conveyed also to all his favourite haunts, to the fields he cultivated, to the grove he planted, to the threshing-floor where he worked, and to the *akrah* where he made merry. When this part of the ceremony is completed, the procession returns to the village and moves in circles round the grave, gradually approaching its goal: at last it stops, and a quantity of rice and other food, cooked and uncooked, is now cast into the hole. The bones are then put into a new earthen vessel and deposited on the rice, and the hole is filled in and covered with the large slab which effectually closes it against desecration.

The collection of these massive grave stones under the fine old tamarind trees is a remarkable feature in Kol villages, and almost an indelible one, for they are found in many places where Kols have not existed for centuries. Besides the grave stones, monumental stones are set up outside the village to the memory of men of note. They are fixed in an earthen plinth, on which, shaded by the pillar, the ghost is supposed to sit. The Kheriahs have collections of these monuments in the little enclosure round their houses, and offerings and libations are constantly made to them.

The funeral ceremonies above described are of a composite order, mingling with the Hindoo custom of cremation, what was in all probability their original mode of burial; but a very profound reverence for the dead pervades them all. I think it is very probable that the Kols originally disposed of their dead differently. The coffin, though put together on the faggots that are to consume it, has projections as if to facilitate transport. Omit the burning and substitute burial, and we have the careful disposal and subsequent adoration of the dead that is practised by the Chinese; but the burning of the body and the long retention of the ashes in a portable form may have been adopted at a time when the tribe could not be certain of continued residence in one place.

Tickell has given at length the Ho legend of the origin of the human race. It is supremely absurd, and very few of the present generation know anything or care anything about it. I have always found such legends changeable and untrustworthy. With no written record to give them permanence, they are altered either to suit new conditions or the fancy of the reciter. Thus though the Kols have known the English for little more than half a century, they assign to them a most honourable place in their genesis. The Assam Abors and Garrows do just the same.

I do not think that the present generation of Kols have any notion of a heaven or a hell that may not be traced to Brahminical or Christian teaching. The old idea is that the souls of the dead become "*bhoots*," spirits, but no thought of reward or punishment is connected with the change. When a Ho swears, the oath has no reference whatever to a future state. He prays, that if he speak not the truth he may be afflicted in this world with the loss of all, health, wealth, wife, children; that he may sow without reaping and finally may be devoured by a tiger; but he swears not by any hope of happiness beyond the grave. He has in his primitive state no such hope, and I believe that most Indian aborigines, though they may have some vague ideas of continuous existence, will be found equally devoid of original notions in regard to the Judgment to come.

It may be said that the funeral ceremonies I have described, indicate clearly a belief in resurrection, else why should food, clothes and money be burned with the body or buried with the ashes? The Kols have given me the same explanation of this that I once before received from the Chulikutta Mishmees in Upper Assam, who have no notion of any existence beyond the grave. They do not wish to benefit by the loss of their friend, which they would do if they were to appropriate any article belonging to him: they therefore give with him all his personalties, all property that he and he alone used and benefited by; but this does not apply to the stock of the farm and household property that all profit by, or even to new cloth, for that might have been procured for any member of the family. It often happens that a respectable 'Ho' has goods of this nature, that he abstains from using even once, because if once used, the article will be destroyed at his death.

The Moondah Oraon races are passionately fond of field sports, and are so successful that large and small game soon disappear from the vicinity of considerable settlements; and they fear not to make a new settlement, consisting only of a few huts, in the jungles most infested by wild beasts. Every year at the commencement of the hot season, they form great hunting parties which are well described in Tickell's memoir. They are also greatly addicted to cock-fighting. They have periodical meets at assigned places where hundreds of fighting cocks are collected. Cruel steel spurs are used, and the combat is always *à l'outrance*, the victims becoming the property of the owners of the victorious birds. This is, I think, the only stake. They are fond of fishing too, and some of them are very expert in spearing large fish.

The arms of the Kols are to this day what they were in the days of "*Rama*"—the bow and arrow and battle-axe. The bow is simply a piece of bamboo, and the string is of the same material. The war arrows have large broad blades doubly and trebly barbed, but they make them of all shapes: poison they do not use. They commence practice with the bow and arrow at the earliest age. In Singbhoom boys three and four years old and upwards, when herding cattle or otherwise engaged, have always their bow, and blunt and sharp arrows; the former for practice, the latter to bring down birds when they have a chance.

In the villages of Chota-Nagpore where the Oraon and Moondah are mixed up together, the difference of character between the two races is not much marked; but if we compare the Singbhoom Hos or Chota-Nagpore Mankees and the Oraons, we see strong contrasts. The Oraon has the lively happy disposition of the Negro. He is fond of gaiety, decorating rather than clothing his person, and whether toiling or playing, is always cheerful.

The Ho or Moondah has more the dignity and reserve of the North American Indian, at least when he is sober. He appears to less advantage when he is drunk, and he is not unfrequently in that state. At all festivals and ceremonies, deep potations of the rice-beer called "*eeley*" are freely indulged in by both sexes. Inspirited by this beverage, the young men and girls dance together all day and half the night; but the dances are perfectly correct, and whenever these meetings have led to improprieties, it is always attributed to a too free indulgence in *eeley*. As a rule, the men are reserved and highly decorous in their treatment of the women; and the girls, though totally free from the prudery that secludes altogether or averts the head of a Hindoo or Mahommedan maiden when seen by a man, have a modest demeanour, combined with frank open manners and womanly grace.

It is said by some, that at the seasons of their great festivals amongst themselves, breaches of chastity are of frequent occurrence; but the mere freedom of intercourse allowed to the sexes is likely to be viewed with unmerited prejudice and misconstrued by their neighbours of different race who place such restrictions upon it, and I believe that this may give rise to false imputations of impropriety. It is, at all events, a fact that illegitimate births are rare. Out of her own tribe, a Ho girl is hardly ever known to go astray, though from the freedom allowed to her and, for a tropical climate, the ripe age at which she is likely to be sought in marriage, she must have to pass through many temptations.

The Hos are acutely sensitive under abusive language that at all reflects upon them, and may be and often are driven to commit suicide by an angry word. If a woman appears mortified by anything that has been said, it is unsafe to let her go away till she is soothed. The men are almost as sensitive as the women, and you cannot offend them more than by doubting their word. It has often seemed to me that the more a statement tells against themselves, the more certain they are to tell the exact truth about it. It frequently happens that a man is himself the first person to bring to notice that he has committed a crime; he tells all about it, and deliberately gives himself up to be dealt with according to law.

The Oraon is, I think, less truthful, he is more given to vagabondising, and wandering over the face of the earth in search of employment; he soon loses all the freshness of his character. He returns after an absence of years, unimproved in appearance, more given to drink and self-indulgence, less genial and truthful than before, with a bag of money that is soon improvidently spent. Those who have never left their own country have far more pleasing manners and dispositions, than those who return to it after years spent in other parts of India or beyond the seas. The fact is, they are not an improvable people. They are best seen in their wild state.

There is no more pleasing trait amongst all these tribes than their kindly affectionate manner one towards another. I never saw girls quarrelling, and never heard them abuse each other. They are the most unspiteful of their sex, and the men never coarsely abuse and seldom speak harshly of the women. This is remarkable on this side of India where you seldom pass through a bazar without hearing women screeching indecent abuse at each other across the street, whilst the men look on. A Kol girl's vocabulary is as free from bad language of this kind as a Bengalee's is full of it.

The young Oraons of both sexes are intensely fond of decorating their persons with beads and brass ornaments. These they entirely discard on embracing Christianity, and the converts may be always recognised by the total absence of all such adornment. The converts do not join in the dances, or festivals, and must not even be seen as spectators, when they are going on. They appear indeed to lose all relish for their old amusements, and shrink with horror at the idea of resuming their discarded ornaments. And as Christianity is rapidly spreading amongst them, and in all probability will continue to spread more and more rapidly every year, it is quite possible that in the course of a few generations, the most marked characteristics of the races I am describing, will have been effaced for ever. It is marvellous with what firmness old prejudices are abandoned, old customs discarded, and even tastes changed, when they become Christians; and there is now a wide-spread feeling amongst the Kols themselves, that this change will inevitably come upon them all.

The Moondah-Oraon are a rapidly increasing people. We may form some calculation as to the rate of increase by the statistics of the Mission. In 1864, the baptised converts numbered 5,923, and in that year there were 195 births to 80 deaths. In 1865 there were 7,828 baptized Christians, and the births during the year were 309 to 86 deaths. The number of professing Christians is probably double the number registered as baptized. I subjoin in a tabular form brief vocabularies of the Moondahs and their cognates, referring to Tickell's memoir for a full notice of the language. I annex notes on the Oraon language with which I have been kindly favoured by the Reverend Frederic Batsch.

APPENDICES.

APPENDIX A.

List of words and phrases to be noted and used as test words for the discovery of the radical affinities of languages, and for easy comparison.

Numerals. One to ten. Twenty. Fifty. Hundred.

Pronouns.	I.	Of me.	Mine.
	We.	Of us.	Our.
	Thou.	Of thee.	Thine.
	You.	Of you.	Your.
	He.	Of him.	His.
	They.	Of them.	Their.

Hand.	Father.	Sun.
Foot.	Mother.	Moon.
Nose.	Brother.	Star.
Eye.	Sister.	Fire.
Mouth.	Man.	Water.
Tooth.	Woman.	House.
Ear.	Wife.	Horse.
Hair.	Child.	Cow.
Head.	Son.	Dog.
Tongue.	Daughter.	Cat.
Belly.	Slave.	Cock.
Back.	Cultivator.	Duck.
Iron.	Shepherd.	Ass.
Gold.	God.	Camel.
Silver.	Devil.	Bird.

Go.	Come.	Die.
Eat.	Beat.	Give.
Sit.	Stand.	Run.

Up	down	before
near	far	behind
who	what	why
and	but	if
yes	no	alas.

A Father.	Two Fathers.	Fathers.
Of a father.		Of fathers.
To a father.		To fathers.
From a father.		From fathers.

A daughter.	Two daughters.	Daughters.
Of a daughter.		Of daughters.
To a daughter.		To daughters.
From a daughter.		From daughters.

A good man.	Two good men.	Good men.
Of a good man.		Of good men.
To a good man.		To good men.
From a good man,		From good men.

A good woman.	Good women.
A bad boy.	A bad girl.

good	better	best
high	higher	highest

a horse	a mare	horses	mares
a bull	a cow	bulls	cows
a dog	a bitch	dogs	bitches
a he-goat	a female goat	...	goats
a male deer	a female deer	...	deer.

I am	Thou art	He is.
We are	You are	They are.
I was	Thou wast	He was.
We were	You were	They were.

Be.	To be.	Being.	Having been.
I may be.	I shall be.		I should be.

Beat.	To beat. Beating.	Having beaten.
I beat.	Thou beatest.	He beats.
We beat.	You beat.	They beat.
I am beating.	I was beating.	I had beaten.
I may beat.	I shall beat.	I should beat.
I am beaten.	I was beaten.	I shall be beaten.
I go.	Thou goest.	He goes.
I went.	Thou wentest.	He went.
Go.	Going.	Gone.

What is your name?
How old is this horse?
How far is it from here to Kashmir?
How many sons are there in your father's house?
I have walked a long way to-day.
The son of my uncle is married to her sister.
In the house is the saddle of the white horse.
Put the saddle upon his back.
I have beaten his son with many stripes.
He is grazing cattle on the top of the hill.
He is sitting on a horse under that tree.
His brother is taller than his sister.
The price of that is two rupees and a half.
My father lives in that small house.
Give this rupee to him.
Take those rupees from him.
Beat him well and bind him with ropes.
Draw water from the well.
Walk before me.
Whose boy comes behind you?
From whom did you buy that?
From a shop-keeper of the village.

APPENDIX B.

Comparative Table of Aboriginal words.

ENGLISH.	DRAVIDIAN.		KOLARIAN.		INDO-CHINESE.		
	Tamul.	Gond, Oraon & Rajmehalee.	Hos or Singbhoom Kols.	Sontals.	Thibetan.	Bodo or Mechi.	Khamti (Siamese.)
One	onru	undi	mi	mia	chik	che	niong
Two	irandu	ranu	bara	baria	nyis	ne	song
Three	munru	munu	apia	pia	sum	tham	sam
Four	nalu	nalu	apania	ponia	zhi	bré	si
Five	angu	saighan	moya	monaya	gna	ba	pa
Six	aru	sarong	turia	turüi	thu	do	pok
Seven	ezhu	yetu	iya	iair	dun	chin	tet
Eight	ettu	anamur	irlia	iral	gyé	ye	pet
Nine	oubadu	...	area	ărĕ	guh	küha	kan
Ten	pata	pada	gelea	gel	chuh	te	sip
I	nan	enan or en	aing	ing	gna	ang	kaü
Thou	ni	nien	am	amg	khe	nang	maü
He	avan	asan or atti	ini	üni	khü	bi	man

We	nam	em or nam	allege	...	gnango	jong	han
You	nin	asü or nina	inkoghi	...	khengo	nang	maü-su
They	avar	asabar or awar	anko	...	khongo	bi	man-ku
Mine	enadu	onghi	iyan	ingrea	gna-yi	ang-ni	kaü
Thine	imadu	ningki	amma	ami	khe-yi	nang-ni	maü
His	avanadu	ona	ini	ünea	kho-yi	bi-ni	man
Our	namadu	emki or mabai	allea	allea	gnango-yi	jong-ni	...
Your	umdu	usghi or nimki	appea	appe	khengo-yi	nang-charni	...
Their	avaradu	ona	enkoa	ankure	khongo-yi	bi-charni	...
Hand	kai	kaik	thi	tihi	sang	akhai	mü
Foot	adi	dappi or kev	katu	kata	kango	yupha	tin
Eye	kan	kank	met	med	mik	mogon	ta
Mouth	vayi	bai	á	mocha	kha	khoügü	sop
Tooth	pal	palk	datha	datha	so	hathai	khiü
Ear	kadu	kheb or kavi	latur	lutur	sa or amcho	khoma	hü
Hair	mayir	robung or chütti	up	up	kin or pra	khanai	pe
Head	talei	tala or kuk	bu	bohu	go	khoro	ho
Father	tandei	wawoo	apang	baba	pha	bipha	po
Mother	tayi or ayi	aval or aya	eang	iyo	ama	bima	me
Man	alsa	allu or malê	ho	horh	mi	hiwa	kun

Comparative Table of Aboriginal words,—(Continued.)

English.	Dravidian.		Kolarian.		Indo-Chinese.		
	Tamul.	Gond, Oraon & Rajmehalee.	Hos or Singbhoom Kols.	Sontals.	Thibetan.	Bodo or Mechi.	Khamti (Siamese.)
Sun	pakalon	dharmi or ber	singi	singi	nisina	shan	wan
Moon	tingal	bilpe	chandu	chundo	dawa	nokabir	lun
Star	vanmin	suku or binka	epil	ipil	kurma	hatot	naü
Fire	nirappu	kis or chik	sengel	sengil	ma	wat	fai
Water	nir	yer	dah	dha	chu	doi	nam
Earth	nilam	kekhat	oti	ot	sa	ha	languim
House	manei	roon or erpa	oa	ora	nang	noü	häu
Horse	kudirei	kondand	sadam	sadham	ta	korai	mää
Dog	nayi	nai	seta	seta	khyi or ayo	ahoi or ma	mă
Cat	pussei or punei	birka	bilai	pusi	byala or süni	moügi	miaü
Fish	min	min	haku	hai	gna	na	pa
Cow	pasu or avu	üdi or oi	gundi	üri	ba	masha	ngo

APPENDIX C.

Comparative Table of Northern and Arian Words.

English.	Sanscrit.	Persian.	Turkish	Hindee.	Panjabee.
One	éka	ék	bir	ék	ek, eko
Two	dwi	do	ìki	do	do
Three	tri	seh	üch	tray or tin	teen
Four	chatur	chahar	dürt	char	char
Five	panchan	panj	besh	panch	panj
Six	shash	shas	altië	cheh	chi
Seven	sapta	haft	yeddi	sat	sút
Eight	ashtan	hast	sekkiz	ath	uth
Nine	navan	nah	dokküz	nava, or nau	nou
Ten	dashan	deh	own	das	das
Twenty	vingsati	best	yirmi	bis, or koree	vee, koree
Fifty	panchásat	punjah	elli	puchas.	punjah
Hundred	sata	sád	yüz	sow	sow
I	aham	man	ben	main	muen
Of me	mama or me	i-man	benin	mujhka	mujhda
Mine	madiya	man or Am	-m,-in	merá	mera

Comparative Table of Northern and Arian Words,—(Continued.)

English.	Sanscrit.	Persian.	Turkish.	Hindee.	Panjabee.
We	vayam	ma	biz	ham	assi
Of us	asmakam, nah	i-ma	bizim	hamka	assi da
Our	asmadiya	ma or an	miz, imiz	hamara	sada
Thou	twan	to	sen	tu	too
Of thee	tava, te	i-to	senin	tujhka	tugh-da
thine	twadiya, távaka	to or at	-n, in	tera	tera
You	yuyam	shuma	siz	toom	tassi
of you	yusmákam, vah	i-shuma	sizne	toom ka	tasi da
Your	yusmadiya	shuma	niz, iniz	toomara	tohda
He	sa	an or oe	ol	wuh	o'
of him	tadiya	i-an	anün	uska	o' da
his	tasya	ash or oe	i, si	us-ka	oéda
They	te	aishan	aular	wè	oèe
of them	tesam	i-aishan	aularüm	un-ka	ohee da
their	tadiya	aishan or shan	larü, leri	un-ka	ohee da

Hand	hasta	dast	el	hat	hŭth
Foot	pada	pay	ayak	pair, paon	pyr
Nose	násiká	beenee	bürün	nāk	nuk
Eye	Chaxû, netra	chashm	güz	ānkh	ukh, neta
Mouth	mukha	dehan	aghuz	mooh	mook
Tooth	danta	dandan	deesh	dānt	dund
Ear	karna	gosh	kúlák	kān	kan
Hair	kesh, bála	moo	múi	bal	wal, kes
Head	sirah, mastaka	sir	bash	sir, kulla	sir, kulla
Tongue	jihwá	zabán	deel	jib	jeebe, zuban
Father	pitá	pedr	bábá	peeta, bap	bap, pita
Mother	mátá	mádr	ama	ma	ma, umma
Brother	bhrátá	brádr	kárdásh	bhai	bhao
Sister	swashá	hamshira	küz kárdásh	bahin	bhyn
Man	mánusha, jana	mardăm	mard	manoos, admee	monookh, admee
Woman	stri	zun	karü	aurut	teemee, stree
Wife	bháryá	zöuja	karü	joroo	bohoo
Child	santána	farzund	chojük	bal, chokra	baluk
Son	putra	pesr	oghül	pootra, beta	putra
Daughter	duhitá, kanyá	dokhtr	küz	pootree, betee	putree

Comparative Table of Northern and Arian Words,—(Continued.)

English.	Sanscrit.	Persian.	Turkish.	Hindee.	Panjabee.
Sun	sûrya	aftab	ghünesh	suraj	sooraj
Moon	chandra	mah	ay	chand	chand
Star	naxatra, táraka	sitara	yildiz	tara	tara
Fire	agni	atash	átash	ag	ăg
Water	ápa, jala	áb	soo	jul, panee	jul, panee
Earth	prithwi, mrittika	zameen	toprak	prithwi, matee	bhomeen
Wood	gahan, káshtha	chob	ágáj	lakrí, kath	kath
House	griha	khana	ev	ghur	ghur
Horse	ghotaka, aswa	asp	át	ghoṛa	ghoḍa
Cow	gábhi, go	gão	inek	gai	gou, goru
Dog	kukkura, swan	sug	küpek	kootha	kootha
Cat	biḍála	gurbah	kedi	billee	billee
Fish	matsya	mahi	balük	muchee	muchee, mas
Of a father	pitûh	i-pedr	bábánün	pitee ka	peethe da
To a father	pitaram	ba-pedr, pedr-ra	bábáyah	pithee ko	peethe nu
From a father	pitûh	az pedr	bábádan	pithee se	peethe, te

Two fathers	pitarau	do-pedran	iki bábá	do pithee	do peethe
Bad father	dushta pitá	pedr bad	......	bud pitha	bad peetha
Fathers	pitarah	padran	......	pithe	peethe
Good man	saj-jana	ek mardum khoob	ayü mard	acha admee, bhala manus	changa manuk
Two good men	saj-janau	do marduman khoob	iki ayü mard	do bhale manus	do change manuk
Good men	saj-janáh	marduman khoob	ayü mardlar	bhale manus	change manuk
Good	sat	khoob	ayü	achha, suth	changa
Better	sat-tara	khoobtar	daha ayü	aur achha	
Best	sat-tama	khoobtareen	au ayü	subse achha	oodumee
I am	asmi, bhavámi	man hastam	olürüm	main hoon	main hon
Thou art	asi, bhavasi	tu hasti	olürsum	tu hai	tu hai
He is	asti, bhavati	oe hast	olür	wuh hai	o' hai
We are	smah, bhavámah	ma hasteem	olürüz	hum hain	assi hain
You are	stha, bhavatha	shuma hasted	olüsünüz	toom hain	tussi hain
They are	santi, bhavanti	anan hastand	olürlar	wee hain	oee hain
I was	ásam, abhavam	man boodam	olürdüm	main tha	main tha
Thou wast	ásih, abhavah	tu boodee	olürdün	tu the	tu the
He was	ásít, abhavat	oe bood	olürdú	wuh the	o' the
We were	ásma, abhaváma	ma boodeem	olürdak	hum the	assi the
You were	ásta, abhavata	shuma booded	olürdünúz	toom the	tassi the
They were	ásan, abhavun	anau boodand	olürdülar	we the	oee the

Comparative Table of Northern and Arian Words,—(Continued.)

English.	Sanscrit.	Persian	Turkish.	Hindee.	Panjabee.
Be	bhava	bash	ol	ho	ho
To be	bhavitum	boodan	olmak	hona	hona
Having been	bhutwá	boodah	olmüsh	hokar, hoke	hoke
I shall be	bhavishyami	man khaham bood	olajagüm	hoga	hoga
I should be	abhavishyäm	man khaham bood	olsüm	honga	honga
I beat	aham hanmi	man zadam	wurüm	main maron	main maren
Thou beatest	twam hansi	tu zadee	wursüm	tu mare	tu mare
He beats	sa hanti	oe zad	wurür	wuh mare	o' mare
We beat	vayam hanma	ma zudeem	wurürüz	hum maren	assi maren
You béat	yuyam hatha	shuma zaded	wurürsünüz	toom maren	tassi maren
They beat	te ghnanti	anan zadand	wurürlar	we maren	oee maren
Beat	jahi	be-zan	wur	mar	mar
To beat	hantum	zadan	wurmak	marna	marna
Having beaten	hatwá	zadah boodah	wurmüsh	markar	markee
I did beat	aham jaghána	man zad boodam	wurürdüm	marahon	marahon
I shall beat	aham hanishyámi	man khaham zad	wurajagüm	maronga	maronga

Comparative Table of Arian Words,—(Continued.)

English.	Pushtoo.	Aboriginal Caucasian.	Cashmeree.	Khas of Nepal.	Singalese.
One	you	ach	akh	ék	ekai
Two	dwá	du	zuh	dwi	dekai
Three	dare	tre	trae	tin	thunai
Four	salor	tsadda	tsoar	chár	hatherai
Five	punz	punts	pánts	pánch	pahai
Six	sh'paj	su	sheh	chhah	hiai
Seven	avo	sut	sat	sát	hathai
Eight	atha	ast	aait	áth	atai
Nine	nah	nu	noun	nou	namai
Ten	las	dos	dah	das	dhahayai
Twenty	schil	biis	wuh	bis	vissai
Fifty	pinzust	du-isa-dos	pantsah	pachás	panahai
Hundred	sil	punc	hat	sai	sēyaí
I	zu	ei	boh	man	mamey
Of me	zma	ima	müne	meró	magey
Mine	zma	ima	meum	......	magey
We	manga	ima	ass	hami hera	matey
Of us	zmuj	imṇa	sone	hami heruko	apey
Ours	zmuj	imṇa	meüm	......	apey

Comparative Table of Arian Worde,—(Continued.)

English.	Pushtoo.	Aboriginal Caucasian.	Cashmeree.	Khas of Nepal.	Singalese.
Thou	ta	tu	tsu	to̱n, ta̱n	thamoosay
Of thee	da ta	tua	choan	tero	thamoosaygey
Thine	sta	tua	theum	......	thamoosaygey
You	taso	vi	tsuhu	timi heru	umbe
Of you	da taso	ya	tahoond	timi heruko	umbegey
Your	staso	ya	tuhaindi	......	umbegey
He	hagha	sega	su	ú	āya
Of him	da hagha	sêga	taha	ùskò	āyagey
His	da hagha	sêga	tamsand	......	āyagey
They	hago	sige	tum	úní heru	awan
Of them	da hago	sigā	tila or tunun	uni heruko	awänegey
Their	da hago	sigā	tuhand	......	awanegey
Hand	las	das	atha	háth	hathey
Foot	......	kur	kor, padu	górá	paya, kakoole
Nose	paza	nasuri	nast	náka	naháye
Eye	stirgha	ānsi	nag, anch	a̱nkha	áha
Mouth	......	asi	aás, kiat	mukha	kate
Tooth	......	dont	dand	dá̱nt	dhathe

Ear	ghwaj	karna	kan	kan	kane
Hair	zoolf	dru	mast, wal	raon	kes, tssakaya
Head	......	sa	kálla	tau, tou	oloowe
Tongue	......	......	jian	......	dhewe
Father	plár	dai	maul	bábá	appa, thatha
Mother	mor	arau	maij	amma	amma
Brother	uror	bla	boi	doju	tya
Sister	khor	sus	benjí	bahini	nanyee
Man	sarrae	mats	mohnyn	manis	miniya
Woman	khadza	istri	zanana, bya	swasní	ganee
Wife	mandinah	......	bya	jo'i	ishteree
Child	balak	......	shur, nechu	......	lamaya
Son	dzoe	sagga	nechu	chóra	pootha
Daughter	jmai	su	kori	chóri	......
Sun	......	......	saria	surj	surya, ouwa
Moon	spazma	......	zun	chánd	handhe
Star	storè	......	tarukh	tárá	istharookawe
Fire	or	ana	agan, nār	ago	gindhere
Water	oba	abu	tresh	pani	wathoore
Earth	......	boom	zameen	prithwi, mati	polawa

Comparative Table of Arian Words,—(Continued.)

English.	Pushtóo.	Aboriginal Caucasian.	Cashmeree.	Khas of Nepal.	Singalese.
Wood	owani	dau	agar	káth	
House	kor	ama	gar, car	ghar	gadhere
Horse	ás	guru	gür	ghora	aspeya
Cow	ghwa	ga	goop	gai	gona
Dog	spaí	kuri	hoon	kukar	balla
Cat	püshee	bisas	broar	biralo	ballelee
Fish	......	......	gad	machha	matsya, maloo
Of a father	da plara	dạị-wa or dā	malu sand	bábá ko	thathagey
To a father	plara ta	dai-e	malis	bábá lai	thathalí
From a father	la plara	dai-da	malinishī	......	thathageng
Two fathers	dwa plaruna	du dai	zu mail	dwi baba	thathadhenna
Fathers	plaruna	dai	mail	bábá heru	thathagey
Bad father	nakar plar	abaru daí	yech maul	naniko bábá	narake thattha
A good man	khah sarrae	mats maista	ek rut mohuyn	ek niko manis	hondhe mineya
Two good men	dwa khaha sarri	du mats maista	zu ruch mohnivi	dwi niko manis heru	hondhe minissu-dhenna
Good men	khaha sarri	mats maista	ruch mohnivi	niko manis heru	hondhe minissu

Good	khah	maista	rut or jan	niko	hondhe
Better	der khah	......	yats rut		
Best	tol khah	......	sitah rut		
I am	zu yaim	ei sum	boh chus		
Thou art	ta ye	tu sis	tsa chuk		
He is	hagha dhè	sega se	su chu		
We are	munga yoo	ima simis	áass chế		
You are	taso yast	vee sik	tohi chewak		
They are	hagha deè	sege sin	tim ché		
I was	zu woom	ei su	boh asus		
Thou wast	ta we	tu suus	tsu asuk		
He was	hagha woo	sega se	su aus		
We were	manga wōō	ima sumis	áass ais		
You were	taso wêê	vee sus	tohi asawa		
They were	hagha wôô	sige sin	tim assis'		
Be	aos	sales	sta-as		
To be	aosdal	......	asan	honee	
Having been	......	......	asmut-asas		
I shall be I should be	zu bah yáim	ei salam	boh yats asan		

Comparative Table of Arian Words,—(Continued.)

English.	Pushtoo.	Aboriginal Caucasian.	Cashmeree.	Khas of Nepal.	Singalese.
I beat	zu wajam	ei veeyansam	boh layan chus	......	mamey ghahanown
Thou beatest	ta wajè	tu veeyansis	tsu layan chuk		
He beats	hagha wajé	siga veeyansi	su layan chu		
We beat	munga wajó	......	aass layan che		
You beat	taso wajo	......	tohi layan chewak		
They beat	hagha wajeè	......	tim layan ché		
Beat	waj	veeyans	layan or maron	......	gahapan
To beat	wajdal	......	layan	......	gahande
Having beat	wajhalee	......	asmat layan		
I did beat	zu wajdam	ei veeyansa	boh layan asus	......	mumey gahanwa
I shall beat	zu bah wájam	ei veeyansalam	boh yats layan	......	mumey gahanowa

Comparative Table of Arian Words,—(Continued.)

English.	Bengalee.	Ooryah.	Maharatta.	Guzeratee.
One	ek	eko	ek	ek
Two	dui	doo-i	don	be
Three	tin	tini	ten	tran, ton
Four	chár	chari	chár	chár
Five	pánch	pancho	pán̲ch	pan̲ch
Six	chhay	chho	sahá	chhă
Seven	sát	shato	sát	sát
Eight	át	atho	át	át
Nine	nay	no-o	nou	nou
Ten	das	dosho	dăhá	dăs
Twenty	bish, kuri	kore-e	vis	bis
Fifty	panchás	ponchaso	pănnás	pachás
Hundred	sata	shoye	sămbhăr	sou
I	ámi	ambhay	mi	hún̲
Of me	ámár, mor	ambhor	májhe	márún̲
Mine	mama, madiỵa	ambhor	májhe	márún

Comparative Table of Arian Words,—(Continued.)

English.	Bengalee.	Oorya.	Maharatta.	Guzratee.
We	ámrá	ambkoo	amhi	apre, hămon
Of us	ámáder, moder	ambha mankoo	ápăs-che, ápás	aprúṇ
Ours	,,	ambha manunkoo	amhálokáche	aprúṇ
Thou	tumi	toombhay	tomhi	túṇ
Of thee	tomar, tor	toombhar	tujhe	thárú
Thine	taba, twadiya	toombhar	tujhe, tomhe	thárú
You	tomrá	toombho man	tomhi lok	tome
Of you	tomáder, toder	toombho manko	tomhá lokáche	tomárú
Your	jushmadiya	toombho manunkoo	tumche, tomhâ lokâche	tomárú
He	tini, se	tahar	to	te
Of him	tár, táhár	tankor	tyáchá	tenu
His	ṭadiya	tankor	tyáchá	tenu
They	tárá, táhárá	samanay	tyálokáchá	teo
Of them	táder, táháder	tahankor	tyálokási	teonu
Their	tadiya	tahankor	tyálokáche	teonu
Hand	hát	hato	háth	háth
Foot	pá	goro	pád	păg
Nose	nāk	nako	nák	nák

Eye	chok	akhi	dăre	áŋkh
Mouth	mukha	mooho	tond	măhrú
Tooth	dānt	danto	dát	dáṇt
Ear	kān	kano	kán	kán
Hair	chul	balo	kes	bál
Head	máthá	motha	doká, sir	máthu
Tongue	jib	jihba	jíbh	jíbh
Father	báp	bapo	báp	báp
Mother	má	ma	máï, áï	máh
Brother	bhái	bhai	bháú	bhái
Sister	bon	bhownee	băhin	ben
Man	mánush	minipo	mánús	mánús
Woman	máyá, má	maikinya	boiká	strí, boiré
Wife	mág, strí	mipo	boikú	pannelí, boire
Child	santán	chha, pila	săntăli, lekre.	bachchhoṇ
Son	chhelya	poo-o	loyk, putro	dikro
Daughter	máyá	jhiyo	lyek.	dikré
Sun	surja	soorjyo	súriyo.	súraj
Moon	chánd	chando	chăndră	chánd
Star	tárá	tora	lakshtră	tárá

Comparative Table of Arian Words,—(Continued.)

English.	Bengalee.	Oorya.	Maharatta.	Guzratee.
Fire	águn	nian	agni, bistu	ágni, ág
Water	jal	paní	pání	pání
Earth	mātí, bhui	proothwee	prithwí, zamin	mitté, zămín
Wood	kát	katho	lăkre, lákúr	lăkron
House	ghar	ghur	ghăr, wárá	ghár
Horse	ghoṛa	gorha	ghorá	ghoro
Cow	goru	gai	gáí	gáí
Dog	kukur	kootha	kutrá	kutro
Cat	biṛāl	birarhee	mánjer	belárí
Fish	mách	machhee	mássá	măchhlí
Of a father	báper	bapur	bápá che	bápnú
To a father	bápke	bapungko	bápás	bápne
From a father	báper thaiṉ	bapungko tharo	bápá pásúṉ	báp pásethi
Two fathers	dui báp	doee bapo	don báp	be báp
Fathers	bápera	bapwanay	bahu báp	bápă
Bad father	manda báp	manda bap	wáet báp	khărāb báp

A good man	ek bhála lok	eka bhala loko	ek changle mánús	ek sáro mánús
Two good men	dui bhála lok	dwi bhala loko	don changle mánúsă	be sáru mánúsă
Good men	bhála lokera	bhala loko monay	changlé mánúsă	sáru mánúsă
Good	bhála	bhala	chángle	sáru
Better	uttamatara	bhala roo bhalo	te apekshá chángle, or te áhúm chánge	bodháre sáru
Best	uttamottama	utkrista	bahut chángle	sonthé sáru, sáru bodáthé
I am	ámi áchi	ambhay höoon	mi áhe	hún chháúṉ
Thou art	tumi ácha	tombhay hooo	tú áhas or tomhi áhet	túṉ chhe
He is	tini áchen	say hooonti	to áhe	te chhe
We are	ámrá áchi	ambhay manay hoo	amhilok áhot	hamon chheyé
You are	tomrá ácha	toombhy manay hooo	tumhilok áhót	tomen chho
They are	tárá áchen	say manay hooon	tya lok áhet	teo chhe
I was	ámi chhilám	ambhay hooi the	me hoto	húṉ hoto
Thou wast	tumi chhilá	toombhay hooi thelu	tu hotásh	toṉ hoto
He was	tini chhilen	say hoi thela	to hotá	te hoto
We were	ámrá chhilám	ambhay maney hoitheloo	amhilok hoto	hămon hotá
You were	tomrá chhilá	toombhay manay hoi-thela	tumhilok hotá	tomeṉ hotá
They were	tárá chhilen	say manay hoithela	tyalok hote	teo hotá
Be	hao	hooo	honá	hoúṉ, thoboṉ
To be	haite	ho-ba	honáche	thowáne
Having been	haiyá, haile	ho-oo	jhále	thayúṉ hotoṉ

Comparative Table of Arian Words,—(*Continued.*)

English.	Bengalee.	Oorya.	Maharatta.	Guzratee.
I shall be	ámi haibo	ambhay haybon	mi eyén	hún thowás
I should be	ámi haitám	......	mi álăch	măne tháú joiă
I beat	ámi mári	ambhay maree	mi márta he	húṉ márúchhoṉ
Thou beatest	tumi máro	toombhay maro	tu máritos	ton márechhe
He beats	tini máren	say maronti	to márito	te márechhe
We beat	ámrá mári	ambhay manay marie	amhilok márito	hămon máriechhyé
You beat	tomrá máro	toombhay manay maro	tumhi márá	tomeṉ márochho
They beat	tárá máren	say manay maroonte	telok márle	teo márechhe
Beat	már	mara	már	maroúṉ
To beat	márite	mariba	márálá	márwáne
Having beaten	máriyá	maree	márle láhe	máreo
I did beat	ámi máriyáchhi	ambhay mareethala	mi márle	me máreo
I shall beat	ámi máribo	ambhay marreebo	mi máren	húṉ máris

APPENDIX D.

Kashmiree Vocabulary and Grammatical Forms.

In consequence of recent discussions in the Society, Mr. L. Bowring, Commissioner of Mysore, was kind enough to let me know that he had many years ago compiled and sent to the Society a Kashmiree Vocabulary. The result has been the discovery of a paper as valuable as the hereditary reputation of the author would lead us to expect, which the Society now loses no time in publishing, and which it has been thought well to put in this place in connection with our Ethnological inquiries. Mr. Bowring's paper gives us a far fuller and better knowledge of the Kashmiree language than anything that we have yet had. The Vocabularies are very full, exact, and well arranged, and the grammatical forms of the verb especially are very fully set forth. It is only necessary (treating the matter ethnologically) to observe that since Persian has been for several hundred years the language of Government, religion and literature in Kashmir, and there has also been a long connection with Hindustan and the Punjab, a vast number of Persian words and phrases, and some Hindustanee and Punjabee expressions have necessarily incorporated themselves in the modern Kashmiree, especially as spoken by the better classes. In fact, that wonderful language Persian infuses itself wherever it comes in contact, and it abounds in Kashmiree just as in the upper class Hindustanee and in fact in Turkish also. Hence a faithful specimen of the Kashmiree of the present day will be found to contain many foreign words. But they are easily distinguishable, still wearing their foreign dress and little adapted to the native forms; and for the most part such words need not be confounded with original native words in such a way as to mislead us regarding the radical affinities of the language.

I have taken the liberty of omitting from Mr. Bowring's vocabularies a few evidently Persian words of a literary, and for the most part compound character, as I thought that these would not serve our present purpose. Some remain as now part of the ordinary vulgar tongue, but looking both to the vocables and to the grammar, I think it will be found that Kashmiree is certainly allied to the Indian languages rather than to the Persian.

Mr. Bowring has, perhaps, in the examples which he has given, put the declension of the noun rather too simply. He has used the uninflected Indian form 'Manush' for man and the Persian word 'Zananah' for woman. He shows, however, that most Kashmiree nouns are inflected to form the plural, and I think it will be found that almost all real Kashmiree nouns are inflected for cases also. Both my own observations and those of Messrs. Edgeworth and Leech, as well as Mr. Bowring's dialogues give the proper Kashmiree form for man 'Mohnyn,' plural 'Mohnivi.' And the following which I take from Leech is, I believe, the true declension of the Kashmiree noun 'Nichu,' a son.

A son, nichu	Sons, nichivi.
Of a son, nichivi-sand	Of sons, nichiven-sand.
To a son, nichivis	To sons, nichiven.
From a son, nichinishi	From sons, nichiven-nishi.

With respect to the variations of the genitive case, Mr. Edgeworth seems to differ from Mr. Bowring, saying that the genitive affix is, like Hindustanee, governed in point of gender by the noun which follows rather than by that which precedes it. So far as I could make out from cursory inquiry on the spot, it seemed to me that in fact the form of this affix is affected by *both* the preceding and the following nouns. Indeed it seems to have the most extraordinary chameleon-like variety of shapes, according to the positions in which the words are placed, and the only conclusion of my inquiries was, that the rules of Kashmiree declension are so complicated, that nothing but careful and scientific study will reduce them to shape.

It may be added that feminines are formed from masculines by inflections, as—

Masculine.	*Feminine.*
Gur, horse.	guir, mare.
Kokur, cock,	kokair, hen.
Tsawal, he goat,	tsavij, she goat.
Batak, drake,	batich, duck.
Kav, male crow,	kavin, female crow.

The language is evidently altogether subject to very many post-inflections, and abounds in affixes and postpositions.

G. Campbell.

Vocabulary of the Kashmírí Language.—By L. Bowring, *Esq., Commissioner of Mysore.*

The following vocabulary was prepared in Kashmírí in 1851, after comparison with another copy in U'rdú.

It may be observed of the Kashmirí that the pronunciation of the letter *ó* is very broad, resembling the *aw* in *awful*, as for instance 'mól,' father, read 'mawl.' The language also affects the compound letter *ts* in lieu of '*ch*,' as 'tsor,' four.

The formation of the plurals of substantives is irregular, but they generally take the affixes '*cha*' and '*chi*.' The genitive of substantives takes its gender from the noun preceding, not from that following as in U'rdú.

The particle نې is not used with verbs. The great number of Sanskrit words existing in Kashmírí is evident, but there are many words peculiar to the language. The character is generally written with Persian letters, but a form of Nágrí is also in use.

Substantives.

Air	ákásh	Boat	nau, shikárí
Apple	tsúnt	Brick	sír
Ass	khar	Book	púth
Arm	nar	Buffalo	moesh
Army	fauj	Bread	tsút
Age	bujar	Breast	vachh
Assistance	yári	Badness	yach
Answer	uttar	Beard	dóṛ
Arrow	tír	Bone	adij
Abuse	lēk	Bill	tont
Bird	pak	Breath	sháh
Brother	bói	Brass	sartal
Boy	lokat	Business	kóm
Branch	lang	Basket	phut, dák
Barley	úshak	Bush	kradzál
Butter	thain	Blood	rath
Blackberry	bar	Bag	thíl
Birth	parsun	Bow	kámán
Bridge	kadul	Blow	chók

Butterfly	didar
Burglary	san
Bee	tilar
Child	bálak
Cucumber	lór
Cherry	glás
Clothes	kapaṛ
City	shahr
Copper	trám
Cow	gáó
Cat	barúr
Camel	únṭh
Chin	hongain
Coat	faran
Ceiling	tálaú
Cotton	kapás
Cheese	cháman
Claim	dáwá
Corner	kón
Colour	rang
Chesnut	búñ
Cedar	deodár
Carrot	gajar
Cloud	abar
Crossbeam	thathar
Chair	sandal
Corpse	mur
Chalk	siap
Candle	soyĕt
Day	dúh
Dew	shabnam
Daughter	kúr
Death	maran
Dog	hún
Deer	loh, rús
Duck	battuk
Dirt	mal
Deceit	bram
Darkness	gath
Dream	supan
Danger	khatar
Drop	phiúr
Dram	henur
Dance	nagmah
Earth	ẓamín
Elephant	hasth
Egg	thól
Eye	úchh
Ear	kan
Eyebrow	bumah
Evil	yach
Edge	buṭh
East	púr
Elbow	khŏn
Enemy	shitar
Exertion	talásh
Fire	tungul, nártungul
Father	mól, băb
Father-in-law	zámtúr
Fruit	mewah
Flower	pósh
Flour	óṭ
Fowl	kukkur
Fox	patsló
Fish	gáḍ
Frog	niñímondij
Food	bat
Field	khyetí
Foot	khór
Forehead	dek
Fear	bayí
Flesh	shun
Firebasket	kángar
Foreigner	bishahrú

Fraud	daghá	Hand	ath
Face	bút	Height	thazar
Feather	par	Heap	dér, anbár
Fever	tap	Hunger	búchí
Fireplace	bukhárí	Health	balan
Friend	mitar	Hedge	vár
Family	shírbóts	Hoof	padur
Ferry	ghát	Honey	mách
Finger	anguj	Horn	hiang
Fisher	gáḍhanj	Hour	gaṛ
Fist	musht	Hemp	bang
Funeral-pile	chentá	Ice	yak
Flea	pish	Insect	kím
Fly	mach	Iron	shistar
God	dé	Indian corn	makhai
Girl	lókat kúr	Interest	súdh
Grass	gás	Interference	*kh*alal, toth
Gram	chholá	Ink	míl
Garlic	ruhan	Juice	ras
Gold	són	Jest	thathá
Goat	tsáwij, tsáwul	Jackal	shál
Goose	ans	Knife	srák
Grain	anáj	Leaf	barak
Garden	bágh	Leg	lang
Goodness	ján	Lip	úth
Greatness	bajar	Length	zechar
Grape	dach	Lie	apuz
Groom	sáis	Life	umar
Game	gindun	Light	gásh
Girth	tang	Letter	achar, harf
Husband	rún	Linseed	alish
Hail	ḍóṭ	Lime	chunah
House	garh, lur	Liver	jigar
Horse	gúr	Lock	kuluf
Head	kalah	Load	bár
Hair	wál	Log	haṭ
Heart	vandah	Lizard	haḍzúng

Moon	zún
Mountain	koh, parvat
Mist	vunar
Month	riat
Morning	subah, prabat
Midday	dopáhar
Man	manush, mohnú
Mother	mój
Mushroom	heḍar
Marriage	khándar
Mosque	mashíd
Money	nakd
Mule	kátir
Mouth	ós
Moustache	gónch
Measure	minun
Medicine	dawá
Milk	dódh
Molasses	gor
Manure	páh
Minute	lazá, pal
Market	koṭh
Mat	vagú
Mine	kán
Monkey	vándur
Mortgage	band̀
Mustard	ásur
Mint	podín
Musquito	mah
Meteorite	trath
Mouse	anmúr
Name	nav
Night	rát
Nephew	bápitar
Niece	bápitar beñí
Nose	nast
Nail	nam
Neck	gardan
Needle	súzan
Nest	ól
Noise	shor, kraknád
Number	ganzrun
Nettle	swáí
Net	zál
North	vutar
Onion	parán
Oil	tíl
Oar	kúr, chapá
Oath	drí
Pumpkin	alah
Pear	ṭank
Partridge	tsar
Pearl	mukt
People	lok
Platter	thál
Pain	dód
Price	mŏl
Pair	joṛá
Poplar	farast
Piece	tukṛá
Peg	mekh
Pepper	marach
Pace	púr
Paper	ká*gh*az
Pen	kalam
Pillar	tham
Pillow	vatrun
Pit	khad
Plough	ālah
Pole	chób
Power	kowwat
Pocketpicking	thappul
Question	prachun
River	daryá

Rain	rúd	Smallness	shikaslad
Rains	barsát	Strength	zór
Rice	tumal	Shadow	sáyah
Raspberry	chanchh	Shoe	paizár
Road	vat	Sleep	nindar
Rat	gagar	Skin	cham
Rump	mandul	Sound	áwáz
Roof	báin	Seed	beul
Relation	rishta	Sugar	shakar
Rope	raz	Stick	lúr
Red pepper	martsuwángan	South	duchan
Rind	diyal	Shop	ván
Rate	mol	Sugarcane	waishakar
Rein	lákam	Staircase	hér
Remedy	iláj	Saddle	zín
Ring	vój	Sorrow	azáb
Rose	guláb	Sack	gun
Rust	khái	Stool	rayat, garusth
Sea	samandar	Spider	zallur
Sun	áftab, saría	Species	ḳism
Star	tárak	Sand	siak
Snow	shín	Saw	lotar
Son	nichú	Scale	trak, háyúk
Sister	beñí	Screw	pech
Son-in-law	heúr	Sheath	kum
Spring	behár	Sheet	chádar
Summer	rathkól	Shield	sipar
Stem	múl	Side	ṭarf
Salt	nún	Silk	pót
Strawberry	kandachh	Sleeve	núr
Street	dúr, kocha	Smoke	duh
Stone	kain	Soap	sabun
Silver	chánd	Spot	dágh
Sheep	gobh	Sting	toph
Snake	sarp	Scorpion	bich
Shoulder	phiúk	Steel	folád
Stomach	yaḍ	Straw	gás

Sweat	gumah
Storm	váú
Spoon	choncha
Thunder	gagráí
Tree	kul
Temple	mandir
Teeth	dand
Tongue	jiau
Thigh	rán
Truth	puz
Time	vakt, vél
Throat	hut
Turban	dastár
Thirst	tresh
Tank	taláú
Tea	cháhí
Tail	dumah
Trade	saudágarí
Toe	khórij anguj
Tomato	ruvangan
Turnip	gogaj
Thread	pan
Tent	khema
Table	mez
Taste	maza, swád
Thorn	kanth
Theft	tsúr
Trust	itimád, pats
Uncle	pitar, chácha
Umbrella	tábdán
Udder	than
Urine	mutr
Use	kám
Venom	zahar
Velvet	makhmal
Vein	rag
Vice	páp
Village	gám
Water	áb, poñ
Wind	háwá
Woman	zenánah
Wife	kolai
Winter	vand
Wheat	kanak
Wood	zun
Wrist	mats
Width	khajar
Well	cháh, krúr
Weight	tolún
West	pachum
Washerman	dub
Watermelon	handwand
Wall	dos
Worm	ámkhiúm
Whore	háfiz
Weed	gás
Wager	dau
Wax	móm
Wheel	hagur
Widow	monḍ
Wing	par
Wire	tár
Wool	wón
Yard	gaj
Year	varíh

Declensions.

Singular.	N.	A man	manush
	G.	Of a man	manush-sund
	Acc.	A man	manush-is
	Ab.	From a man	manush-nishin
Plural.	N.	Men	manash
	G.	Of men	manash-sund
	Acc.	Men	manash-is
	Ab.	From men	manash-nishin
Singular.	N.	A woman	zenání
	G.	Of a woman	zenání-hund
	Acc.	A woman	zenání
	Ab.	From a woman	zenání-nishin
Plural.	N.	Women	zenánah
	G.	Of women	zenánah-hund
	Acc.	Women	zenánah
	Ab.	From women	zenánah-nishin

Examples of Plurals.

Beñí	a sister	Beñícha	sisters
Bói	a brother	Báí	brothers
Mól	a father	Mail	fathers
Mój	a mother	Májí	mothers
Nichu	a son	Nichii	sons
Kul	a tree	Kuil	trees
Barak	a leaf	Barakchi	leaves
Gám	a village	Gámchi	villages
Gás	a grass	Gáscha	grasses
Jánwar	an animal	Jánwarchi	animals

Adjectives.

Active	takṛá	Blind	un
Blunt	munḍ	Blue	niúl
Boiling	tut, bahar	Black	karhún
Broken	phuṭmuṭ	Bitter	tsok, chok

Bad	yach
Cheap	sug
Clever	gaṭul
Clear	sáf
Coarse	viuṭ
Crooked	hul
Cold	turun
Certain	pats
Deep	sun
Dear	drug
Dark	anigut
Doaf	súr
Dumb	kul
Dead	múdmud
Double	zuh
Dry	huk
Dirty	malburut
Drunk	muṭ
Easy	ásán
Empty	*k*hálí
Expert	fázil
First	pathiúm
Former	bronṭh
Fat	viuṭ
False	ápuz
Frightened	khochún
Fine	zayul
Full	barit
Fond	ṭóṭh
Good	ján
Great	bód
Glad	khúsh
Greedy	lúlachí
Green	sabz
Generous	dátah
General	ạ́m
High	thud
Hard	dúr
Hungry	buch
Heavy	gubh
Hot	garm, ushan
Ill, bad	yach
Low	past, tsut
Long	dsiút, khul
Little	kam
Less	kehna
Last	brunṭhun
Lame	lung
Loprous	hitrilad
Lazy	sust
Light	lut
Loose	diyul
Left	hul
Lower	tal
Many	sitáh
Mad	dewána
Middle	sum
New	nó
Naked	nathnun
Old	purón, buḍh
Proud	kibar
Putrid	dudriyomut
Poor	gharíb
Quick	tikán
Ready	tayyár
Right	sind
Ripe	papiúmúd
Raw	khám
Small	lúk
Sweet	miúṭ
Stupid	nádan
Straight	siud
Square	chankunjal
Sharp	tej

Slippery	pishul	Weak	liyad
Thirsty	treshut	Well	ján
Thin	lissá	White	safíd
Tight	tang	Wet	tar, udar
Ugly	yach	Young	jawán
Upper	piaṭh		

Declension.

N.	A good man	ján manush	*Singular.*
G.	Of a good man	ján manush-sund	
Acc.	A good man	ján manush-is	
Ab.	From a good man	ján manush-nishin	
N.	Good men	jánchi manash	*Plural.*
G.	Of good men	jánchi manash-sund	
Acc.	Good men	jánchi manash-is	
Ab.	From good men	jánchi manash-nishin	

Comparison.

Good	Ján
Better	Yuts ján
Best.	Sitáh ján

Verbs.

To awake	votun	To Burn	zálun
„ Avoid	bachun	„ Blow	phok diun
„ Ascend	khasun	„ Bury	gárhun
„ Advance	bron khasun	„ Buy	miúl hiún
„ Ask	prutsun	„ Come	iyun
„ Be	sompanun	„ Cut	tsatun
„ Be able	hekkun	„ Call	nádun
„ Bring	ánun	„ Conquer	jítun
„ Begin	lagun	„ Choose	tsárun
„ Bite	tsátun	„ Cover	vatun
„ Believe	patskarun	„ Chew cud	drámun karun
„ Boil	pakinwun	„ Drink	chiun
„ Beg	mangun	„ Die	marun

To Dwell	basun
,, Do	karun
,, Decrease	kamgachhun
,, Draw	lamun
,, Drive	patrozun
,, Drown	phatun
,, Expel	kaḍit tsumun
,, Erase	kaḍun
,, Enter	andar atsun
,, End	makoláwun
,, Find	labhun
,, Fight	laḍun
,, Fly	uphún
,, Fall	paṛun
,, Fasten	lágun
,, Forget	mashun
,, Frighten	kotsunáwun
,, Go	gasun
,, Give	diun
,, Gamble	záras gindun
,, Hear	bozun
,, Increase	baḍun
,, Join	melanáwun
,, Kill	márun
,, Know	janun
,, Kick	lat diun
,, Lose	hárun
,, Live	zindásun
,, Leave	chhoṛun
,, Laugh	ásun
,, Learn	hichun
,, Hide	khaditrozun
,, Lift	tolun
,, Leap	khanun
,, Lie	apuz vanun
,, Meet	melun
,, Melt	galun

To Move	alaráwun
,, Open	mussurun
,, Play	gindun
,, Put on	gandun, chháwun
,, Put off	mutsurun, wálun
,, Pain	dod karun
,, Place	tháwun
,, Pass	guzaráwun
,, Plague	dek karun
,, Pour	ḍalun
,, Push	dhakdiun
,, Read	páṛhun
,, Roast	buzun
,, Run away	tsalun
,, Reap	fasl tsatun
,, Reckon	gansrun
,, Recollect	yad karun
,, Return	phir diun
,, Repel	nibar kadun
,, Retire	pat nerun
,, Ride	khasun
,, Rise	vathun
,, Row	vayun
,, Rouse	uzanáwun
,, Run	dáúwun
,, Rub	mathun
,, Stick	lagun
,, Swim	tsátwáyun
,, Swell	hunun
,, Sweep	dún
,, Suckle	cháwun
,, Sing	gewun
,, Spit	taktráwun
,, Sell	kunun
,, Sit	bihun
,, Show	hawidun
,, Send	sozun, ludun

To Strain	chhánun	To Take	hiun
„ Seek	tsáḍun	„ Taste	tsuhun
„ Sow	váwun	„ Teach	hichunáwun
„ Strike	márun	„ Throw	trevitsunun
„ Stand	istádrozun	„ Touch	lágun
„ Seize	ratun	„ Vomit	khai karun
„ Shut	bandh karun	„ Weave	vonun
„ Say	vanun	„ Weigh	tolun
„ See	uchhun	„ Wait	prárun
„ Smell	mushakhiun	„ Wish	yatsun
„ Sleep	shongun	„ Wash	chhalun
„ Speak	vanun		

Conjugations.

Sompanun, to be.

Present.		*Imperfect.*	
I am	buh chus	I was	buh ósus
Thou art	tsuh chukuh	Thou wast	tsuh ósukuh
He is	suh chuh *or* chó	He was	suh óús
We are	as chih	We were	as óús
Ye are	tahí chiwuh	Ye were	tahí ósuwuh
They are	tim chih	They were	tim óús

Perfect.

I have been	buh ósus osmutun
Thou hast been	tsuh ósukuh osmutun
He has been	suh óús osmutun
We have been	as óús osmutun
Ye have been	tahí ósuwuh osmutun
They have been	tim óús osmutun

Pluperfect.

I had been	buh ósus sompunwatun
Thou hadst been	tsuh ósukuh sompunwatun
He had been	suh óús sompunwatun
We had been	as óús sompunwatun
Ye had been	tahí ósuwuh sompunwatun
They had been	tim óús sompunwatun

Future.

I shall be	buh heksompanit
Thou shalt be	tsuh hekaksompanit
He shall be	suh hekisompanit
We shall be	as hekáúsompanit
Ye shall be	tahí hekiúsompanit
They shall be	tim hekáúsompanit

To be	sompanun
Being	sompanit
Been	sompun

Vanun, to speak.

Present.

I speak or am speaking	buh chus vanán
Thou speakest	tsuh chukuh vanán
He speaks	suh chuh vanán
We speak	as chih vanáú
Ye speak	tahí chiwuh vanáú
They speak	tim chih vanáú

Imperfect.

I spoke	mi vun
Thou spakest	tsuh vanut
He spoke	suh vun
We spoke	as vanwutun
Ye spoke	tahí vanwutun
They spoke	timáú vanwutun

Perfect.

I have spoken	mi chum vanwutun
Thou hast spoken	tsuh chuh vanwutun
He has spoken	tim chá vanwutun
We have spoken	as chá vanwutun
Ye have spoken	tahí chuh vanwutun
They have spoken	timáú chuh vanwutun

Pluperfect.

I had spoken	mi ós vanwutun
Thou hadst spoken	tsuh ósí vanwutun
He had spoken	tim ós vanwutun
We had spoken	as ósus vanwutun
Ye had spoken	tahí ósú vanwutun
They had spoken	timáú ós vanwutun

Future.

I shall speak	buh hek vanit
Thou shalt speak	tsuh hekak vanit
He shall speak	suh hekí vanit
We shall speak	as hekáú vanit
Ye shall speak	tahí hekiú vanit
They shall speak	tim hekáú vanit

Potential.

I may speak	buh vanah
Thou mayest speak	tsuh vanak
He may speak	suh vaní
We may speak	as vanáú
Ye may speak	tahí vaniú
They may speak	tim vanáú

Speak	van
Speaking	vanán
Spoken	vanwutun

CONJUGATION OF THE PASSIVE VOICE OF MÁRUN TO STRIKE.

Present.

I am struck	buh gasa márah
Thou art struck	tsuh gasak márah
He is struck	suh gasa márah
We are struck	as chih márah gasán
Ye are struck	tahí chuh márah gasán
They are struck	tim chih márah gasán

Imperfect.

I was struck	buh gós márah
Thou wast struck	tsuh gók márah
He was struck	suh gáú márah
We were struck	as gayé márah
Ye were struck	tahi gáú márah
They were struck	tim gayé márah

Future.

I shall be struck	buh gatsa márah
Thou shalt be struck	tsuh gatsak márah
He shall be struck	suh gatsa márah
We shall be struck	as gatsáú márah
Ye shall be struck	tahí gatsiú márah
They shall be struck	tim gatsáú márah

PRONOUNS.

Personal.		*Possessive.*	
I	buh	Mine	miún
Thou	tsuh	Thine	chhón
He, she	suh	His	tasun
We	asi, mi	Our	miún
Ye	tahí	Your	chhón
They	tim, timáú	Their	tasun

Relative and Interjective.		*Indicative.*	
Who?	kus?	This	ih
Which?	kyá	That	uh, suh
Whoever	yus	These	yum
Whatever	yih	Those	tium
He who	yus		

Miscellaneous.

Self	páné	Another	duyum
Such	yithúí	Any	kánh
All	sárí	Every	yusaká
Same	sárú	Own	panun
Other	bék		

Declension of Pronouns.

N.	I	buh	N.	We	mi
G.	Of me	miún	G.	Of us	as in singular
Acc.	Me	mi	Acc.	Us	
Ab.	From me	mi nishin	Ab.	From us	

N.	Thou	tsuh	N.	You	tsih
G.	Of thee	chhon	G.	Of you	as in singular
Acc.	Thee	tsih	Acc.	You	
Ab.	From thee	tsih nishin	Ab.	From you	

N.	He	suh	N.	They	tim
G.	Of him	tasun	G.	Of them	as in singular
Acc.	Him	humis	Acc.	Them	
Ab.	To him	humis nishin	Ab.	To them	

N.	This	Ih	N.	These	yum
G.	Of this	yimsun	G.	Of these	yuhund
Acc.	This	yimis	Acc.	These	yiman
Ab.	From this	yimis nishin	Ab.	From these	yiman nishin

N.	That	uh, suh	N.	Those	tium
G.	Of that	yusun	G.	Of those	tinhund
Acc.	That	humis	Acc.	Those	timan
Ab.	From that	humis nishin	Ab.	From those	timan nishin

Myself	buh páné
Of myself	buh pánas

&c.

Adverbs.

Above	piaṭ	Below	tal
Always	doháí	Backwards	pat
Almost	jaljal	Except	siwáí
Also	bíyih	Exactly	thík
As	yiut	Enough	thayú
Already	wuini	Far	dúr
Alone	kunui	From	piath, nishin
Altogether	sárí sán	Forwards	brúnt

How	kiut	Still	támat
How much } How many }	kótá	Then	til
Hither	yúr	Thus	ithui
Inside	andar	There	tati
Immediately	jhaṭpaṭ	Thither	hór
Near	nakh	Therefore	imbápat
Now	vuin	Together	sán
Nothing	kechnú	Very	sitáh
No	nah	When	yil
Outside	nebar	Where ?	kati
Perhaps	dewuh	Why	kyázi
Quickly	jalpáhan	Yes	őn, áú
So	ithui	How	kitpóthin
Slowly	lut	sA }	yithipóthin
Suddenly	yekáyek	So }	tithipóthin

Prepositions.

According	ithuí	In	andar
After	pat	On	piaṭ
Among	mauz	Towards	ṭarf
Before	brúnt	With	satin
Besides	varáí	Without	siwá
For sake of	bápat		

Conjunctions.

And	ta	If	hargáh
Although	hargáh	Either	yá
But	lekin	Or	yá
Because	yudvane		

Interjections.

Alas !	afsús !	Lo !	uch !
Ho !	hatá !	What !	kya !

Cardinal Numbers.

One	ak	Seventeen	saddah
Two	dzuh	Eighteen	aṭhdah
Three	tré	Nineteen	kunuwúh
Four	tsór, chór	Twenty	wúh
Five	páns	Twenty-one*	ekwúh
Six	shah	Thirty	truh
Seven	sat	Forty	chatjí
Eight	áth	Fifty	pansa
Nine	náú	Sixty	sheṭ
Ten	dah	Seventy	satat
Eleven	káh	Eighty	shít
Twelve	báh	Ninety	namat
Thirteen	trowáh	Hundred	hat
Fourteen	chaudah	Two hundred	zahat
Fifteen	pandah	Thousand	dahshat, sás
Sixteen	shurah	Lakh	lach

---

*22	dzitówúh	49	unwanzah
23	trawúh	51	ekwanzah
24	cháúwúh	52	dowanzah
25	pántsuh	53	trewanzah
26	shawwúh	54	chauwanzah
27	satowúh	55	panswanzah
28	aṭhowúh	56	shahwanzah
29	untruh	57	satwanzah
31	ektruh	58	aṭhwanzah
32	daitruh	59	unhath
33	tchtruh	61	ekhath
34	chaitruh	62	dohath
35	pánstruh	69	kunsátat
36	shahtruh	71	eksatat
37	sattruh	72	dosatat
38	aṭhtruh	79	kunshít
39	kuntazi	81	ekshít
41	ektazi	89	kunánamat
42	as above	91	eknamat
43	as above	99	namánamat
44	as above		
45	as above		
46	as above		
47	as above		
48	as above		

Ordinal Numbers.

First	godniuk	21st	ekwúhiúm
Second	duyum	22nd	dzitowuhium
Third	treyum	23rd	trawuhium
Fourth	tsurum	24th	cháúwuhium
Fifth	panchum	25th &c.	&c.
Sixth	shayum		
Seventh	satum		
Eighth	aṭhtum		
Ninth	nawum		
Tenth	dahiúm		
Eleventh	káhiúm		

Sentences.

What is your name?	chhón náú kyá chŭh?
What is the name of this village?	yit gámas kyá chŭh náú?
How far is it to Kashmir?	Kashmír támut kótá chŭh dúr?
How many houses are there in this village?	yit gámas kuts garh chuh?
Who is the head man?	mokaddam kus chuh?
What is the time?	kótá chuh dŭh?
Three o-clock.	sihpahar chuh.
Bring that.	uh anun.
Take away this.	ih niun.
What crops are grown here?	yithi kyá fasl chuh sompanín?
Are the pears ripe or unripe?	ṭank chó paminmud ki na khám chuh?
Go away.	gats.
Come here.	vol yúr.
Come quickly.	jald volah.
What does this man want?	ih monhyú kyá chuh mangán.
Ask him.	humis prichú.
I cannot say.	buh chus sasna vanit hekán.
I shall go to-morrow.	buh gats phagá.
It rained yesterday.	rát volun rúd.
It is very hot.	sitáh garm chuh.

The road is good.	vat chuh (*or* chavuh) ján.
The road is bad.	vat do. yach.
One must ascend that hill.	yit kohas piat baniá khasun.
What is the price of this?	yit kyá chuh kímat?
It is dear.	drug chuh.
It is cheap.	sug chuh.
You ask too much.	tsuh chukuh sitáh mangán.
Are there any manufactures here?	yithi baniá ki tyár karun?
Is cloth woven?	kapar baniá vanun?
What pay do you get?	tsuh kyá chuh talab inelan?
Is the Kardar a good man?	Kárdár chó ján monhyu?
I wish to find out.	buh chus yatsán zi maálúm kar.
Is he able to carry that load?	hekyá uh bór tulit?
My horse is lame.	miun gur lung chuh.
Can you shoe him?	tsuh hekak yimis guris nál lágit?
What rent do you pay for this shop?	yit vánas kot chukuh diwan kiráya tsuh?
Six rupees a year.	shah rúpí varíhas.
He began to get tired.	suh lug thakne.
They began to fight together.	tim lég pánawin harhar karani.
Can you read and write?	tsuh hekak likhit, parhit?
A little.	kam kam.
How do you know?	tsuh kitpóthin zának?
In what way will you repair this?	tsuh kitpóthin karan ih durust
In what month is saffron gathered?	kat retas andar chih kongposh [tsaṭán?
In Kártik.	Kártikas andar.
What colour is best?	kyá rang chuh sáríkot ján?
If he takes it what will you do?	hargáh ih heki timsritit, tsuh kyá karakadah?
Has he gone before, or is he following?	suh chuh brúnt gomut, kin-pat chuh áwán?
Why are you making such a noise?	tahí kyá zi chúr yút krakanád karán?
Put on this dress and put off that.	ih kaparu mutsar, uh tsun nóil.
I went with him.	buh chus gomut humis satin.
He walks without shoes.	suh chuh paizár siwái pakán.
When he comes tell me.	yili suh yi tili gasi mi khabar.
Is it near or far?	nazdík chó, kinh dúr chuh?

You always delay.	tsuh chukúh dóhí tsér karan.
We are almost ready.	as chih thikán thikán tyár.
I am hungry and thirsty.	buh chus pháké bi treshut.
Don't eat raw apples.	khám tsunt ma khiú.
I have ate enough.	thaiú, khiaú.
Where is my servant?	miun naukar kati chuh?
Is he here or there?	yithi chó, kinh tathi chuh?
It is still raining.	vunyas tányat chuh válán.
Shall you sleep inside or outside?	andar shongak kinh nibar?
This dog is exactly like mine.	yih hún chuh menis húnis hiú.
I have already heard that story.	mi búz suh kissa brúnt.
There is a bridge opposite.	brohun kani chuh kadul.
Do as I say.	yithipóthim buh dapán chus, tithi póthin kariú.
Write accordingly as I do.	menis lekhinas hiú likhiú.
Are you alone?	tsuh chukuh kunezun?
He fell from his horse.	suh piau guri piaṭ visiṭ.
Throw down that blanket.	uh kamal sun bonkun trevit.
Come up here.	yúr khas hiúr.
How far is it from here?	ithi piat kótá chuh dúr?
It is five kos.	páns króh chuh.
My brother and I went home.	ak buh bi miún bóí gaye garh.
Either you or he will be punished.	yá tsuh nat humis meliwuh sazá.
Why should I be punished?	mi kyá zi diú sazá.
Because you are a thief.	awé bápat zi tsuh chukuh tsúr.
Unless you have witnesses you will be imprisoned.	hargáh tsuh gawá ashinah, ta kaid sompanak.
This horse is better than that.	ih gur chuh humsin kotján.
What do you call that basket?	hut fiatis kya chuh vanán?
Don't be frightened.	kots muh.
He ought to have done so.	timis guts ih karun.
Can you swim?	tsuh hekak tsánt vayut?
Listen! show me the road.	hatá? mi háú vat.
You must do it.	tsuh gatsi zarúr karun.
Taste this peach.	ih tsunun gatsi tsuhun.
I cannot find my coat.	miún kurtah chuh nah melán.
Look behind that wall.	hut dewáras pat kạni uchhú.

He lost Rs 50 in gambling.	hum hárí záras andar pantsáh rúpí.
I won Rs. 100 „ „	mi ziún „ „ hat „
A snake bit him in the leg.	humis dítsnas sarpan langas tiop.
She laughed much.	humi us sitáh.
We seized 10 thieves.	asi rit dah tsúr.
They all escaped.	timáú tsail sárí.
They shall leave this country.	tim tsalan yihu mulk.
I will punish them.	buh dimak adh timan sazá.
Can you lend me a rupee ?	tsuh hekak asi rúpiyahak wozum dit ?
What do you teach these children ?	im shiúr kyá chiwak hichanáwan ?
Let him come, why do you stop him ?	yiu ih kyá zi chuwan raṭan ?
I beat him soundly.	mi dint humis sitáh már.
His house has been burnt.	humis lug garhas nár.
He will be buried to-morrow.	phagá ihi daffan karanah.
Choose one of these apples.	yimáú tsuntáú andar tsuhun ak tsunṭánah.
Cover that pan.	hut ḍegchas piaṭ thavin sarposh.
Send me some fruit.	asi mishin ladiu kinh mewah.
He answered me falsely.	tim vuṇasi mishin apuz jawáb.
Hang up these clothes.	ih kapar tsinun awezán.
What are you doing ?	tsuh kyá chukuh karan ?
I am cutting corn.	buh chus kanak tsaṭán.
Are these cows chewing the cud ?	ih gáú chuh drámun karán ?
Go and see.	gatsit vuch.
Feed them with grass.	yim khiáwúk gás.
Give them water to drink.	yim chúviúk tresh.
Has the room been swept ?	at kothis duwah kinh nah ?
Can this be washed ?	ih yiyá chhalanah ?
I have two horses.	mi chuh dzuh gur.
He had three wives.	timas ásah tre koleyih.
I shall have plenty.	mi nishin ási ih sitáh.
I rode 10 kos without stopping.	buh gós dahan krohun guris kia lákim varáí.
What is to be done ?	kyá gatsi karun ?
They are drunk.	suh chuh mut.
We are poor.	as chih kangál.
This room is 12 ft. long, 10 ft. wide,	ih koth báh páwah dsut, dah páwah

and 9 ft. high.	khúshadah, bi chuh náú páwah thúd.
He was very lazy.	suh ós sitáh sust.
Give me rather less than one seer.	mi gatsi ak sír akich kih kom diún.
Weigh this ghee.	ih ghiáú tuliun.
How much honey for a rupee?	rúpía kótá chuh mách?
Change this rupee into pice.	yit rupía aniu tiunk.
Is there any batta taken?	kinh chuh hewán rúpía vat?
Give that blind man, that lame man and that leper each an anna.	humis anis ta humis langis ta humis hitriládas, akak áná diú.
Tare care how you carry that.	uh chíz gatsi khabardarí san niun.
I shall be very glad.	buh gatsa sitáh khúsh.
All the people came to see.	sárí lok áye uchhini.
Is this the same horse or another?	ih chuh suhí gur kinh bék chuh?
Every man was killed.	pratakáh gáú márah.
His father and mine are cousins.	humsund mól bi miun mól chih pánaion bói bói.
His uncle is rich.	humsund pitar chuh dáúlatmand.
Her mother is poor.	humsanz mój chuh kangál.
Your horse is lame.	chhón gur chuh lung.
My servant is ill.	miún monhyú chuh bemár.
Put this and that together.	ak ih bi ih gachi vátun.
This is my own watch.	ih chuh mi panin gar.
Why was I beaten?	buh kyá zi gós márah?
Shall I be beaṭen?	buh gatsa márah?
Why should I give you anything?	buh kyá zi dimái tsuh kih?
You should go quickly.	chhon gatsi jald gatsun.
There are rocks above and below.	koh chuh piaṭ ti tá tal ti.
This language is rather difficult.	ih zabán chuh kentsa mushkil.
With practice it will become easy	ádat satin gatsi ásán.
Never mind, speak every day.	ki parwar chunah duhí van.
Shall I go with or without my horse?	buh gatsah garheth knih nah?
Why do you follow me?	tsuh kyá zi chukuh mi patpat wán?
I want alms.	buh chus bechán.
Perhaps it will rain.	dewah válik.
I was wet through.	buh ós sitáh baranah.

Dry my clothes in the sun.	miún kapar hoknáwú tápas. [phiat.
He and his brother were drowned in the river.	suh bi tasun bóí daryávas andar
The mahárájá is very kind to artisans.	Mahárájá chuh karigaran piat sitáh miharbání karan.
They are never fined.	amis chun zehtí chit iván hinah.
He sent me a good 'ziafat.'	tim laz asi zabar ziáfat.
I laughed and she wept.	mi us ta tim wud. [hund.
This shawl is not worth Rs. 400.	ih doshálah chuh nah tsorhatun
This is not the first time.	ih chuh nah godiniúk dó.
The Government takes half the produce.	sirkár chuh nisf paidaish hewán.
I and you and he will go together.	ak buh bí tsuh bi suh gatsánikwatén.
You will never come back.	tsuh guk nah biyi zá yór.
The people here are very dirty and poor. [Kashmír?	yithik lók chih sitáh mail talryi chih kangál.
How many boats are there in	Kashmíras andar kotsa náú chih?
About two thousand.	aṭsaṭ chih dósás.
Do they pay any tax?	kinh chih mahsúl diwán?
If he ever do so, beat him.	hargáh suh biyi ithui kare, adh márun. [wot tárit.
If you can jump over this ditch.	hargáh tsuh hekak yit khandakas
I cannot jump over it.	buh hek nah tarit. [tan?
Can you shoot birds flying?	tsuh hekak wuphun janáwar márl-
Is there any game in these hills?	yit kohas chó kinh shikár?
Yes, a great deal.	áú, sitáh.
Of what kind?	kyá kyá chuh?
There are bears and deer.	hápat chó kinh rús chuh.
How do you know?	tsuh kitpothin zának?
I am a sportsman.	buh chus shikárí.
What do the bears eat?	hápat kyá chih khiawán?
Indian corn, walnuts and fruit.	makhai chih khiáwán, dun chih khiawán, kinh mewah chih khiawán.
Are there any white bears?	kanu chah safíd hápat?
Not here, but there are beyond.	ithi chuh nah, ammá wehin chuh
In what district?	kut pergannahs andar?

On this or on that side of the hill?	kohas ihpár kinh chuh kinh apár kinh chuh?
Beyond it.	apáré.
What kind of fish are there in the river?	daryávas andar kami reng chih gád?
A great many kinds.	sitáhí reng chih.
Do people catch them or not?	low chih gád ratan kinh nah?
Attend to what I am saying.	ih kinh tsuh buh vanánchus, tat piaṭ tháú dhián.
If you do not, you will repent it.	hargah nah karak, adh pashtáwak.
If you do not go, I will beat you.	hargáh nah gasak, adh marut.
Had you done as I told you, this misfortune would not have happened.	yithi póṭhin mi dah piumáú, hárgah tithi póihin karihiu, adh ih hauwinan kánthi balái.
If I were rich, I would repair this house.	hargah buh daulatmand ásah, adh karahah yit kothas marammat.
If he had gone there, he would undoubtedly have been killed.	hargáh suh ór gatsaheh adh bilá-shak gatse suh márah.

APPENDIX E.

*Language of Dravidian Aborigines. Notes on the Oraon Language.—
By the Rev.* F. Batsch.

Nouns.

The language is very defective in nouns. It is evident that the Oraons have lost much of their own language, and that they have made up their losses from the languages of the people amongst whom they have dwelt, chiefly Sanskrit and Hindustani. They have no original religious terms, no abstract ideas, no words for actions of the mind or thoughts.

Gender.

In Oraon there are two genders, the masculine and the feminine, but there are very few nouns of the latter.

Whether the noun is a masculine or feminine is only to be found in the termination of the verb. In the declension, the gender is not or only very seldom expressed.

Declension.

There are all the usages of the Hindi language to be found in the Oraon. The oblique cases are also formed by postpositions.

Note. Pronunciation of the Roman characters as used in writing the Oraon words.

à	like	a	in	father	e	like	e	in	peg
u	„	u	„	rule	o	„	o	„	so
ì	„	i	„	police	ai	„	ai	„	aisle
a	„	a	„	roman	au	„	ow	„	owl
u	„	u	„	full	ch	„	ch	„	church
i	„	i	„	still	ch as in German doch, loch				

SINGULAR.

Nom.	kukos, the boy.
Gen.	kukosgahi, of the boy.
Dat.	kukosge, for to the boy.
Acc.	kukosin, the boy.
Abl.	kukosgusti, from the boy.
Instr. (?)	kukusanti, from or by the boy.
Loc.	kukosnu, on, in, upon the boy.
Agent.	kukosim (?)
Voc.	ana ko, oh boy.

PLURAL.

Nom.	kukor.
Gen.	kukorgahi.
Dat.	kukorge.
Acc.	kukorin.
Abl.	kukurgusti.
Instr.	kukoranti.
Loc.	kukornu.
Voc.	ana koe.

SINGULAR.

Nom.	kukoi, the girl.
Gen.	kukoigahi.
Dat.	kukoige.
Acc.	kukoidin.
Abl.	kukoigusti.
Instr.	kukointi.
Loc.	kuknu.
Agent.	kukoidim.
Voc.	an koi.

PLURAL.

Nom.	kukoier.
Gen.	kukoiergahi, etc.

SINGULAR.

Nom.	chad, the boy.
Gen.	chadasgahi.
Dat.	chadge.
Acc.	chadin, or chadasin.

Abl.	chadgusti.
Instr.	chadanti.
Loc.	chadnu.
Agont.	chadasim.
Loc.	ana chad.

PLURAL.

Nom.	chadar.
Gen.	chadargahi.

etc.

The plural is mostly expressed in the termination of the verb, the noun remaining unaltered in the singular and plural.

NOUNS.

Masculine.		*Feminine.*	
tangdas	son	tangṛi	daughter
kukos	boy	kukoi	girl
belas	king	belṛi	queen
meũt	husband	mukka	woman

NOUNS.

mercha	firmament	chebda	ear
chechal	earth	tatcha	tongue
binko	star	cheka	hand
biṛi	sun	chochal	bone
chando	moon	pall	tooth
pairi	morning	chesar	shoulder
ulla	day	chocha	back
màchà	night	kul	belly
ucha	darkness	umbalcho	liver
āl	man	?	heart
meth	male	?	lungs
mukka	female	cheso	blood
kuku	head	ched	foot
kes, chuti	hair	chosga	leg
chan	eye	angli	finger
kapṛe	forehead	eroch	nail
moy	nose	gurchi	heel
boi	mouth	màka	knee
gale	cheek	bàri	arm

thapṛi	palm of hand	bercha	cat
gunṛi	cow	lakra	tiger
ado	ox	haṛha	wolf
eṛa	goat	tsigalo	jackal
paṭha	lamb	cher	fowl
allah	dog	cokro	cock

Pronouns.

En	I	nām	we (both)
nin	thou	em	we (more than two)
ās	he	nim	you
ād	it	ar	they
ād	she		
ne	who		
end	what		

Declension of pronouns.

	Singular.	*Plural.*
Nom.	En, I &c.	Em, we, &c.
Gen.	enghai, of me	emhai.
Dat.	engage	emage
Acc.	engan	eman
Abl.	engusti	emgustim
Instr.	enganti	emanti
Loc.	engnu	emanu or emanum
Agent.	enim	emim
Nom.	nin, thou	nim, you
Gen.	ninghai	nimhai
Dat.	ningāge	nimāge
Acc.	ninin	nimin, nimanun
Abl.	ningusti	nimgustim
Instr.	ninanti	nimanti
Loc.	ninganu	nimganu
Agent.	ninim (?)	nimim (?)

Nom.	ās, he	ar, they
Gen.	āsgahi	ārgahi
Dat.	āsge	ārge
Acc.	āsin	ārin
Abl.	āsgusti	argustim
Instr.	āsanti	aranti
Loc.	āsganu	argnu
Agen.	âsim	arim.

The dual may be formed, but does not really exist,—as

nām	irab, we both	nim	irib, you both
nām	irbgahi	nim	irbargahi
nām	irbge	nima	irbarge
nām	irbatin	nim	irbarim
nām	irbgusti	nim	iribgusti
nām	irbanti	nim	iribanti
nām	irbnu	nim	iribnu

Postpositions.

gane,	with	chocha,	after
gusti,	from	mechha,	above
gusan,	unto	kuti,	beside
ge,	to, for	hiri,	near
anti,	by, through	kaṭha,	beyond
nu,	upon	gechha,	far
num,	in	menya,	up
kīnya,	beneath	mund,	before

Adjectives.

The adjectives, which are only a few, take no part in the declension.

Nom.	sanni alas, little man
Gen.	sanni alasgahi
Dat.	sani alasge
Acc.	sani alasin
Abl.	sani alasgusti
	etc. etc.
Nom.	sanni mukka, little woman
Gen.	sanni mukkagahi

Dat.	sanni mukkage
Loc.	sanni mukkasin
Abl.	sanni mukkasgusti, etc.

Comparison.

Pos.	sanni, small
Comp.	adinti sanni, smaller
Superl.	ad hurminti sanni, smallest

Pos.	koha, great
Comp.	adinti koha, greater
Superl.	ad hurminti koha, greatest

ADJECTIVES.

paṉru,	white	gaṛi,	deep
mochāru,	black	oṭṭa,	heavy
cheso,	red	nebba,	light (not heavy)
hariar,	green	marchia,	dirty
pīyar,	yellow	kuri,	hot
dīgha,	long	kurna,	warm
pudda,	short	kiri,	cold
mōṭ,	thick	baríar,	strong
sarhua,	thin	jukki,	little
chaika,	lean	chaiga,	wet
kuba, benko,	crooked	chaika,	dry
		kiṛa,	hungry
ujgo,	straight	didiṛna,	satisfied (full)
mechha,	high	nidi,	empty
phuda,	low	ninka,	full
maldan,	ugly	chandrna,	sleepy
sobhdas, koṛe,	beautiful	ejrna,	watchful
		landi,	slow
beṉs,	good	kitka,	rotten
malbeṉs,	bad	panjka,	ripe
malkoṛe,	ill	chena,	unripe
pachgi,	old	ghutum otaro,	round
joch,	young	tissa,	sour
sanni,	small	phāṛi,	pure
bhircha,	hard		

Numerals.

onta, one
en̲r, two
mun̲d, three
nāch, four
pantche, five
soi, six
sate, seven
aṭhe, eight
nawe, nine
dase, ten

There are no ordinals.

tāṛa, half
onghon̲ thaun̲a, once
pán̲r en̲r, twice
pán̲ṛ mund, thrice
pánr nách, four times
etc.

In numbering human beings, these are the following numerals:

ort ālas, one man
irib ālar, two men
núb ālar, three men
naib ālar, four men
pantche ālar, five men
etc.

Verbs.

The auxiliary to be, mannáge.

Indicative Mood.

Present.

I am &c.

En ra : adan rain
nin ra : aday ra : adi
ās ra : adas ád ray ad rai
em ra : adam raim
nim ra : adar ra : aday
ār ra : anar ar ra : nay

Imperfect.

I was.

En ra : achkan ra : achan
nin ra : achkay ra : achki
ās ra : achas ād ra : acha
em ra : achkam
nim ra : achkar ra : ach kay
ār ra : achar ād ra : achay

Perfect.

I have been.

En	manjkan	be : edan	en	manjkan	be : en
nin	manjkai	be : eday	nin	manjki	be : edi
ās	manjkas	be : edas	ád	manjki	be : i
em	manjkam	be : edam	em	manjkeem	be : em
nim	manjkar	be : edar	nim	manjkay	be : eday
ār	manjkar	be : enar	ad	manjkay	be : enay

Pluperfect.

I had been.

En	manjkan	ra : achkan	en	manjkin	ra : achan
nin	manjkai	ra : achkaij		manjki	ra : achki
ās	manjkas	ra : achas	ad	manjki	ra : acha
em	manjkam	ra : achkam		manjkam	ra : achkam
nim	manjkar	ra : achkar		manjkay	ra : achkay
ār	manjkar	ra : achar		manjkay	ra : achay

Future.

I shall or will be.

En	manon	
nin	manoy	
ās	manos	ad mano
em	manom	
nim	mannor	
āṛ	mannor	

Future completive.

I shall have been.

En	manj chachon,
nin	manj chachoy
ās	manj chachos
em	manj chachom
nim	manj chachor
āṛ	manj chachor

IMPERATIVE MOOD.

En	manon,	let me be.
nin	mana	manai, be thou.
ās	mana	ad mani, let him, etc. be.
em	mannom	
nim	mannor	
āṛ	mannor	

POTENTIAL MOOD.

Present.

I can be.

En	manna oṉgon,
nin	mana oṉgoi
ās	manna oṉgos
em	manna oṉgom
nim	manna oṉgor
ār	manna oṉgor

Imperfect.

I might, could, &c. be.

En	manna oṉgdon
nin	manna oṉgday
ās	manna oṉgdas
em	manna oṉgdam
nim	manna oṉgdar
āṛ	manna oṉgmar

Perfect.

I may have been.

En	manna ongkan	be : edan
nin	manna ongkay	be : eday
ās	manna ongkar	be : edar
em	manna ongkam	be : edam
nim	manna ongkar	be : edar
ār	manna ongkar	be : enar

Pluperfect.

I might, could, &c. have been.

En	manna ongkan	ra : achkan
nin	manna ongkay	ra : achkay
ās	manna ongkar	ra : achas
em	manna ongkam	ra : achkam
nim	manna ongkar	ra : achkar
āṛ	manna ongkar	ra : achar

CONDITIONAL MOOD.

Present.

If I be.

Te	en	manoṉ,	em	manom
	nin	manoy	nim	manor
	ās	manos	ār	manor

Imperfect.

If I were.

Te en	holle,	em	holle
nin	holle	nim	holle
ās	holle	āṛ	holle

INFINITIVE MOOD.

manna, being

mannāge, to be

Kálage, to go.

INDICATIVE MOOD.

Present.

	Masc.	*Fem.*	*Dual.*
En	kālakdan,	kālagin,	nām irbatim kālakda
nin	kālakday,	kālakdi,	
ās	kālakdas, ad	kālgi,	
em	kālakdam,	kālagem,	
nim	kālakdar,	kālakday,	
āṛ	kālaknar,	kālaknay,	

Imperfect.

En	kālakkan	kālakkam
	kālakkay	kālakkar
	kālakyas	kālakyar

Perfect.

En	kerkan	be : edan
	kerkay	be : eday
	kerkas	be : edas
	kerkam	be : edam
	kerkar	be : edar
	kerkar	be : enar

Pluperfect.

En	kerkan	ra : achkan
	kerkay	ra : achkay
	kerkas	ra : achas
	kerkam	ra : achkam
	kerkar	ra : achkar
	kerkar	ra : achar

Future.

En	kāun	kāom
	kāoy	kāor
	kāos	kāor

Future completive.

En	kāla chachor	kāla chachom
	kāla chachoy	kāla chachor
	kāla chachos	kāla chachor

IMPERATIVE MOOD.

En	kāun	kālon	kāum	kālom
nin	kaoy	kālakaloi	kāor	kāla
	kāos		kāor	

POTENTIAL MOOD.

Present.

I can go

En	kāla ongon,	kāla ongom
	kāla ongoy	kāla ongor
	kāla ongos	kāla ongor

Imperfect.

En	kāla ongdan	kāla ongdam
	kāla ongday	kāla ongdar
	kāla ongdas	kāla ongnar

Perfect.

En	kāla ungkan	be : edan
nin	kāla ungkay	be : eday
as	kāla ungkas	be : edas
em	kāla ungkam	be : edam
nim	kāla ungkar	be : edar
āṛ	kāla ungkar	be : edar

Pluperfect.

En	kāla ungkan	ra : achkan
nin	kāla ungkay	ra : achkay
ās	kāla ungkas	ra : achkas
em	kāla ungkam	ra : achkam
nim	kāla ungkar	ra : achkar
āṛ	kāla ungkar	ra : achar

CONDITIONAL MOOD.

Present.

If I go.

Te en	kāun,	em	kāum
nin	kāe	nim	kāor
ās	kāus	āṛ	kāor

Imperfect.

Te en	kerkan	em	kerkam
nin	kerkay	nim	kerkar
as	kerkas	ār	kernar

PATICIPLE.

kalke
kālar
kālnosim

INFINITIVE MOOD.

kāna, going
kālage, to go

Nanáge, to do.

INDICATIVE MOOD.

Present.

En	nandan	nandam
	nanday	nandar
	nandas	nandar

Imperfect.

En	nanjkan	nanjkam
	nanjkar	nanjkar
	nanjas	nanjar

Perfect.

Enim	nanjkan	be : edan
ninim	nanjkay	be : eday
āsim	nanjas	be : edas
emim	nanjkam	be : edam
nimim	nanjkar	be : edar
ārim	nanjkar	be : enar

Pluperfect.

Enim	nanjkan	ra : achkan
ninim	nanjkae	ra : achkay
āsim	nanjkas	ra : achas
emim	nanjkam	ra : achkam
nimim	nanjkar	ra : achkar
ārim	nanjkar	ra : achar

Future.

En	nannon	em	nannom
nin	nannoy	nim	nannor
ās	nannos	āṛ	nannor

Future completive.

En	nanjchachon	em	nanjchachom
nin	nanjchachoy	nim	nanjchachor
ās	nanjchachos	ār	nanjchachor

IMPERATIVE MOOD.

En	nannon	em	nannom
nin	nannoi	nim	nanor
ās	nannos	ār	nannor

VERBS.

to beat	laona
to drink	ona
to sleep	chandrna
to walk	ekna
to swim	ogna
to plough	oyna
to cut	choina
to sow	cháchna
to eat	mochna }
to eat	ona }
to ride	argna
to fall	katrna
to rise	cho : na
to see	eṛna
to hear	menna

to speak	kochna karna
to sing	páṛna
to blow	úrna
to dance	nalna
to sit	okna
to tie	chotna
to go	kána
to cook	biitna

Adverbs.

below	kiṇya
noar	hiri
within	ekatara
whence	ekaiants
how	ekane
not	ambo
yes	hae
whence	ekaianti
whither	ekatara
alone	oatoch

Conjunctions.

and	dara
then	antle
but	pahe
or	bhel
because	igune
also	hon̠
when	ekabiri
if	je

The Lord's Prayer.

He embai je mercha nu ra: aday. Ninghai náme pavitr mano, Ninghai ráji bar: o; ninghai suuwak ekane mercha nu, aneho chochal nu ho mano. Emhai ulla ullanta asma ina emáge chia. Antle emhai dosan muaf nana, ekane omho emhai dosnanurin muaf nandan. Antle oman pariksha nu amba cha: a, pahe burainti chhar a ba: a Ráji, sáwang antle mahatm sadau sadau ninghai rai. Amin.

Creed.

En bishwás nandan Dhames embas nu, ás je mercha dara chechalgahi sángias sirjanhāras taliás, antle ásgahi ortostonka tangdas. Prabhus Jisus Christusnu, je Dharmatmanti Kulnu barchhas dindam Mariamauts kundrus, Pontius Pilatus tarti dukhan chedas, Krusnu kilras keras, ketchas keras, mándras keras, antle naraknu itiás, ulmundnu ketch ka gusti ujias dara chochus mercha nu argias, antle sawangias tambas Dharmeshgahi mandi cheka tara uk : as be : edas ; eksanti ás ujnárin antle ketch karin nisáb nanáge phen bar : os.

En bishwás nandan dharmatma nu : Dharmir Christáner gahi go honda nu dhar mir gahi salha me, pápgahi chhema, med gahi jia cho : ona antle jug jug gahi jia nu. Amin.

Ten Commandments.

1. Dharme nimhai Dharme entol konnek anum dosar Dharmesin amba man : a.
2. Indri im juthi gahi dewt a puja amba nana.
3. Dharme ninghai Dharmes gahi namin begar bujhra : am amba ana.
4. Dharmes gahi ulan paoits niáge amba modr a.
5. Ninghai ágo babásin mahá tmchia.
6. Alawein amba chetár chia.
7. Nanna mukkargane amba naña bekamma drál tarah amba mana.
8. Chalal amba chara.
9. Phásiar amba ana, ninghai orsi porsir un phásiar gawáhi amba chia
10. Ninghai orsi porsir gahi erpa erpanta tálach amba nana.

APPENDIX

Brief Vocabulary of the Moondah and

English.	*Moondah.*	*Ho.*	*Kherriah.*
Man	horo	ho	hibo
Woman	era	era	kanseldo
Boy	coora	cooa	baboo
Girl	corsi	cooi	buij
Head	bohu	bo	boko
Hair	ub	ub	ulloi
Ear	lutur	lutur	lutur
Eye	med	met	mud
Mouth	......	a	tamode
Tooth	data	danta	goíneh
Hand	tihi	tih	tih
Foot	kata	kata	katta
Bone	jang	jang	......
Blood	myam	myum	enjam
Egg	billi	......	......
To-day	tiping	tiping	mupoo
Night	......	nida	eedib
Sky	sirma	sirma	o
Sun	singi	singi	borho
Moon	chandu	chundu	lerung
Star	epil	epil	sencom
Heat	lolo	lola	lolo }
Fire	singil	sèngil	tìngson }
Water	dah	dah	dah
Wind	hoyo	hogo	kogo
River	......	......	......
Stone	......	......	......
Tree	daru	daru	......
Village	......	......	......
House	ora	ora	o
Snake	......	beeng	bungham

F.

cognate Languages of the Kolarian type.—By Lieut.-Col. DALTON.

Putoons or Juang.	Sonthal.	Bhumiz (Latham.)	Coour (Dr. Voysey.)
juang	horh	horro	hoko
mukha	......	......	suttan
lunda			
lundi			
bocob	buho	buho	
juta (H)	ub	ub	ap
lutur	lutur	lutur	
emor	met	met	meht
tamon	mocha	alang	ah
goneh	dátha	dátta	
......	thi	thi	
......	kata	kata	
har (H)	jang	jang	
iyam	myum	myũn	
susuté	billi	pito	
missing	teheng	tising	
berote	níndhá	nídhá	
akas (H)	sirma	reiumil	
suruj (H)	singi	singi	
lerung	chandu	chandú (H)	
konjinda	ipil	ipil	ipil
lalai	sengel	sengel	singhél
dah	dah	dah	da
koyo			
noi (H)	garra	garra	
olag	dirrí	dirrí	
sumsing	dáré	dárú	dȧrao
jaon (H)	athú	hathúgé	
......	órá	ora	oarru
bubung	bing	bing	

APPENDIX G.

Language of the Kolarian Aborigines ;—Grammatical construction of the Ho language.—By Lieut.-Col. TICKELL.*

I hope due allowances will be made for the imperfectness of the grammatical details here given, when it is remembered that the Ho language has no written character, nor does there exist a person, native of the Kolehan or otherwise, who could give me the slightest assistance on this point.

It would be trite to observe that grammar is as inherent and essential to all languages, even the most barbarous, as a vocabulary itself. By first learning a number of the words and sentences arbitrarily, the system on which they are founded may be detected in due time by patient comparisons of them, even when the speakers themselves are unable to give the inquirer the least information on the construction of what they are saying. With this difficulty once mastered, it is inconceivable with what ease the most (apparently) complex and difficult languages become familiar.

The sounds of the Ho language are exceedingly pure and liquid, without strong aspirates or gutturals, and may be well rendered by the English alphabet, or still better the French one, as that admits of the slight nasal inflection which prevails in many words in the Ho dialect.

Let the following conventions be made to the sound of the vowels, in the ensuing dialogues, &c.

á ———	as in	"father," "rather,"
é ———	,,	"prey," "été,"
ĭ ———	,,	"skip," "trip,"
ee ———	,,	"sheep," "peep,"
ȳ ———	,,	"fly," "try,"
aï or aÿ——	,,	longer sound as in "aye, aye?"
ŏ ———	,,	"bone," "stone,"
oo ———	,,	"fool," "stool,"
†n̦ (nasal n)	,,	"Ton" "Fanfaron," (French.)

* Reprinted from As. Soc. Journal, Vol. IX. p. 1063.

† Also g, as the French liquid g, in Cologne, Boulogne.

The long acute vowel sounds, such as *oo* and *ee*, also the letter *r*, are pronounced too liquidly and subtilely to be easily imitated by a stranger, and in some words the inflections of the vowels are inconceivably complex and mellifluous. The general euphony or cadence of the language is sprightly and cheerful; if the subject be of a complaining nature, it subsides into a strange chaunt, the sentences being linked together by such see-saw sounds, as "ná-do na-do enété ná-do" which have no meaning, but serve to connect together the speaker's ideas.

When two or more words come together, the former ending, and the latter beginning with similar vowels, they are joined by ellipsis. as "Hola'lé seniéna," instead of "Hola allé seniéna," *we went yesterday.*

Article.

There is none, (properly speaking), definite or indefinite.

Noun.

There is no distinction of genders, marked or influenced by termination, it being determined by the sense or meaning of the word, whether referring to a *male* or *female* being. Besides *man* and *woman*, "erril" and "èra," *boy* and *girl*, "koá" and "koŏee," names of relations, and those of a few domestic animals, all other nouns are distinguished in their gender by prefixing "Sandee" *male*, or "Enga" *female*, as in Persian or English ومادن ریچ نرریچ *he-bear, she-bear.*

A noun has three numbers, singular, dual, and plural, as in Greek.

The nouns can scarcely be said to have declension, as the terminal does not vary either according to number or case, although a distinguishing adjunct, which may be called a 'Pronoun article,' from its nature and use, is added.

	Singular.	Dual.	Plural.
Nom.	Sètá, *a dog.*	Seta king, *two dogs.*	Sèta ko, *dogs.*
Gen.	Sètá-á, *of a dog.*	Seta kingya, *of two dogs.*	Seta koà, *of dogs.*
Ab.	Seta-té, *from a dog.*	Seta king tè, *from two dogs.*	Seta ko tè, *from dogs.*

The dative, accusative, and vocative cases do not differ from the nominative, being only known from their position in a sentence.

In composition, the noun in an accusative case takes the first place in the sentence, if the nominative be a pronoun; otherwise the noun-nominative precedes, the accusative follows, and the oblique or dative case comes immediately before the verb, sometimes immediately after it. "En ho kajikeeáï áÿa èra," *that man said to his wife*, "Dendka oé tootigoikeea," *Dendka shot the bird.* "Eeán hōn do chowlee seta emadÿa," *my son gave the dog some rice.*

ADJECTIVE.

The adjective does not alter in termination, either in number, case, or gender; and always precedes the noun it qualifies. As "Boogee ho," *a good man;* "Boogee ho-á," *of a good man;* "Boogee ho lo té," *with a good man*, &c. There are no degrees of comparison, but as in Hindustani the qualifying words *very*, or *most of* all, are prefixed to denote grades of quality, as "Etka," *bad*, "Ená té neeá o etka," *this is worse than that.* "Sabee ré nee o etka minna," *this is worst of all.* "Boogee lèka èra," a *pretty woman.* "Boogee lèka èra ko," *pretty women.*

PRONOUN.

The first personal pronoun has four numbers, the singular, dual, plural, and plural comprehensive. The others only the three first, as noticed in the noun-substantives.

The possessive pronouns are the same as the personal, with the genitive inflection *á* added.

PERSONAL PRONOUNS.

	Singular.	Dual.	Plural.	Pl. comprehensive.
1*st.*	Eeng *or* aïng, *I*	Alleeng, *we two*	Allé, *we*	Aboo, *we all*
2*d.*	Um, *thou*	Abben, *you two*	Appé, *you*	"
3*d.*	Aÿ *or* áÿo, *he*	Aking, *they two*	Ako, *they*	"

In speaking, if the person include the person addressed, himself, and every one present, as nominatives or agents, he uses the plural comprehensive. If he exclude the person addressed, he employs the first person plural, as "Hola aboo seniéna," *yesterday we went* (i. e. you and all of us.) "Hola allé seniéna," *yesterday we went* (i. e. not you, we alone.)

The personal pronouns in the nominative case both precede and terminate the verb, optionally with the speaker, as, I *speak*, "Eeng kajitanna" or "Eeng kajitannaïng" or "Kajitannaïng."

I go, "Eeng senotana," or "Eeng senotannaïng," or "Senotannaïng."

And to give energy to the sentence, the pronoun is repeated, with the connect "do" between them, as "Eeng do eeng kajitanna," *'Tis I who speak*," Um do um kombookenna," *Thou alone statest it.*

The most difficult part of their construction is in the dative and accusative cases, which are absorbed in the verbs they are governed by, in a manner unknown to other languages, being placed in the centre of the verb, after the root, and before the tense terminal.

As, *I speak to thee*, "Eeng kaji*me*tanna;" *he spoke to me*, "áÿo kajiked*ing*ia;" *he spoke to them*, "kajiked *koäï*;" *the tiger saw me* "koola do nelded*ing*ia;" *he killed him*, "áÿo goïked*áÿ*a." Here I have underlined the oblique or accusative pronoun, where it comes in, just before the tense terminal of the verb.

Possessive Pronouns.

	Singular.	Dual.	Plural.	Pl. comp.
1*st*.	Eenga* or áïngia, *my*	alleengia	alléa	abooá
2*d*.	Umma, *thy*	abbena	appéa	„
3*d*.	Aÿa, *his*	akingia	akoá	„

These always precede their substantives.

Demonstrative Pronouns.

Singular	Dual.	Plural.
Nee *or* inee, *this*	neeking, *these two*	niko, *these*
Neeá *or* ineeá, *of this*	neekingia, *of these two*	neekoá, *of these*
Neeté, *or* ineeté, *to*, *with*, &c. *this*	neekingté,	neekoté,

---

En, *that*	enking, *those two*	enko, *those*
Ená, *of that*	enkingá, *of those two*	enkoá, *of those*
Enté, *by*, *from with &c. that*	enkingté,	enkoté,

"Nee" *this*, is sometimes used idiomatically by a person referring to himself. If a Kole were to be asked what countryman he was? he would answer, "Ho nee gé," *I am*; or literally, *this is a Kole*. Of what clan are you? Answer, "Poortee neegé," *I am a Poortee*.

Interrogative Pronouns.

Okoï, *who?*	chikan, *which?*	chiá, *what?*
Okoiá, *whose?*	chikaná, *of which?*	

Relative Pronouns.

Relative pronouns are very vague, the sentence being generally so rendered as to obviate the necessity of them, thus, instead of saying, *The man who went*; a Kole would say, *The gone man*, "Senien Horo."

* Pronounced, as 'mignon,' 'Ligne,' &c. in French.

But at times "Chikana," *whatever*, and "Ena," *that*, are used relatively, as "Chikana um kajeeá, èna eeng áïooma," *what you say, that I will listen to.*

Verbs.

Verbs are either active or neuter. There is no passive voice.

The Infinitive mood is formed by adding *téá* to the root.

The present participle by adding *tan* or *té*.

The Past participle by affixing *kedté*.

In the active or transitive voice, the Present tense Indicative mood adds to the root "*tanna*," in the neuter voice, "*akanna*."

Imperfect tense there is none, the Present tense being used, and its Imperfect signification understood by the context.

The Perfect tense is formed by adding in the active voice, "*kidda, keea, kenna, lidda*, or *tadda*," to the root. In the neuter voice, "*lena*," or "*ièna*," sometimes "*kenna*."

There is no Pluperfect tense, but greater completion is expressed by conjugating the verb "chabteá," *to finish*, added to the root; much the same way as "chookna" in Hindustanee.

The Future is formed by adding to the root *eea* or *oá*, or sometimes simply *á*, in which latter case the sound of the root is prolonged. Except "nooiteá," *to drink*, which makes "noonooá;" and "roteá," *to gore* (as a bull) "roroá."

The Imperative is formed by adding (in the 2nd person singular) to the root, "*mèn*" and "*omén*" or "*ÿmén*," if the root end with a consonant. In the other persons *ká* precedes the pronoun, and the simple root of the verb, which will be more clearly shown in conjugating. In a negative sense, "*alum*" or "*alo*" is prefixed to the 2nd personal pronoun, *á* being added to the root; if in the 3rd person, singular, dual, or plural "*aloka*" is prefixed to the pronoun, and the root alone of the verb is used.

The Subjunctive mood is vague and imperfect. In the Present and Future tenses "*rèdo*" is added to the root, sometimes together with the word "*honang*," "*derang*," or "*torá*" (signifying conditionality) affixed.

The Past tense is formed in the same way; indeed there appears to be no Past Snbjunctive tense; but sometimes the conditional terminal "*rèdo*" is added to the Past perfect Indicative.

This word "*rèdo*" admits the vowel to be affixed to it, or to come immediately before it and after the root.

Conjugation of the verb "Kajĕeteá," *to speak.*

Infinitive Mood.

Present tense—Kajĕetéa, *to speak,*

Present Participle—Kajitan, or Kajienté, *speaking,*

Past Participle—Kajikedté, *having spoken.*

Indicative Mood.

Present tense.

Sing.				Dual. Plural.	
1st. Person,	Aïng,	Kajitanna,		Alleeng—Allé,	Kajitanna, *I &c. am speaking.*
2d. ,,	Um,			Abben—Appé,	
3d. ,,	Aÿo,			Aking—Ako,	

Perfect tense.

1st.	Aïng—Alleeng—Allé,	Kajikidda, Kajilidda *or* Kajitadda. *I &c. spoke or have spoken.*
2d.	Um— Abben—Appé,	
3d.	Aÿo— Aking— Ako,	

Future tense.

Aïng, Um, &c. &c. &c.—Kajeea, *I &c. &c. will speak.*

Imperative Mood.

Sing.	Dual. Plural.
Eeng Kakajee, *Let me speak.*	Kajeeaboo *or* Abookakajee, *Let us all, &c.*
Um Kajeemén, *Speak thou.*	Kajeeben *or* Abbenkakajee, *Speak you, &c.*
Ayo Kakajee or Kakajee o káï, *Let him speak,*	Kajeealling *or* Allingkakajee, *Let us, &c.*
	Kajeeallé *or* Alléokakajee *Let us, &c.*
	Kajeeako *or* Akokakajee *Let them, &c.*
	Kajeeaking *or* Akingkakajee, *Let them, &c.*

Negative.

Sing.	Dual. Plural.	
Alokáïng kajeea, *Do not let me speak.*	Alo k'aboo kajeea.	*Do not let us &c. &c. speak.*
Alum kájeea, *Speak not.*	Alo k'allé kajeea.	
Alo kaï kajeea, *Do not let him speak.*	Alla'bben kajeea.	
	Al'appé kajeea.	
	Alo ka'ko kajeea.	
	Aloka'king kajeea	

Subjunctive Mood.

Present tense.

Eeng Kajeerèdo, *If I speak.*
Um Kajeeredo, *If thou speakest.*
Aïo Kajeeredo, *If he speak.*

Aboo, Allé, Abben, Appé, Ako, Aking, } Kajeerèdo, *If we &c. speak.*

Perfect or Pluperfect.

Eeng, Um, &c. &c. &c. Kajeekedrèdo, *If I &c. &c. &c. had spoken.*

Conditional, or Potential.

Eeng Kajëäïng honang, *I would speak.*
Um Kajeeum honang, *Thou &c.*
A··o Kajeea honang, *He, &c.*

Allé &c. &c. Kajeea honang, *We might or would speak.*

Note. As has been before explained, in all these tenses and persons (except in the Imperative) the pronoun may be either prefixed, or affixed, or both.

The same Verb, Conjugated with its Objective pronoun.

Indicative Mood

Present tense.

Eeng or Aÿng	Kajeeing tanna,	*I speak to myself.*
,,	Kajee metanna,	*I speak to thee.*
,,	Kajee áïtanna,	*I speak to him.*
,,	Kajee' létanna,	*I speak to ourselves.*
,,	Kajee' ling tanna,	*I speak to us two.*
,,	Kajee' ben tanna,	*I speak to you two.*
,,	Kajee' pètanna,	*I speak to you.*
,,	Kajee king tanna,	*I speak to them two.*
,,	Kajee kotanna,	*I speak to them.*

The same exactly for all the other persons, and tenses, &c.

Perfect tense.

Aïng, Um, Aÿó, &c. &c. &c.	Kajikedingiá.	I, thou, he, &c. &c. &c.	*spoke to myself.*
	Kajiked'mia.		*spoke to thee.*
	Kajikedáïá.		*spoke to him.*
	Kajikede'lia.		*spoke to ourselves*
	Kajiked'lingia.		*spoke to us two.*
	Kajiked'bena.		*spoke to you two.*
	Kajikedpéá.		*spoke to you.*
	Kajikedkingiá		*spoke to them two.*
	Kajiked'koá.		*spoke to them.*

Examples of this construction, especially in the Imperative mood, will be given in the Vocabulary, so need not be further dwelt on here.

It is scarcely possible to reduce the verb "*to be*" to conjugation, unless we suppose the varied forms in which it is used as inflections of separate verbs, wanting in many tenses. For "*to be*" is expressed by different verbs, according to its allusion to time, a person, or a thing; and its relation to mere existence or to the nature of existence. In short, there is no auxiliary verb "*to be*" which can be independently conjugated. The unchangeable word "minna," or "minnakana," is applicable in the present tense alone, to denote a *state* of existence, as "Eeng, um, aÿó, &c. menna, or minnakana," *I am, thou art, he is*, &c. But in past and future tenses some other verb denoting *presence*, as the verb "*to come*," "*to reside*," &c. must be employed.

But the verb "*to be*," when implying the *nature* of existence, can be rendered in the past and future tenses, as well as the present, by adding to the participle or adjective, *oá* in the future, and *iena* in the past, as "eeng laga akanna," *I am tired*; "eeng lagaoá," *I shall be tired;* "eeng lâgièna," *I have become tired;* "eeng rènga akanna, or renga akannaing," *I am hungry;* "eeng rengaoá or rengaoing," *I shall be hungry;* "eeng rengaièna," *I was hungry. Oá* and *iena*, it is to be remembered, are inflections of the future and past tenses in all neuter verbs.

Again the verb "*to be*" can be simply represented in the future and past tenses, when speaking of a *thing*, by the word "hobawa," *it shall or will be*, and "hobiena," *it has been;* also in the present, "hobowtanna," *it is.* This mode of expression commonly refers to the success or accomplishment of any project. In the English idiom we should say for "hobawa," *it will do*, or *it will answer;* "hobiena," *it is all over*, or *has succeeded;* "hobowtanna," *it is going on.*

That boy will be a thief, could not be rendered, "En koá do komboo hobawa," but "En koá do komboo oá."

Your business will be done to-morrow, not, "Umma kajee gappa oá," but, "Umma kajee gappa hobawa."

This will never do, "Ka hobawa;" *go away, it is all over* "Marsenomén hobiéna."

In English and other languages, state, nature or condition, is rendered by affixing or prefixing the various tenses of the verb "*to be*" to the adjective, as to be hungry, *I am hungry*, *I was hungry*; "*to be glad*, *I am glad*, *&c. &c.*" But in the Ho dialect the adjective itself becomes a neuter verb, and is conjugated by affixing to it the different inflections denoting time and mood—*to be hungry*, "rengatéá;" *I am hungry*, "renga akannaïng;" *I was hungry*, "rengaiénaïng;" &c.

NEUTER VERBS.

After what has been said, it would be unnecessary to give any example of the conjugation of neuter verbs. It only requires to be remembered that their present terminal is "akanna" instead of "tanna;" and their past inflection "iĕna," instead of "kidda, tadda, lidda, or eea," all of which latter are transitive forms.

Some verbs are both neutral and transitive, as "chabateá" *to finish*. They have therefore both inflections. In the transitive form "chabatea" is frequently added to the root of some other verb, to denote completion; but it may also be used alone: in the neuter form, it is of course confined to the third person.

EXAMPLES.

Yōmchabakiddaí, *He ate it all up.*
Bȳchabakidallé, *We finished (making) it.*
Kajeechabȳmén, *Finish speaking.*
Gappa miang chabawa, *It will be done to-morrow or next day.*
Nádo chabiéna, *It is now finished.*

The word "hereá" is placed between the root and terminal of a verb to denote positiveness or certainty; as when the speaker means to state something as an incontrovertible fact, as, "Kajee hereákiddaï," *most assuredly he spoke.* "Oodoob hereámén," *speak positively.*

The causal form is rendered by putting "chee" between the root and terminal—as "landateá," *to laugh*, makes "landacheeteá" *to cause to laugh*; "aïoomtea," *to hear*, "aïoomcheetea," *to cause to hear*, as in Hindustani *á* is inserted (with a few exceptions) for the same purpose, as Hunsna, Hunsána; Soonna, Soonána, &c.

Continuity (in the Imperative mood alone) is expressed by adding "akán" to the root, as "doobmén," *sit down*, "doobakánmen," *remain sitting*; "Aïoom mén," *listen*, "Aïoomakánmén," *continue listening.*

Finally, the thoroughly performing an act, is often rendered by adding the verb, "jōmeteá," *to eat*, to the root of the expletive verb, as "neljoomkidallé," *we all saw it (thoroughly)*; "aïoomjōmmén," *listen (attentively)*; "Geetee jōm-meén," *sleep (soundly)*. And should the verb be of a violent nature (referring to some violent act) the particle "táb" between the root and inflection gives force to the meaning, as "Goïtabkiddaï," *he slew him (outright)*; "Toltab kidallé," *we bound him* (forthwith); "Neertabmén," *Run (quickly) fly!* so "Ooiteá" is *to jump*, and "Ooitabtea," *to bound (as a tiger)*.

Ká before the pronoun gives the verb a negative form, as has been before explained in describing the Imperative mood.

There is no verb "*to have*," possession being denoted in the same manner as in Hindustani. *I have*, "Eengtra minna"—"Méré pas hȳe."

From the foregoing remarks may be gathered, that in the active or transitive voice—

The present terminal is,	"*Tanna.*"
The past,	"*Kidda, tadda, lidda, kenna* or *keea.*"

In the Neuter Voice—

The present terminal is,	"*akênna.*"
The past,	"*ièna* or *lèna*;"

In either Voice—

The conditional, subjunctive, or potential mood terminate in } "*redo*" or "*kedrado,*"

All these terminals being of course subject to the inflections of their pronouns, which are, as has been said, as often affixed as prefixed.

A nondescript species of Verb is used in rendering the sentence "*what shall or can I, (thou, he, &c.) do?*

Future and Present.

Ch'eeng chikȳa,		*I,*	
Chee'm chikya,		*Thou,*	
Chee chikȳa,		*He,*	
Cheeboo chikya,		*We all,*	
Chee'lé chikya,	*what shall or can*	*We,*	*do?*
Chee'pé chikȳa,		*You,*	
Chee'ben chikȳa,		*You two,*	
Chee'ko chikȳa,		*They,*	
Chee'king chikȳa,		*They two,*	
Chee'ling chikȳa,		*We two,*	

Past tense.

Chee'ng chikakidda, *what could I have done?* &c. &c. &c.

The verb "*to be able*" is rendered by "Dȳtea" in its moods and tenses, as "Niádo eeng bȳdȳa," *I can make this*; "Umdokadȳa," *you cannot*; "K'áĭ dȳoá," *he will not be able.*

Many little exceptions and variations occur to these general rules, which it would be impossible to become familiar with, without constant practice in their arbitrary use; but the foregoing remarks comprise all that would be of practical utility. The constant elision and confluence of words beginning and ending with vowels must be remembered, and that the particle *do*, has no meaning whatever. This will render the examples above given to the different rules simple and illustrative.

For Sale.

A series of 122 Photographs of Inscriptions in the Ancient Canarese Language, taken from stone and copper Shashanas in the Mysore Presidency. By Major Henry Dixon, H. M.'s 22nd Regt. M. N. I. Single copies, in cloth leaved album of 60 pages, half-bound morocco, Rs. 115.

For six copies, each, ...	Rs.	105
For ten or more copies, each,..................	,,	100

The Society has received 50 copies of Professor Herman Schlagintweit's Isotherical Chart of India, for gratuitous distribution to those members who may apply for copies.

PUBLICATIONS

OF THE

ASIATIC SOCIETY OF BENGAL

For Sale at the Society's Premises, No. 45, Park Street.

	RS.	AS.
Aborigines of India, by B. H. Hodgson, Esq., B. C. S., ...	3	0
Asiatic Journal, from Vols. XII. to XXIV. i. e. from 1843 to 1855, Vols. I. to XI. and Vols. XXV. to date, prices as per title page, ...		
Ditto Researches, from Vols. VI. to XII. and Vols. XVII. to XX. each at, ...	10	0
Ditto ditto Index, at, ...	5	0
Catalogue of Birds in the Museum of the Asiatic Society, by E. Blyth, Esq., Curator, ...	4	0
——— of Curiosities in the Museum of the Asiatic Society, by Babu R. L. Mitra, ...	0	8
——— of the Books and Maps in the Library of the Asiatic Society, by ditto ditto, 1856, ...	3	0
——— of Sanscrit Books and MSS. in ditto, ...	1	0
——— of Books and MSS. in Arabic, Persian and Urdu,	1	0
——— of the Fossil Remains of Vertebrata from the ewalik Hills, the Nerbudda, Perim Island, &c. in the		0
Museum of the Asiatic Society of Bengal, by H. Falconer, Esq. M. D., F. R. S., G. S. and L. S., ...		0
——— of the Recent Shells in the Museum of the Asiatic ociety, by W. Theobald, Jr. Esq., ...	3	0
——— of Mammalia in the Museum of the Asiatic Society of Bengal, by E. Blyth, Esq., ...	2	0